the EMPTY NESTER'S
FINANCIAL HANDBOOK

by

Mark E. Battersby

Macmillan Spectrum/Alpha Books

Macmillan General Reference
A Simon & Schuster Macmillan Company
1633 Broadway
New York, NY 10019

Library of Congress CIP data 97-071170

ISBN: 0-02-861754-1

Publisher: Kathy Nederhaus

Production Editor: Suzanne Snyder

Production Team: Eric Brinkman, David Faust, Heather Pope, and Karen Teo

Indexer: John Sleeva

Book Design by Margaret Dunlap

Manufactured in the United States of America

10 9 8 7 6 5 4 3 2 1

CONTENTS

INTRODUCTION

Eventually, or is it hopefully, the kids move out. Now you are an "empty nester." No longer tied down with the day-to-day responsibilities of raising the children, you can now spread your wings and begin to do all of the things that you have always wanted to. You can travel whenever and wherever you want—if your job and your finances permit, of course.

Often overlooked by empty nesters is their financial status. Yes, in all likelihood, you will have extra money available once the children have left the nest. But will it be enough to let you enjoy the kind of lifestyle that you want? More importantly, will your financial situation enable you to retire when you are ready and continue to live in the manner that you desire?

In the chapters ahead, we are going to be taking a look at how you, as an empty nester, can enjoy your lifestyle as well as afford it. We're also going to show you how you can afford the empty nester lifestyle while, at the same time, planning and investing for your retirement. You may even find that many of the retirement planning strategies that we'll outline will actually enhance your enjoyment of your empty nester lifestyle.

Your Goals

In the early stages of your empty nester status, you must decide what type of lifestyle you enjoy. Do you enjoy travel, staying at home, dining out or your hobbies? Early in your days as an empty nester you must also decide where you want to live—and how. Surprisingly, the answers to these questions can be found when you begin thinking about what the future holds for you.

No, you don't need a crystal ball in order to predict your financial future. Obviously, no one can predict the future with any degree of certainty. What every empty nester should do is allow themselves to dream and set goals for the future based on those dreams.

In order to have "realistic" dreams, you, the empty nester, should immediately take stock of your present assets. What is your home worth? What savings or investments have you managed to accumulate thus far in life? What other assets do you have? You may be surprised at how much you have managed to accumulate before the nest emptied out.

Now comes the hard part: You must decide how you are going to use your current assets as a base and accumulate enough additional capital to finance the goals you've decided on. That is your retirement plan.

Most empty nesters are all too well aware of how difficult it is to accumulate savings by simply "putting it away." After all, there is always something more important than savings. Thus, we'll explore the difference between savings and investing and try to show how investments can be both a hobby and financially rewarding. We'll explore the largest and most important asset of every empty nester—their home. That home can provide shelter from both the elements as well as from the tax collector. It's such a good tax shelter, in fact, that you may even want to acquire a second home, a vacation cottage or condominium in a resort area.

Those unique tax breaks for homes can also help propel an empty nester into the role of landlord. Rental property, as you will see in the chapters ahead, often makes a good investment. And, while it may not be your cup of tea, puttering around, fixing up or even renovating properties may provide enjoyment for any empty nester so inclined.

Naturally, any new endeavor requires a safety net. Your new empty nester lifestyle is no exception. A diminished need for life insurance may be countered by a greater need for health insurance or long-term care insurance. Today, the question is not so much how big a safety net do you require, but how much of a safety net can you afford? We'll attempt to answer that question in Chapter 4.

Among the risks faced by every empty nester is that of a return migration—when the grown children decide to return to the nest. Fortunately, thanks in part to our tax rules, that return migration by recently departed children need not be a financial drain on the empty nester, at least with proper planning. It doesn't take a crystal ball to foresee the inevitability of a return migration in today's economy.

Enjoying and Profiting from the Lifestyle

An empty nester who is suddenly faced with the time and resources for hobbies or other enjoyable activities can often utilize those activities as a springboard to additional income, tax breaks and even a retirement business—one that will generate income long into retirement.

Although our tax rules have eliminated most of the so-called "tax shelters" that were, in the past, used by the wealthy to legally hide income from the tax collector, an empty nester can create their own perfectly legal tax shelter. A unique provision of our basic income tax laws, the Internal Revenue Code, allows every empty nester to convert a hobby into a "tax business."

With a tax business such as greyhound racing or breeding, crafts, farming or woodworking, additional tax write-offs are created. At the same time, those inevitable losses that result from so many hobby-related, spare-time activities can be used to offset income from other sources, such as a job or investments.

Even collectibles, if properly handled, can provide an enjoyable investment vehicle for empty nesters. Capitalizing on collectibles to help fund the retirement plan is an excellent alternative investment as well as an enjoyable pastime.

Savings Versus Investing

As already mentioned, it is the rare empty nester who can achieve his or her retirement goals simply by putting a few dollars away each pay period. With a basic understanding of how investments actually work and a knowledge of the potential for growth offered by the various types of investments, every empty nester can safely and quickly accumulate funds for retirement. How much should be accumulated and how quickly will be determined by each empty nester based on his or her own unique circumstances.

The obvious goal is to accumulate the funds they feel are necessary in order to enjoy the type of lifestyle they've envisioned for their retirement. Investments may also provide enough additional income to fund today's empty nester lifestyle as well.

There is a tremendous number of both savings and investing options available today. Few of us are experts in all of them. However, once again, a basic knowledge of investments and how they work and the circumstances that they are meant for can help guide any empty nester to the particular type or types of investment best suited to their goals—and their temperament.

In Chapter 12, we'll explore the basics of such investments as stocks, bonds and mutual funds. We'll even take a look at the extremely risky futures and risk options. Despite the amazing run-up in stock prices in recent years, stocks may not be the right investment for your retirement portfolio. On the other hand, perhaps stocks combined with other investment options are the only way to achieve the goals that you have set for yourself.

Since Uncle Sam wants a percentage of everything you make, be it from your labor or your investments, it only makes sense to use those tax laws to your own advantage. That means taking full advantage of tax deferment. Today, tax deferment comes in a variety of shapes and sizes, all perfectly legal under our tax rules.

What is tax deferment? If, for example, you put one dollar into a savings account before income taxes have been taken out, it is worth more to you. By the same token, if that dollar earns interest, it will grow a lot faster if that interest is free from taxes even if only until you withdraw it. Thus, using before-tax dollars and tax deferment to increase your investment income makes a great deal of sense.

Although not always resulting in tax savings, investment strategies as simple as allocating your retirement portfolio to achieve the results—and a tax bill you can afford—can "grow" your investment portfolio far faster than simple savings or even routine investing.

Everyone Wants to Help

That's right, as you progress through the pages of this book, you will discover a number of sources that will help you achieve your retirement goals. Even your own employer usually offers fringe benefits that can be of tremendous help in building your retirement portfolio. Naturally, there are a number of potential pitfalls, some of which are explored in Chapter 17.

Others willing to help, often for a fee, include professional investment advisers, bankers, lawyers and other professionals such as insurance agents. Surprisingly, you may discover that the best investment advice you will receive is part and parcel of the fees connected with investments in mutual funds. Every mutual fund has investment advisers ready to help you.

The Past is Prologue

Just as this book will help you plan for and cope with a return migration, it should also help you remember the past, your own family, the family that raised you. Today's economic climate is forcing more and more elderly to turn to their families for financial support or assistance.

We'll explore the moral dilemma presented by friends and family members who might require support. We'll attempt to show some of the options that you can help other family members with—or make use of yourself if you wait too long to begin your own retirement planning.

And lastly, the subject of estate planning is an integral part of retirement planning. As you will see, there are many immediate tax savings to be realized from properly planning your estate, who you are going to leave what to, now rather than later. And, of course, there is also the added benefit of having your assets go where you want them to and with a minimum bite taken out for estate taxes.

Why Now and What Now?

All empty nesters find themselves faced with a unique opportunity. The kids are gone along with their insatiable demands on your time, savings and income. Now you can begin to enjoy the lifestyle of an empty nester. But now is also the time that an empty nester should be thinking about the future.

Fortunately, it is possible for most of us to enjoy the lifestyle of an empty nester while, at the same time, planning and saving for the future. In fact, the planning strategies, techniques and investment vehicles we outline in this book may help you better enjoy your empty nester lifestyle—now and tomorrow. And best of all, as you will see in the pages ahead, it is possible to enjoy as well as profit from your retirement plans.

Chapter 1

THE NEWLY EMPTY NEST

If you are like most empty nesters, about now you are probably just beginning to think about how much golf you will play. Perhaps you fantasize about all of the exotic places that you can now visit. Or maybe you simply imagine how enjoyable it will be to sit in the shade and catch up on 20 years' worth of reading.

In reality, however, now that the nest is empty, you should be thinking about retirement. Fortunately, thinking about and planning for retirement need not put a damper on enjoying your newly discovered lifestyle as an empty nester. In fact, retirement planning may actually enhance your present financial situation, giving you more money now as well as after retirement.

Maximum Enjoyment, Minimum Income

By some standards, having enough money is the only key to a successful lifestyle. But bank accounts and investment portfolios should be viewed simply as tools for future enjoyment, not as some distant goal. In other words, an empty nester who sets out exclusively to achieve financial security upon retirement may or may not achieve that goal. Incorporating the need for retirement savings into your lifestyle as an empty nester is more realistic. In other words, small sacrifices now can mean enjoyment both now and after retirement.

The Myth: Financial Planning Is Only For Those With Money

Wrong! Financial planning is for those who want to have a lot of money—or at least enough to retire on comfortably.

Life presents each of us with a seemingly endless series of choices. Even something as ordinary as the beginning of a routine workday offers many options.

You can choose to get up early, arise at your customary hour or even to sleep late. Your choice, once made, closes some options but opens new ones.

The early riser trades sleep for an array of possibilities. What to do and in what order? Exercise vigorously? Read the morning paper? Take a long walk? Go to work early? Shower? Watch television news? Eat breakfast?

As the day goes on, the choices multiply and so do the decisions that you must make. In addition to these routine daily decisions, each with its own trade-off, there are less frequent but bigger choices: marriage, family, religious beliefs, lifestyle and many, many more.

All choices, large or small, help give us a sense of freedom that enriches our lives. Yet each one causes a consequence because it requires a trade-off: Selecting option A means you will consume some resource (your time, emotional energy or money) that otherwise could have been spent on option B.

Not too surprisingly, all too often the resource consumed is money. At first glance, trade-offs involving money seem as straightforward as any. Children learn that the same 50 cents cannot buy both a candy bar and a soda. It will purchase only one of these items, so a choice must be made.

Many parents give their children weekly allowances to acquaint them with this reality and afford them experience in making their own financial trade-offs. By adulthood, you know too well the choices imposed by money. The dollar amounts may be bigger—you may, for example, be deciding between a new kitchen and a new car, each costing $20,000—but the nature of the trade-off still seems the same as candy versus soda.

On closer examination, however, financial trade-offs for the empty nester turn out to be more complex and challenging than the simple money choices made by children. Why?

Financial trade-offs reach into the future. The choices that you face now are never solely between alternate ways to spend your money today. Whether you realize it or not, as part of the bargain you are also trading off various ways to spend money in the future. Thus, the choice is not simply between using $20,000 to buy a car or a new kitchen. A third alternative, for example, is to use the $20,000 to pay for several years' living expenses when you are retired.

The Choices of Empty Nesters

Children leaving the nest open up many more options. Just consider work as one option. Why would you want to work more now that the nest is empty and, theoretically, routine living expenses are lower?

Midlife crises often prompt career changes among people at this point in their lives. A second income may be particularly helpful in enjoying the empty nest while, at the same time, rebuilding your coffers depleted by family demands, education or other family-related expenses.

Many employers actively seek part-time employees because they don't need to provide benefits and can gain a great deal from the experience and skills of seasoned workers. For your part, a part-time, second job may be a way to get your feet wet in another trade or profession.

Of course, working for someone else is not the only avenue you can take. Becoming a self-employed entrepreneur is gaining in popularity among empty nesters and others with fewer demands on their time and budgets.

You might, as just one possibility, take advantage of the reduced demands on your time and finances to turn a hobby into a moneymaking venture, do consulting or venture into something completely new. You can also tie that desire for a new trade, profession or a business of your own into the retirement planning that you should be undertaking.

Education

Many empty nesters are living proof that it is never too late to learn. In fact, empty nesters are moving into classrooms in large numbers, pursuing degrees or just taking courses out of personal interest.

Volunteerism

There are many ways to utilize your newfound time as a volunteer. Approximately 25 percent of men and women over 50 volunteer according to the U.S. Census Bureau. Their combined efforts are the equivalent of 500,000 full-time workers.

To enjoy your empty nester lifestyle in this manner and to become a part of this growing and much-needed segment of our society, you will have to reach out. Remember the need for volunteers is greater than ever before.

Leisure

Leisure may have the strongest appeal for you. There are hundreds of ways to spend leisure time: travel, crafts, carpentry, fishing, golf, movies, reading. This list is endless. What do you enjoy? What new leisure activities do you want to try? This is your opportunity for fun and enjoyment.

Remember, though, whatever you do, do it with thought. In other words, think about how much time you'll be allocating to leisure and the types of activities that bring meaning and pleasure into your life.

Also, give a great deal of thought to whether you want to spend your leisure time alone, with your spouse or with those family members who have recently fled the nest? There is no right choice. It is important to decide how much of your leisure time you want to spend in solo activities and how much time with someone else.

Empty Nests Are Conducive to Relationships

Although most people become empty nesters as one-half of a couple, a large segment today's empty nesters are single, divorced or widowed. But, since married couples form such a large segment of the empty nester population, it pays to devote some thought to your spouse.

Oddly enough, marital relationships are rarely addressed by those entering into the empty nest phase of their lives. First, there never seems to be enough time to discuss these issues. Second, marriage is a personal subject. Third, those couples who have been doing fine for the last 20 years may see no reason to discuss their relationship.

Obviously, an empty nest means change—and that includes changes in many a marital relationship.

This period of transition is a time to reflect on why you married your spouse. In the early years of marriage, you never had enough time to be together as a couple because of careers, additional education and starting a family. Now is your chance to rediscover your spouse.

Remember, however, that continuing in a splendid marital relationship, until now, has never required spending all of your free time together. Each of you is an individual. Your new lifestyle as an empty nester requires you to look at your need for privacy and your current work environment.

Without the distractions of other family members, most empty nesters seek privacy. Do you—or your spouse—need some area that is just for you? Look at your home and determine what space can be allocated as yours. Perhaps an area can be converted into a den, computer room, work shop, library or art studio.

Aside from physical space, ask yourself if you need some private "mental space." Do you need to do some things alone without accounting for every minute of your time?

And Then There Are Taxes

Empty nesters frequently find themselves facing higher tax bills. The loss of dependent exemptions and deductions for family medical bills, insurance, and the like frequently cause the tax bill to escalate. Of course, those higher tax bills are usually a result of having to spend less on family expenses. The empty nester is in the enviable position of having money available that is no longer necessary to support the daily living of the recently departed family.

Faced with extra income, the need to begin thinking about that fast-approaching retirement and the desire to enjoy that new lifestyle, why not think about combining all goals to reduce that tax bill?

That's right, there are a number of methods to utilize the extra money that is usually available to empty nesters, many of those strategies will help ensure a financially secure retirement.

Balancing The Empty Nest Lifestyle

In physics, equilibrium is a state of complete balance between opposing or conflicting forces. Financial equilibrium represents the same type of harmony where money and lifestyle are concerned.

In order to achieve financial equilibrium, you must be able to strike a balance between your financial resources and your spending goals. You must also successfully make trade-offs between life's current expenses and those that will need to be borne in the future.

To have reached a state of financial equilibrium is to be reasonably prepared for whatever curves life will throw at you. That may require you to seek some risk protection.

Some events in life are unpredictable and highly unlikely to occur, but when they do occur their effect can be devastating. For example, the likelihood that you will die before retirement age is statistically very low. But the financial impact on the family and dependents (yes, empty nesters have dependents) of a wage earner who dies prematurely can be overwhelming. This is why life insurance may be needed.

Reaching Financial Equilibrium

Financial equilibrium is a lifelong concept. In the short-term, basic income and outgo may be out of synch at different times in your life and for different reasons. Households typically go through a cycle of financial deficits and surpluses, first borrowing to purchase a home and cars, later paying down those debts and eventually accumulating investment assets out of surplus income.

When the kids leave home and the mortgage gets paid off, empty nesters are typically able to increase their savings to help fund retirement needs. Unfortunately, too much spending on their lifestyles over the years may have severely narrowed the range of financial options available to them as they grow older.

Reducing Expenses For Later Enjoyment

If you are out of balance, consuming too much today and shortchanging your future goals, how do you move toward financial equilibrium? You might earn more money. Another step, more realistically, is to reduce current expenses. For many of us, a relatively small cutback in consumption translates into a big increase in savings. Plus, there are quite a few strategies that can not only help cut taxes and reduce current expenses, but also help you better position yourself for a financially secure retirement.

Your Home

While we'll explore the value of your home and explain more fully how a home can help provide that financially secure retirement in later chapters, consider the impact on your lifestyle of "trading down" that home.

Our income tax laws offer two highly advantageous financial planning options for homeowners who have built up substantial equity in their primary residences. If used appropriately, these allowances may enable you, as an empty nester, to "trade down" to a less expensive home and, at the same time, free-up cash to add to your retirement portfolio.

The first tax provision allows empty nesters to take a one-time exclusion of up to $125,000 in capital gains—the profit realized from the sale of the primary residence. Unfortunately, it is a one-time exclusion that can only be used by those empty nesters over the age of 55. We'll delve into how this legal loophole can help in Chapter 3.

CALCULATING THE GAIN ON SALE OF PERSONAL RESIDENCE

Selling price, old house	$190,000
Less: Selling expenses	(15,000)
Fixing-up expenses	(10,000)
Adjusted selling price	$165,000
Original cost, old house	$ 50,000
Closing fees, original purchase	2,000
Improvements	11,000
Cost basis	$(63,000)
Gain on sale	$102,000

The second provision enables an empty nester to defer taxes on some or all of any remaining capital gains above the $125,000 exclusion by purchasing a replacement home.

To be eligible to defer the capital gains on the sale of a primary residence when you buy a new residence, you must meet the following requirements:

■ You must buy and occupy your new residence within 24 months before or after selling your old residence.

■ The price of the new residence must be equal to or greater than the adjusted sales price of your old residence. The adjusted sales price is the selling price less direct selling expenses, any fix-up expenses related to the sale and, if applicable, the one-time $125,000 exclusion.

■ You must not have deferred a gain on the sale and replacement of your primary residence within the last two years unless you did so as the result of a job transfer or to accept a new job in another location.

Thus, empty nesters can sell their residence and postpone any tax bill on the gains merely by purchasing a more expensive replacement residence. If the move is to be into a smaller residence costing less than the price received for the old home, the empty nesters must be 55 years old or older to shelter up to $125,000 in capital gains.

FIGURING COST BASIS OF NEW HOME

Purchase price	$186,000
Purchase costs	4,000
Less gain deferred from previous home sale	(102,000)
Cost basis of new home	$ 80,000

Moving Away

Once the kids are on their own, many empty nesters express their desire to "change the locks before the kids change their minds" and decide to move back in. In reality, few empty nesters actually want to burn their bridges that quickly. Even the act of moving to another, less expensive, more convenient or more suitable location is a choice in which one should consider both personal and family issues.

Who among us wants to pull up stakes and move away from relatives, lifelong friends or even their communities? A smaller, more easily maintained new home in a community more conducive to the lifestyle of empty nesters need not mean a long-distance move.

In fact, before you make any final decisions, you should visit the area where you are thinking about relocating at different times. In considering whether to relocate, you should also determine what the new taxes will amount to each year.

In addition to estimating taxes, you should prepare a budget outlining what you expect to spend on housing, food, utilities, taxes, auto insurance, medical care, recreation and the like. If your move will result in higher commuting expenses, also consider them.

This preliminary budget is the first step in preparing the financial plan that will help you maximize your status as an empty nester while, at the same time, allocating funds for retirement.

Next, we'll explore the basics of retirement planning before delving into the many ways of accumulating retirement savings—many of them quite enjoyable.

Chapter 2

EMPTY NESTERS MUST SAVE

According to the recently conducted Workplace Plus Survey for the Employees Council on Flexible Compensation, the average American in 1992 socked away $2,688 for retirement. Two years later, that figure had plunged 34 percent to $1,776. Why? Are we saving less because we assume that we'll have to work well beyond age 65? Even if that is the case, the fact is that the more that you save now, the more options that you will have later. And, what better opportunity to save than that presented to those suddenly facing an empty nest?

It takes discipline and motivation to sacrifice today and set aside money for tomorrow. However, even without sacrificing the immediate goal of enjoying your empty nester status, it is still possible to put money away for retirement. The first step is to establish goals.

Establishing Goals

Goals are your financial objectives or targets. Each goal will have its own time horizon—the period over which you will accumulate money for that goal and the period over which it will be spent. You can start developing your own goals simply by making a list, then revising and refining it as you go.

The first time, outline your goals in qualitative terms only, then begin to revise them. The revisions should make your goals increasingly specific and measurable. In fact, you should be able to revise each goal two or three times without actually stating it in terms of a particular dollar amount. Instead, express your goal as a percentage of your current income or your current living expenses. Thinking of your goal in terms of today's dollars makes it easy to compare it to your present level of income and investments.

Your goals will usually fall into one of two categories: accumulation goals and income replacement goals. With an accumulation goal you are targeting an amount of money that will be needed on a certain date.

An income replacement goal, on the other hand, aims to generate a stream of income starting at some point and continuing into the future. As a result, the time horizon of an income replacement goal itself has two parts: an initial period when you build up the required amount of money and a subsequent period when the money is spent.

Of these, planning for retirement represents the biggest challenge because your retirement time horizon extends decades into the future, creating a number of uncertainties. The length of the retirement time horizon is unknown because you can't predict your retirement date with any degree of certainty. Plus, you have no way of knowing your life expectancy.

The extended time horizons make forecasts less reliable. As a result, your retirement goal and the strategies that you will develop in order to reach that goal are a "first shot" that will have to be revised many times as the future unfolds.

While you were busy raising a family your goals might have been to

■ Pay for the kids' college educations.

■ Build a "rainy day" fund for emergencies.

■ Make sure that my spouse and children have enough money if I die.

■ Retire with enough money to live comfortably.

■ Buy a much bigger house.

Today, your preliminary goals might look like this:

■ In case of my death, replace 50 percent of my income in today's dollars until my spouse reaches age 65.

■ Build a "rainy day" emergency fund to cover six months of living expenses. Accumulate one-third of the required amount over each of the next three years.

■ Accumulate enough money in five years for the down payment on a house costing twice as much as our current home.

■ Retire at age 65 with 80 percent of our current income in today's dollars for 25 years. Be prepared to retire at age 60 with 70 percent of our income in today's dollars for 30 years.

NOTE: TODAY'S DOLLARS VERSUS FUTURE DOLLARS

One way to keep things simple is to plan in terms of today's dollars, or what something is worth this year, not what it might cost after 10 or 20 years of inflation have taken their toll. The cost in today's dollars is easy to relate to your present level of income and savings. Future living expenses will climb higher over the years in all likelihood, but then so too will your income and

your capacity to save. By stripping inflation out
of these planning equations and concentrating on
purchasing power, you will have a more understand-
able gauge of the real resources needed in order
to meet your goals.

Reaching Those Goals By Planning

Achieving financial security requires planning and sacrifice; the only way that you are
going to be successful in reaching your financial goals is to save regularly and invest
wisely. The only way to save regularly is to spend less than you earn. The only way to
spend less than you earn is to plan ahead and, if necessary, forego some nonessential
purchases.

The more specific and realistic you are about your financial goals, the greater are your
chances of actually achieving them. Of course, you must establish your goals before
devising the strategies, or detailed plans, that you will use to achieve them. Obviously,
devising strategies, particularly ones that you may enjoy, requires more effort and dili-
gence than creating the goals. In other words, it's a lot easier to say "I want to retire by
age 55," than it is to actually be able to design a plan to accomplish that goal.

Setting priorities is an important part of successful goal setting. You need to prioritize
your goals so that the pursuit of one goal doesn't interfere or detract from the pursuit
of another goal. For example, many people rank securing adequate insurance coverage pretty far down the list of priorities, yet adequate coverage is essential to financial
security.

Since insufficient insurance may jeopardize years of accumulated savings, adequate
insurance coverage should be a top priority as you will see in Chapter 4.

Devising a plan for a financially secure, worry-free future is like putting together a jig-
saw puzzle that, once assembled, will give you a clear picture of financial self-sufficiency
and security. Because lifestyles are becoming so diverse, one person's puzzle will look
quite different from another's.

Now is the time to ask yourself these critical financial questions:

- How much money will I really need in order to maintain the lifestyle I want and
  where will it come from?

- What can I do now that the nest is empty to make sure that I have enough?

- What will Social Security provide?

- How can I get started?

■ Do I really want to eventually quit work altogether?

■ What investment, tax, savings, credit and insurance strategies will help me put together the best worry-free plan?

And, above all,

■ Can I enjoy the many heretofore undiscovered benefits of my empty nester lifestyle while, at the same time, still successfully planning for retirement?

Where do you start planning?

Begin With The Records

In order to find where you actually stand in your quest for a worry-free, financially secure retirement, you first need a good record-keeping system. This record-keeping system will allow you to prepare a statement of assets and liabilities as well as a personal budget. All of these will help start you down the right financial planning path—while, hopefully, better enjoying the trip.

Financial Statements

Statement of Your Personal Assets and Liabilities

Preparing this statement is not only an excellent tool that can help you understand where you stand today but also a good way to gauge your financial progress along the road to retirement. The statement should list assets at their current fair market values (what they are worth if you were to sell them today). Try to be realistic, especially when valuing real estate and personal property, such as jewelry or a sailboat—areas where many people are prone to overvalue.

If you have some common stock or real estate that has appreciated considerably in value, remember that your net worth might not be a high as it now appears once you sell those assets. Why? You may have to pay tax on their appreciated value.

Personal financial statements are important in showing any individual's financial well-being. Two types of statements should actually be prepared. The first is the statement of personal assets and liabilities (personal balance sheet) that we've just explored. This will summarize your assets and liabilities and determine your net worth.

> NOTE: Your net worth is the amount by which your assets (your savings, investments, property owned) exceeds your liabilities (debts owed). Periodically determining net worth helps you to gauge your financial progress towards those goals that you have—or will soon—set for yourself.

Once an up-to-date statement of personal assets and liabilities or personal balance sheet has been prepared, you can make plans to increase your net worth. The first step in increasing that net worth and accumulating the money needed for retirement is to decide how much you can afford to put away for that fast-approaching retirement.

The second statement needed at this time is a personal budget that summarizes where your income comes from and how it is to be spent.

A Personal Budget

Budgeting is crucial to measuring your day-to-day finances. The purposes of budgeting are (1) to define possible problems in spending patterns, (2) to identify opportunities to overcome these problems and (3) to help you plan realistically to improve your spending habits.

Whatever form your own budget reconciliation takes, remember to leave a comfortable margin for unexpected expenses. There are always unexpected roadblocks, roadblocks that you can't possibly be expected to predict. That is just one reason why the personal financial statements and the personal budget are—or should be—an ongoing, never-ending process. We'll discuss the flock returning to the nest and other potential problems as we go along.

A budget is an essential part of any successful financial plan because it provides a moving picture of your financial situation. But remember, your budget should carefully balance the various needs of your newfound status as an empty nester.

Obviously, a budget that cuts too close to the bone or leaves too little room to enjoy your empty nest status will not work. And you don't need an accountant to prepare your personal financial statements. But you will need to gather your financial records.

The Tools You Will Use

Saving Versus Investing

Saving money can be as easy as not spending it. Investing, on the other hand, means taking money that you have saved or not spent and doing something with it in order to earn a return or make a profit. Things go much easier when you can separate these two steps.

Separating saving and investing means that it may be possible to make saving routine. Saving can be made routine—perhaps with automatic deductions from your paycheck. Once saved, the money can wait temporarily in the bank until you decide how to invest it. The investing process, on the other hand, requires more time and possibly even help from a professional adviser.

By separating savings from investing, you can make sure (1) you are setting money aside in a disciplined, regular way and (2) your investments are chosen carefully and with due consideration for your overall financial goals.

Investments

Sorting out and understanding the numerous investment alternatives available to you is actually far easier than you may think. Although we'll delve more deeply into these and other investments later in an effort to show you which types are best for your particular retirement strategy, for now, let's begin by examining the main categories of investments.

Interest-Earning Securities

These are usually divided into two categories: bonds (fixed income) and cash equivalent (CDs and money-market accounts).

Fixed income investments, including Treasury, municipal, and corporate bonds, are interest-earning securities with maturities greater than one year after their issue date. Backed by the "full faith and credit" of the Federal government, Treasury bills and notes are considered the safest bonds. Next in safety are municipal bonds.

While municipal bonds are not guaranteed by Uncle Sam, they are backed by state and local governments or by specific revenue sources. And although cities and towns can default, or fail to pay their debts, they rarely do.

Least secure are corporate bonds. Why? Because these bonds are usually only backed by the company that issues them, their degree of safety is directly related to the company's health. If a firm goes bankrupt, the bonds can become worthless. Thus, bonds issued by financially strong blue-chip corporations are the safest type of corporate bond.

To help investors evaluate the risk of corporate (and municipal) bonds, some companies, notably Standard & Poor's and Moody's, rate bond quality. Junk bonds are on the opposite side of the safety coin. They have lower ratings and are high-risk investments.

Cash equivalents are investments considered to be of such high liquidity and safety that they are virtually as good as cash. In addition to CDs and money-market accounts, other cash equivalents are money-market mutual funds and Treasury bills.

Stocks

Most people think of stocks as a synonym for investments. Yet, paradoxically, many Americans never take advantage of stock ownership because they consider them too risky. But empty nesters should consider stocks as part of their investment portfolio. After all, stocks can provide both regular income (in the form of dividends) and inflation-beating appreciation (increases in value over time).

Real Estate

Owning real estate is perhaps the most complicated form of investing. Evaluating a property's potential for income, appreciation and its tax ramifications is very difficult. On top of that is the need to monitor and—if you buy the property yourself—manage the property once it is purchased.

Some people opt for passive real estate ownership through a limited partnership, which considerably simplifies the process of real estate investing. But it in no way safeguards your investment from real estate slumps.

The easiest way for empty nesters to participate in the real estate market is to buy shares of real estate investment trusts (REITs), (which are discussed later) but return may be far less than you could attain by buying individual property.

Naturally, all investment categories will be discussed later in greater detail along with a number of alternative investments that provide enjoyment, tax write-offs and profits.

For now, however, every empty nester should understand the importance of setting goals, planning and the basic tools available for achieving those goals. Now let's think about how you can both enjoy and profit from your empty nest—or even from a second home.

Chapter 3

ENJOYING AND PROFITING FROM THE EMPTY NEST ITSELF

In this chapter you will learn how to make the most of that newly empty nest. While the enjoyment aspect of your empty nester lifestyle is up to you, benefiting financially from that empty nest or even acquiring and profiting financially from another empty nest, such as a vacation home, means understanding our income tax rules. First, let's look at how you can get all of the tax deductions that your use of your home entitles you to.

Profiting from Business Use of the Home

It should be remembered that, as with most of our tax rules, no empty nester is automatically entitled to deduct any of the expenses of using his or her home for business purposes. That's right, unless those expenses are attributable to a specific portion of the home (or a separate structure) that is used exclusively on a regular basis as either (1) the principal place of any business carried on by empty nester or (2) as a place of business that is used by patients, clients or customers in meeting or dealing with the taxpayer in the normal course of business, there can be no home office or shop deduction.

If the empty nester is an employee working for someone else, the business use of the home must also be for the convenience of the employer. The allowable deduction is computed on Form 8829.

Generally, a specific portion of the empty nester's home must be used exclusively for the purpose of carrying on a trade or business in order to satisfy the tax law's exclusive use test. That requirement is not considered to have been met if the home office or shop area is used for both business and personal purposes, such as a den that doubles as a guest room.

However, an exception is provided by our tax rules for what the IRS calls "a wholesale or retail seller" whose dwelling unit is the sole fixed location of the trade or business. In these situations, the ordinary and necessary expenses allocable to space within the dwelling unit that is used as a storage unit for inventory are tax deductible. That is, those expenses are deductible provided that the space is used on a regular basis and is a separately identifiable space that is suitable for storage.

The U.S. Supreme Court (*Soliman*) ruled that actually determining whether a particular business location is a taxpayer's principal business location means comparing that location to all of the taxpayer's business locations. This is because only the most important, consequential or influential location can be the principal location.

In other words, a doctor practicing at a number of hospitals as well as running his or her practice from home must decide which location is the principal location of his or her practice. If the bulk of the doctor's time is spent at one hospital, it makes no difference whether office space is provided by that hospital or not, chances are that it will be his or her principal business location.

> NOTE: RESIDENTIAL TELEPHONE
>
> An empty nester with a qualifying home office or shop is specifically denied a business tax deduction for basic telephone service charges on the first line in his or her residence. Additional charges for long-distance calls, equipment, optional services (e.g., call waiting) or additional telephone lines may be tax deductible.

Office Deductions for Employees

In order for employees to qualify for the home office deduction, they must meet the requirements cited above. What's more, the exclusive use of that home office must be for the convenience of their employer.

However, regardless of whether or not an employee meets the requirements, an employee is denied a home office deduction for any portion of the home that is rented to the employer (except for expenses such as home mortgage interest and real property taxes that are deductible regardless of whether the office space is qualified business usage).

Generally, an employee's home office expenses must be taken as a miscellaneous itemized deduction subject to the 2 percent floor on Schedule A. However, self-employed empty nesters are permitted to claim their allowable home office deductions on Schedule C (Schedule C-EZ, the easy tax form for small businesses, may not be used in this case).

> NOTE: LIMIT ON HOME OFFICE DEDUCTION
>
> The home office deduction is limited to the gross income from the activity, reduced by expenses that are deductible without regard to business use (such as home mortgage interest) and all other deductible expenses attributable to the activity but not allocable to the use of the unit itself.

> Thus, a tax deduction is not allowed at least to
> the extent that it creates (or increases) a net
> loss from the business activity to which it
> relates. Any disallowed deduction may be carried
> over, subject to the same limit in carryover
> years.

Your Home as an Investment

If you are anything at all like most empty nesters, at this stage of your life you probably already have most, if not all, of your net worth tied up in real estate—your home. However, generally speaking, your principal residence should not be considered part of your investable assets. In fact, its value should not be counted in determining the allocation of your assets that we'll discuss in Chapter 15. The reason? You have to live somewhere.

Think about it. If you were to sell the house, you would have to reinvest in another house or you would have to set aside funds to generate enough income to pay rent. The exception: If the value of your house is significantly in excess of your present or near-future requirements. In that case, the excess value may be considered as an investable asset allocated to real estate.

Suppose, by way of illustration, that you are within a few years of retirement and plan to move to a less expensive house. In this case, you may not need to allocate any additional funds toward investments in hard assets.

Don't Forget Mortgage Interest

Under our tax rules, owning a home can result in favorable tax treatment—but you have to look for it. The reason is the long-standing philosophy of our lawmakers that says people who buy homes deserve some sort of tax benefit. But, with the Federal deficit looming large in Washington, D.C., those lawmakers do not want to lose too much tax revenue.

One significant tax break that homeowners receive is the right to deduct all or a portion of their mortgage interest on their income tax returns. The interest on any mortgage loan signed on or before October 13, 1987, is fully tax deductible on your return. This general rule of full deductibility holds true regardless of whether the debt is a first or second mortgage, a home-equity loan or a refinanced mortgage.

If, however, you purchased a new home, refinanced an existing mortgage or incurred additional mortgage debt after October 13, 1987, the tax law divides your tax deductible mortgage debt into one of two categories: acquisition debt and home-equity debt.

Acquisition debt is a loan secured by your primary or second home and which is incurred when you buy, build, or substantially improve your home. Acquisition debt is limited to $1 million ($500,000 if you are married and file separate income tax returns).

What if you refinance an existing mortgage? In that case, acquisition debt includes only the debt that is outstanding at the time of the refinancing and only up to the ceiling of $1 million. You may still deduct interest on the amount of debt in excess of the old mortgage, of course, so long as the additional debt is used to substantially improve your home or if the excess debt itself qualifies as home-equity debt.

Home-equity debt is best described as a loan that is also secured by your primary or secondary home. But, in contrast to acquisition debt, you don't use the proceeds to buy, build or substantially improve your primary or secondary residence. The maximum amount of home-equity debt you may have—and hope to deduct the interest on—is limited to $100,000 ($50,000 if you're married and file separate returns). The exact amount of tax deductible interest depends, to a large extent, upon the fair market value of your home and the amount of acquisition debt that you currently have outstanding.

Property Taxes

Local, state and even foreign real property taxes are generally deductible only by the person upon whom they are imposed and then only in the year in which they were paid or accrued. Real property taxes are taxes imposed on interests in real property and levied for the general public welfare. Such taxes do not include taxes assessed against local benefits.

In other words, the taxes that you pay on your property to a local taxing authority, municipality or governing body are tax deductible. If those taxes take the form of a special assessment, even to provide some local improvement that will benefit everyone, our Federal tax rules won't permit them to be deducted.

It should be noted that local property taxes are probably the most misunderstood taxes you will encounter. Local property tax assessors usually compute your property tax bill for you, telling you only what you owe. Those who bother to check that property tax bill, or the assessment that it was based on, frequently find errors.

With time available, empty nesters might be well advised to take a trip to their local property tax assessor's office and check their property's assessment records. The first step is to check for obvious errors in property dimensions, building materials or even the type of structure that the assessor believes that you have on your property.

Horror stories exist about taxpayers checking their assessments to find multistory parking structures built on small residential plots and extra-large dwelling units located on minuscule plots—at least according to the local property tax assessor. Such errors are easily corrected by bringing them to the assessor's attention.

The assessment on your property should also be compared to the assessments on other similar properties in the neighborhood. Property tax assessments, after all, are supposed to be equitable, based only on the property's value.

Energy Conservation Subsidies

Subsidies for energy conservation measures—the value of any subsidy provided (directly or indirectly) by a public utility to a customer for the purchase or installation of energy conservation measures for a dwelling unit are specifically excluded from the customer's gross income. In other words, there is no income tax on energy conservation subsidies.

By definition, energy conservation measures are considered to be any installations or modifications that are designed to reduce the consumption of electricity or natural gas or to improve management of energy demand.

Converting Your Property for Profit and Tax Deductions

Many empty nesters look at their newly empty nest and begin thinking about renting a portion of it out to raise money for their retirement. That may be all well and good from a practical standpoint and the local zoning authorities may even approve. The biggest stumbling block, however, may come when you attempt to offset that rental income with the expenses associated with renting the property.

Unfortunately, special rules limit the amount of tax deductions that may be taken by an empty nester in connection with the rental of a residence or vacation home that is also used as the empty nester's residence.

If the property is rented for less than 15 days a year, no tax deduction may be taken for any expenses nor must the rental income be included in taxable income. Naturally, deductions, such as those for mortgage interest, property taxes or casualty losses, are not affected by this rule.

A Vacation Home for Empty Nesters

When it comes to vacation homes, you have to ask yourself these questions: What do I really want from my vacation home? A place the family can gather now that the nest is empty? A place the family and I can use whenever we like? A place I know that I can always escape to? Or is my primary consideration simply keeping costs down?

If getting away from the maddening crowd is your primary goal, then tax consequences are a secondary issue. If that extra income is important, you have to take full advantage of our often confusing tax rules. However, in either case, you must understand the rules in order to avoid an unexpected tax bill.

As far as the IRS is concerned, your second home is either a vacation home used exclusively by you and your family, rental property or some combination of the two. A vacation home you use personally most of the time gets much the same tax treatment as your first home, even if you rent the property to others for as many as 14 days each year.

If your vacation home is treated as a second home, you may deduct your mortgage interest and property taxes as itemized deductions on your income tax return. You may not, however, deduct other expenses such as repairs and utilities. And the same restrictions that apply to the deductibility of mortgage interest on your first home apply to the second.

When it comes to income taxes, the difference between a personal vacation home and rental property are great and the tax laws are very precise about which is which. If you intend to rent your second home and take advantage of the tax deductions that renting brings you, these distinctions are important to you.

The tax law says that you may classify your second home as rental property as long as you do not occupy it for more than 14 days in the year or for more than 10 percent of the total number of days that it is rented at fair market value for the year, whichever is greater.

Rental Residence or Vacation Home

Special rules limit the amount of deductions that may be taken by any individual or an S corporation in connection with the rental of any residence or vacation home, or a portion thereof, that is also used as the taxpayer's residence.

MINIMUM RENTAL USE. If the property is rented for less than 15 days during the year, no deductions attributable to such rental are allowable and no rental income can be included in gross income. Deductions allowed without regard to whether or not the home is used for business or the production of income, such as those for mortgage interest, property taxes or a casualty loss, are not affected by these limitation rules.

MINIMUM PERSONAL USE. If the house is not used by the empty nester for personal purposes for (a) more than 14 days during the tax year or (b) more than 10 percent of the number of days during the year for which the home is rented at a fair market rental, whichever is greater, the limitation of the tax laws do not apply. However, the deductibility for expenses still may be subject to the hobby/loss rules—that is, in those cases if rental of the residence is not engaged in for profit. (Chapter 7 delves into the hobby/loss rules in more detail.)

Deduction Limits

If the property is rented for 15 or more days during the tax year and is used by the tax-payer for personal purposes for the greater of (a) more than 14 days or (b) more than 10 percent of the number of days during the year for which the home is rented, the rental deductions may not exceed the amount by which the gross income derived from such activity exceeds the deductions otherwise allowable for the property, such as interest and taxes.

According to the IRS, expenses attributable to the use of the rental unit are limited in the same manner as that prescribed under the hobby loss rules (i.e., the total deductions may not exceed the gross rental income and the expenses are further limited to a percentage that represents the total days rented divided by the total days used). However, the U.S. Tax Court has rejected this formula (affirmed by higher courts).

It is the Tax Court's position, not the IRS's, that mortgage interest and real estate taxes are not subject to the same percentage limitations as are other expenses because they are assessed on an annual basis without regard to the number of days that the property is used. As a result, the formula employed by the Tax Court computes the percentage limitation for interest and taxes by dividing the total days rented by the total days in the year.

NOTE: RENTAL PROPERTIES

In 1991, individual investors—including single people, married couples and the estates of deceased people—owned 92 percent of the nation's rental properties.

A vacation home is deemed to have been used by the empty nester for personal purposes if for any part of a day the home is used

1) for personal purposes by the taxpayer, any other person who owns an interest in the home or the relatives (spouses, brothers, sisters, ancestors, lineal decedents and spouses of lineal descendants) of either;

2) by any individual who uses the home under a reciprocal arrangement whether or not a rent is charged; and

3) by any other individual who uses the home unless a fair rental is charged.

Notwithstanding the foregoing, if a taxpayer rents the home at a fair rental value to any person (including a relative listed above), for use as that person's principal residence, such use by that person is not considered personal use by the taxpayer. This exception applies to a person who owns an interest in the home only if the rental is under a shared equity financing arrangement.

The term "vacation home" means a dwelling unit, including a house, apartment, condominium, house trailer, boat or similar property.

Something to Think About: Reverse Mortgages

Reverse mortgages loans are a relatively new form of mortgage that will allow you to eventually convert the equity in your home into installment payments that could provide you with monthly income for life. By taking out a reverse mortgage, you borrow against your property but, instead of getting the proceeds in a lump sum, they are paid to you in installments.

As an alternative, you may have the option of getting the proceeds from the reverse mortgage in the form of regular payments for a predetermined period of time (say 10 years) or in the form of a credit line against which you can withdraw money when you want it. When you die or move from your home, your reverse equity mortgage immediately becomes due.

Since there are no monthly payments due for a reverse mortgage, you do not need a salary or other earnings in order to qualify. The amount of monthly income you can obtain from a reverse mortgage depends on several factors, including your age, prevailing interest rates, and, of course, the value of your property.

Although reverse mortgages are available to borrowers age 62 or older, the monthly income is much higher for older borrowers. An 85-year-old taking out a reverse mortgage, for example, might expect roughly five times the monthly payment that would be available to a 65-year-old borrower on property valued at the same amount.

While available in most states, reverse mortgages are relatively new and are not widely used. But they are an option that every empty nester might want to consider at or after retirement.

A Sale-Leaseback of Your Home

Another strategy that you might want to consider in your later years is the sale-leaseback of your home. A sale-leaseback transaction is typically arranged between retiree-parents and their children. The parents sell their home to the child (or a partnership of two or more children) and then arrange to lease the home and continue to live there.

In a sale-leaseback transaction, the parents often will use their $125,000 capital gains exclusion and finance the transaction by taking back a mortgage. The sales price, mortgage interest and monthly rental fee must all be at market rates for the transaction in order to meet the IRS rules.

A Warning: These transactions involve important tax and estate planning issues; expert advice and assistance is mandatory.

Taking full advantage of your home, not only making the most of available tax deductions, but also aggressively benefiting from our tax laws and the new financial strategies available to you, can help ensure your financially secure retirement. Benefiting from your home should play an important role in your financial planning.

Next, we'll take a look at the safety net that every empty nester needs to protect his or her nest, nest egg, and retirement.

THE SAFETY NET

Every empty nester needs a safety net, not only to ensure a financially secure retirement but also to help them survive financially until it is time for retirement. A large part of that safety net consists of insurance—in all its many flavors, colors and price ranges.

The keys to dealing most successfully with the insurance aspect of your newly discovered empty nester lifestyle and the necessity to guarantee you the lifestyle that you are aiming for are simplicity and cost control. Your goal is to determine the insurance coverage that you need in order to protect yourself, your family (recently departed or soon to return) and your nest egg against financial disaster, but to spend as little as possible doing so. The savings can be added to your retirement nest egg.

Life Insurance

Life insurance offers important advantages as a way to protect your survivors from the loss of your earning capacity. First, the payment of a death benefit is guaranteed by the life insurance company, meaning that you can be assured that the money will be there when you die. The insurance industry is heavily regulated and insurance companies have an excellent record for reliability in paying death benefit claims.

The cost of life insurance protection is likely to be small at the time that you need it most—when your family is young. Depending on your age, the annual premium for life insurance can be as low as a small portion of a penny per dollar of coverage. That means buying life insurance for risk protection is a highly efficient use for your money.

Remember, too, that life insurance proceeds are free of income tax. If your spouse is the beneficiary of your policy, the proceeds are also free of any estate tax at your death. With no tax bite taken from the policy proceeds, all of your insurance dollars will go toward providing support for your survivors.

The advantage of life insurance for survivor protection—low-cost and guaranteed tax-free death benefits—make it almost essential if you have dependents. Remember, however, not every empty nester needs life insurance.

The Downside of Life Insurance

An empty nester with no dependents and enough money to meet funeral expenses probably doesn't really need life insurance. You may not need life insurance if you already have sufficient resources to support yourself and your spouse (or companion) in retirement—something every empty nester should be aiming for.

Of course, life insurance can be used for purposes besides survivor protection, its advantages in these cases can be less compelling. For instance, insurance can provide cash to help your family pay taxes on your estate or it can serve as a long-term deferred investment.

Before buying insurance for these purposes, however, you should consider less expensive alternatives. You may be able to plan for sufficient estate liquidity in a more cost-efficient way than by purchasing life insurance. Similarly, you may discover that the cost of investment-oriented life insurance outweighs its tax advantages.

Selecting Life Insurance Policies

If you decide that life insurance is needed and affordable, you should understand the basics. Life insurance comes in two basic variations: term and permanent. Term insurance provides pure no-frills protection for a particular period of time, usually a year. The price, or premium, reflects the risk to the insurance company of your death during that period. When the term is over, the price of renewing the term life insurance policy usually goes up. That's because the likelihood that you will die—and thus the likelihood that the insurance company will have to pay—has increased with your age.

Term insurance offers no buildup of cash value, no matter how long you continue to renew your policy. By its nature, term insurance is cheap for younger people but grows very expensive after you reach the age of 60.

Term Insurance

Term policies are straightforward and fairly easy to evaluate based on their premium per $1,000 of death benefits. The two major types of policies are annual renewable term and level term.

Annual renewable term premiums increase each year. Level term, in contrast, charges a rate that is initially higher than the rate for annual renewable term. However, the level term rate remains fixed for a term of 5, 10, 15 or even 20 years. At the end of that time, the cost of reentry, or renewing for another fixed term, rises significantly. That increase may be reduced somewhat through a conditional exchange option if you can demonstrate that you are still in good health.

COMPARING TERM INSURANCE AND PERMANENT INSURANCE

TERM INSURANCE	PERMANENT INSURANCE
Features	
"No-frills" death benefit	Death benefit plus cash value
Better if you need protection	
For 10 years or less	For more than 10 years
Annual premiums	
Lower but will increase	Higher but generally fixed
Insurance company financial strength	
Less Important	Very important
Commissions and sales costs	
Not significant	It pays to shop

You can compare the cost of level term versus annually renewable term insurance by summing the present value of the annual premiums for each policy over a particular period.

Thus, adding up the five years' total premiums for a five-year renewal term policy versus the amount you would pay for five years of coverage with annual renewable term insurance will provide answers about which is most cost-effective.

In recent years, many insurance companies have priced level term policies very attractively as compared to annually renewable term life insurance. If you know that you need or want coverage for a particular period, say 10 years, a level term policy for that period may be your best option.

One important feature offered by many term policies is convertibility. This allows you to convert the policy into permanent (usually whole life) insurance without the need for a medical examination. If your health deteriorates in the future, the convertibility feature can assure you that you have access to permanent insurance at reasonable cost.

Another feature is the waiver of premium in the event of a disability. You pay extra for this feature and it may or may not be worth the money, depending on the insurance company's definition of disability.

Although term insurance is a standard commodity, don't assume that all insurers will charge the same prices, or that group rates are necessarily better. In some instances, coverage under a group policy may cost more than an individual policy sold through an agent.

The insurance company needs to price the policy on the mortality experience of the entire group. If you are younger and healthier than the average group worker, you may be able to do better purchasing an individual policy.

Naturally there are exceptions. Some group policies offer favorable rates and, in addition, may offer you the opportunity to buy coverage above the basic level. If you need additional insurance, you should first check rates and terms of your group policy.

Permanent Insurance

Whole Life

Whole life is the traditional form of permanent insurance and remains the largest selling policy of this type. The premium and death benefit typically are guaranteed, although the death benefit may increase over time.

Whole life gradually builds a cash value that can be borrowed against or withdrawn if you cancel your policy. The insurance company usually guarantees a certain minimum level of dividends or earnings credited to the policy, but in most cases, they will exceed the guaranteed level.

Universal Life

Universal life policies offer flexible premiums and, in turn, flexible death benefits. Universal life rates are sensitive to changing interest rates. Rates offered by the company are changed annually and guaranteed for the next year.

If you like the current rate of return provided by the universal life policy, you can invest more into the policy. If you don't, you may be able to skip the premium or pay only a minimum amount. However, the policy may lapse if you have not paid sufficient premiums to keep the cash value greater than the provider charges for expenses and mortality costs.

Variable Life

These policies amount to little more than mutual funds with a life insurance wrapper. They typically offer empty nesters several fund-like investments with stocks, bonds and money market funds as alternatives. Premiums are generally fixed and a relatively small death benefit is guaranteed.

Returns from variable life polices—and the growth of cash value and the death benefit—depend on the performance of the underlying funds, not on the insurance company's overall investment performance.

Joint Policies

These policies involve the lives of two or more persons. They can be attractive because their premiums are often less than the total premiums for separate insurance policies on each individual. So-called "first-to-die" policies pay a benefit on the first death among the covered individuals. They are used by two-income couples who need survivor income replacement in the event of either spouse's death.

Another use for joint policies is for business partners who want the death benefit to provide the cash needed to purchase the ownership interest of any partner who dies. Second-to-die policies, also known as survivorship insurance, usually pay a benefit on the death of the second of two covered individuals. They are used most often by couples to cover estate taxes on the death of the second spouse.

In contrast, permanent insurance, also known as cash value insurance, is designed with the assumption that you will keep the policy for life. The insurance company sets a fixed annual premium much higher than what is needed to cover the risk of your death in the initial years of the policy. The excess amount is used to fund a cash value that grows over the life of the policy. You can take out the cash value in the form of policy loans or by surrendering the policy and canceling your coverage.

Compared to term insurance, permanent insurance is more expensive at any given age. As you get older, however, the annual cost of retaining your fixed premium, permanent policy will eventually become less than the premiums that you would have to pay for a comparable amount of term insurance.

Investing in Insurance

For any type of permanent insurance, the attractiveness of a particular policy depends on a number of factors such as the insurer's investment returns, the sales and administrative costs, mortality expenses (the longer its policyholders live, the better) and the insurance company's lapse rate (the more policyholders who cancel, the worse).

In order to project the future performance of any policy that you may be considering, an insurance agent will prepare a policy illustration using various assumptions about each of the variables.

Because insurance companies invest primarily in bonds, the cycles of interest rates and bond returns are particularly important in determining their investment performance. (In the case of a variable policy, returns depend on performance of the underlying investment funds.)

If the assumptions presented by the insurance company are all reasonable, the projection can give you a good picture of how the policy will perform at different levels of interest rates. (Always ask to see what would happen if rates dropped.) However, if the projection is based on guesses that mortality experience or investment returns will improve, the policy illustration may be nothing more than wishful thinking.

Broker Vs. Agent

Far more important than illustrations to an empty nester are the insurance company's past history of performance and its claims-paying ratings. Because you expect to own a permanent life insurance policy for many years, you want the insurer to be financially sound. (This may be less of a consideration with a variable life policy because the fund assets are legally separate from the insurance company's own portfolio and not greatly affected by its financial soundness or overall investment returns.) Look for policies from companies that are highly rated for claims-paying ability by several rating agencies, such as A.M. Best Co. (A+ or better), Standard & Poor's Corp. (AA or better) and Moody's Investor's Services (A or better).

> NOTE: Buy convertible term insurance to cover your basic survivor protection needs. Rarely will an empty nester find it necessary to convert some or all of their coverage to a permanent insurance policy—unless it's part of their investment strategy.

INSURANCE RATING AGENCIES

A.M. Best Co., Oldwick, NJ 08858; (908) 439-2200

Duff & Phelps, Chicago, IL 60603; (312) 368-3157

Moody's Investor's Services, New York, NY 10017; (212) 553-1658

Standard & Poor's Corp., New York, NY 10004; (800) 221-5277

Weiss's Research, Palm Beach Gardens, FL 33410; (800) 289-9222

Most publish directories ranking all insurance companies. These directories may be found in most major libraries.

LIFE INSURANCE IN FORCE

(in millions of dollars) as of 12/31

	Ordinary	Group	Industrial	Credit
1915	16,650	100	4,279	
1930	78,576	9,801	17,963	73
1945	101,550	22,172	27,675	365
1950	149,116	47,793	33,415	3,844
1955	216,812	101,345	38,682	14,493
1960	341,881	175,903	33,563	29,101
1965	499,688	308,078	38,818	53,020
1970	734,730	551,357	39,644	77,392
1980	1,760,474	1,578,355	35,994	165,215
1985	3,247,289	2,561,585	28,250	215,973
1990	5,366,982	3,753,506	24,071	248,038
1995	6,835,239	4,608,746	20,145	208,491

Source: American Council of Life Insurance

Something to Think About For the Future

Quite recently, a number of insurance companies have begun to offer policyholders an option to receive part of the proceeds of their policies during their life. Naturally, this unique option is limited to those circumstances where a catastrophic illness or permanent confinement to a long-term care facility affects the policy owner.

These so-called "living benefit" riders can be added to existing polices or included with new ones. Today, approximately 200 companies offer this option.

Under these riders, the policy owner can receive from 25 percent to 100 percent of the policy death benefit; the exact amount depends on life expectancy (usually 12 months or less) and state regulations. Plus, according to the Internal Revenue Service, the proceeds will not be considered income for Federal income taxes.

Health Insurance

Health coverage is always important. Life and disability insurance are important for empty nesters in their 40s or 50s, but the need often diminishes as they near retirement. Long-term care coverage, while it probably won't be needed until well beyond retirement, is immensely cheaper if you buy it while your are still in your 50s.

Medical insurance, however, is a must both now, and in the years ahead in order to secure your retirement. The cost of health care is so high, and has been rising so rapidly, that the lack of health coverage jeopardizes your retirement nest egg if you fall victim to a serious illness or accident.

If you have employer-sponsored health coverage—either through your company or your spouse's—making the most of it now can free up resources for your worry-free retirement plan. Begin by taking a look at the coverage that you and your spouse have now. You may be able to save thousands of dollars each year by managing health insurance benefits more efficiently. For example, by avoiding double coverage for working couples, costs can be cut drastically.

It is getting increasingly more difficult to collect 100 percent of a medical claim, even when both spouses work and each has health insurance at work. In the past, one policy might have picked up where the other left off. But that's less common now, so it could be downright wasteful to keep funding the overlap.

Now is the time to study exactly what you will get from each health care policy and what you will lose by dropping either one. Before you cancel any insurance, however, find out the conditions under which you'll be allowed to rejoin the group if your other health care coverage is ever in jeopardy.

Select a balanced menu from the benefits "cafeteria" of your employer. Many employers offer an insurance benefits menu, allowing their employees to choose among different types of coverage. Take advantage of this flexibility to select the coverage that best meets your needs. In fact, you and your spouse can make different choices to avoid overlapping coverage and free up funds for your 401(k) plan or other retirement savings.

Individual Health Policies

If you and your spouse don't currently have health coverage through an employer, you'll need an individual (nongroup) health policy. The cost of such coverage drops dramatically as the deductible amount that you are willing to shoulder goes up.

To illustrate, a major medical policy that calls for 20 percent co-payments on the first $5,000 of medical bills (and no co-payments after that) and a $250-per-person deductible (up to $1,050 per year) would cost about $250 for a 47-year-old, nonsmoking couple. The same policy with a $500 deductible would cost $215 per month. Raise the deductible to $1,000 and the premium falls to $185. With a $2,500 deductible, the policy would cost $148.

Since your out-of-pocket costs will likely be capped at no more than $3,000 to $5,000 per year regardless of the deductible that you choose, it makes sense for healthy empty nesters and individuals to go with a high deductible and stash the cash premium savings in a bank account. That reserve would be used to pay any uncovered expenses with any balance being socked away in your retirement account.

Making a Choice

Compare out-of-pocket costs. Suppose that you are offered a choice between two policies. One carries a zero deductible—meaning that you would never be required to pay out-of-pocket charges—and costs you $150 per month in premiums. The other option is paid for entirely by your employer but has a $300 deductible and requires you to pay 20 percent of any remaining charges. Which policy would you choose?

Most people are inclined to pick the first option to avoid unexpected, out-of-pocket expenses. yet the second option is probably a better deal and would leave you with a nice chunk of immediate cash to enjoy your newly discovered lifestyle—or to sock away for retirement.

At $150 per month, you would lay out $1,800 a year in premiums for the first policy. You would have to incur medical expenses of $7,800 to spend that much a year on the second policy.

COMPARING THE COST OF LONG-TERM CARE COVERAGE

AGE	LEVEL PREMIUM PER YEAR
30s	$ 100
40s	200
50s	800
60s	1,500
70s	3,000
80s	4,000

Source: Shopper's Guide To Long-Term Insurance, National Association of Insurance Commissioners, Kansas City, Missouri

The Cost of Long-Term Care

Insuring long-term care can leave you financially crippled. And if you think that Medicare will be there after retirement, think again.

Many empty nesters believe that Medicare will pick up their nursing bills; in reality, it actually pays only for the first 100 days in so-called skilled nursing facilities—and then only if admission follows a hospital stay. According to the American Health Care Association, Medicare pays less than 2 percent of all long-term care-related expenses.

Nursing home costs can range from $35,000 to more than $60,000 a year—per person. The amount varies considerably depending on the quality of services and your geographic location—and fees are rising at a rate that is higher than inflation!

The Health Insurance Association of America estimates the average nursing home stay at about 2.5 years and home care services (which can include physical therapy, administration of drugs and food preparation) are no bargain either.

With these cost levels, planning for long-term care becomes a necessity for every empty nester who hopes to provide for quality care and, at the same time, conserve even a modest estate for their heirs. Evaluating your long-term care options in today's environment comes down to these basic choices:

- Do nothing. That is, assume the risks that you won't need long-term care, or if you do need it, then you will be able to pay the cost out of current income and investment assets. To the extent that either is insufficient, look to Medicare for assistance.

- Transfer the risk to an insurance company by purchasing a long-term care insurance policy. Like any insurance policy, this involves paying annual premiums to obtain the insurance company's guarantee of some level of coverage.

- As a third alternative, you might combine the two options above by choosing a long-term care policy with coverage exclusions, with lower daily benefits or one that pays benefits only after certain waiting periods have elapsed.

Long-Term Care Insurance

Given the complexities of Medicare planning and the risk to financial security that long-term care poses, buying long-term care insurance may be the easiest alternative for most people. However, whether you should sign up for long-term care insurance now depends largely on your age.

People under age 50 are best advised to do nothing because many retirement planning experts believe broader and better solutions, public or private, probably lie ahead.

Others, however, argue that buying policies when you are under age 50 and thereby locking in lower rates makes good sense.

> NOTE: Depending on the policy, current long-term insurance premium rates for a 55-year-old can be as much as four times that for a 45-year-old.

It's becoming increasingly more common for large companies to offer group long-term care policies to their employees, so check out your employer's benefit plans. Some professional associations also offer this type of insurance. You can often purchase coverage for relatives, such as aging parents, as well as for you and your spouse. An excellent idea to help keep the empty nest empty.

What to Look for in a Long-Term Policy

Ideally, a long-term care policy should offer the widest possible number of options, including nursing homes in three categories of medical care: skilled homes; intermediate homes which provide rehabilitative therapy; and custodial homes, which offer little more than practical nursing. The best policies also pay for care at home, adult day care centers and brief intermittent care at a nursing home, also known as "respite" care.

The policy should offer these benefits in nearly equal amounts. A policy that covers nursing home care for a year, but home care for only a month or so, forces you to opt for institutionalization or to skip benefits.

Most insurance companies now cover home care, but some charge extra for it or reduce payments over time. Plans may pay for home care only after you've been in a nursing home for a period of time and then only for as many days as you were there.

Some long-term care policies require hospitalization for three days before benefits begin, yet the need for care is often the result of a deteriorating condition such as arthritis, which may not put you in the hospital at all. The best policies require only that a doctor certify the need for care.

Always look for a guaranteed renewable policy. Certain states forbid insurance companies from canceling your long-term care policy because of either your age or deteriorating health. Make sure that your coverage will continue as long as you want it to and that your premiums can't be increased unless the company increases them across the board.

Drawbacks to Long-Term Care Insurance

Almost all policies have one major drawback—they indemnify you a fixed-dollar amount, generally $30 to $200 per day, no matter how much you're actually paying for services. In contrast, hospital and major medical insurance pays all or a high-percentage of each bill.

Long-term care policies also usually include deductibles in the form of a waiting period. The number of days you must pay for yourself before your benefits begin and how long the benefits continue will greatly influence the premiums that you pay.

Most insurers offer at least two choices of waiting periods—typically, anywhere from 20 to 100 days. Selecting a 100-day waiting period can reduce your premiums by as much as 30 percent. So, you probably want to choose as long a waiting period as you can afford.

At the other end though, more is generally worth paying for. Since the majority of policyholders will need care for less than a year, benefits that quit after one year or so may cost only half as much as those for continuing for the six-year maximum that most policies currently offer. The extra charge, however, can mean the difference between your solvency and bankruptcy for the minority whose confinement continues for years.

Medicaid as an Option

Medicaid is a state-run program designed primarily to help those with low income and few or no resources. It provides a safety net of sorts for retirees—but only those in the most dire situations. Yet, about 61 percent of retirees rely on Medicaid to cover at least a portion of the cost of custodial care.

While the Federal government helps pay for Medicaid, each state has its own rules about who is and who isn't eligible and what is covered. You're eligible for Medicaid if your health care costs absorb about all of your income and you've used up all but $1,000 to $4,000 of your assets, excluding your home. The exact amount varies by state.

Exempt assets typically include personal property, one automobile and life insurance of less than $1,500.

Disability Insurance

Disability income policies are intended to replace a certain portion of your earnings when you can't work as a result of sickness or injury. In order to collect a benefit, you must be disabled and you must also have suffered a loss of earned income.

Premiums are usually based on the amount of monthly benefit and a variety of other factors, including how soon the benefit payments start after you become disabled, how long benefits will continue and how disability is defined by the policy.

Terms and conditions for policies issued by different companies tend to be more or less standardized than those used on other types of personal insurance policies. They typically feature many coverage options and riders that can add to the cost of basic disability income protection.

Some of these options merit consideration by empty nesters. One is a provision that raises benefits along with inflation once you become disabled and start to receive monthly checks. Another alternative option gives you the right to convert your disability income policy at a certain age into a long-term care policy that will provide benefits if you must enter a nursing home.

Other provisions, however, are not necessarily a good deal. One example is known as the return-of-premium rider. This provision offers a rebate of a portion of the premiums you have already paid, say 60 percent, if you have no disability claims over a certain period of time, typically five years. The idea may sound appealing but most insurance professionals would advise caution.

The extra cost of the return-of-premium rider can make it a bad investment. All these varied policy features and options mean that disability income policies are complex and difficult to compare.

Disability income policies can also be difficult to buy. The company that is happy to sell you as much life insurance as you want, will be wary when you apply for disability insurance. You will have to take a medical examination and answer questions about your medical history. Your application may even be rejected because of an existing medical condition that could lead to disability. Or the company may issue the policy but exclude coverage for disability caused by an existing medical condition.

And don't forget, before issuing a disability income insurance policy, the insurance company will want to confirm the amount of your earned income at the time that you apply for the policy and your record of steady employment over the years.

If you make a claim, the company will require proof of your loss of income before it pays. This caution reflects the real concern among insurance companies that some policyholders can find it more attractive to try to collect disability benefits than to continue working.

Coverage may not be as expensive as you think. However, if it is so expensive that getting a disability policy would be a burden, then you might want to consider whether you qualify—now or at some later date—for benefits under one of the entitlement programs such as Supplemental Security Income, food stamps, Aid to Families with Dependent Children, etc. Remember, though, if you have assets or future income to protect, disability insurance is coverage that you can't afford to overlook.

That Safety Net, Today and Tomorrow

We've covered a number of types of insurance that can help empty nesters while they are enjoying their new lifestyle and building their retirement nest eggs. We've also out-lined insurance that can be purchased to protect family members who need protection. Most importantly, we've alerted you to the need to consider the need, after retirement, for insurance. Next, we'll delve into Social Security in an attempt to show you how it can fit into your retirement plans now—and whether it will be there for you later.

EMPTY NESTERS AND SOCIAL SECURITY

The purpose of our Social Security system, stated in the broadest terms, is to "provide for the general welfare." To this end, Social Security provides a wide range of programs, including retirement (old age) insurance, survivor's insurance, disability insurance, hospital and medical insurance for the aged and disabled, black lung benefits, supplemental security income, unemployment insurance, as well as a variety of public assistance and "welfare" services.

Although there is a great deal of controversy over the continued existence of Social Security as we know it today, it will, in all likelihood, continue to play an extremely important role in the lives of every empty nester as they speed down the road toward retirement—or later, after retirement.

Why bother with Social Security now? After all, you've only recently discovered a new lifestyle as an empty nester and are just beginning to enjoy it. It is depressing enough that you've got to begin thinking about—and planning for—your retirement, but at least you've been promised that retirement savings will be, in part, enjoyable.

Social Security provides a safety net for you now as well as offering a number of benefits that you can take advantage of later. Those benefits may well reduce the burden of saving and investing now. In other words, with Social Security as a safety net, now and later, you can combine your new lifestyle and retirement planning without too much unnecessary stress. And, don't forget that you may want the nest to remain empty. That means knowing what safety net exists for your dependents or those who may become your dependents.

The Future of Social Security

There is little doubt that Social Security will be around and will still be paying benefits when most empty nesters are ready to retire. But there is also little doubt that Congress will be forced to change the Social Security system sometime within the next decade or so. The result is likely to be less purchasing power for retirees and other beneficiaries than would be projected from the system today.

The reason? Social Security faces a looming financial shortfall because of changing demographic patterns. Over the next 35 years, the baby-boom generation (those born from 1946 to 1964) will retire, while the smaller contingent of "baby busters" meets the Social Security payroll taxes.

Forty years ago, 16 workers were contributing to Social Security for every recipient drawing benefits. Today, that ratio is 3.3 to 1. Forty years from now there will be only two workers paying for each retiree. The result will be bigger retirement bills and fewer workers to pay them.

Congress completed an overhaul of Social Security in 1983, pushing the normal retirement age to 67 by the year 2010, instituting tax on some Social Security retirement benefits and raising Social Security taxes so they now generate a surplus each year. These surpluses are earmarked for a trust fund that is expected to swell to $3 trillion and then be depleted by the year 2029 as it is liquidated to pay benefits for retiring baby boomers.

However, amounts credited to the trust fund are actually being invested in U.S. Treasury bonds and used to finance the government's budget deficits. When it comes time to spend the trust fund for retirement benefits, the government will have to raise taxes in order to generate the cash needed to retire the bonds and provide the Social Security Administration with money to pay benefits.

With no changes in the current levels of benefits and taxes, Social Security will eventually fall short in its ability to pay promised benefits. Estimates of the shortfall vary, but it seems at this point likely to be between 20 and 35 percent. Congress is expected to close the shortfall by raising taxes and cutting benefits.

Among the ways that benefits could be trimmed: reducing cost-of-living increases, raising the normal retirement age to 70 and introducing a "means test" that would phase out benefits for upper income retirees.

What does this mean for empty nesters? Don't count on Social Security to replace the same portion of your income that it replaces for those in your earnings bracket who are retiring today. But, remember, Social Security will survive and, chances are, it will play a large role in your future retirement—not to mention continue in its present role as a safety net for the unexpected.

What Will You Get from Social Security?

How much can you realistically expect to receive from Social Security? Obviously, an empty nester must have some answer to this question in order to plug it into their financial plans or for use in setting their retirement goals.

Aside from the uncertainty facing the Social Security system, the key factor in determining any benefit you may receive is how much you make during your working career. The formula for calculating those future benefits is complicated, but in general, it's based on your earnings over most of your working lifetime.

You become eligible for Social Security when you've earned 40 work "credits." Basically, you pick up four credits for every year worked, which means that you qualify for retirement benefits after 10 years of work. Credits are based on earned income, which is income from a job or self-employment, not savings or investments. The amount needed for each credit increases each year.

Unfortunately, earning more credits does not boost your benefits. Earning more money does. To figure your benefit, the Social Security Administration will start with your earnings for 35 years (up to each year's maximum, which is the top amount to which Social Security applies), adjust those figures for inflation, then calculate a yearly average. Your benefit will be a percentage of that average. The lower the income, the higher the percentage.

Social Security replaces approximately 42 percent of income for the average wage earner and 25 to 28 percent for maximum earners ($65,400 in 1997). Since the top benefit is based on that maximum-earner figure, those who earn more will see a smaller portion of their earnings replaced by Social Security.

What does it take in order to qualify to receive the maximum benefit when you retire? You will need to earn the maximum wage—so you pay in the maximum tax—for 35 years. But, don't worry. If you're a little below the maximum for a few years it won't drop your benefit by much because the benefit amount is a long-term average.

NOTE: AN ESTIMATE OF YOUR BENEFITS

For an estimate of the Social Security benefits that you will receive at retirement (a figure based on your earnings history), you can request a personalized benefits estimate from the Social Security Administration. Call (800) 772-1213 and request Form 7004-SM (Request for Earnings and Benefits Estimate Statement).

About six weeks after this form is returned, you'll receive your estimate in the mail. Remember, however, your projected benefits will be in today's dollars, not inflation-adjusted dollars.

The form is fairly easy to complete, except when it asks you to provide an estimate of future average yearly earnings. If you already make more than the Social Security maximum, don't worry. Put down

what you earn now and the Social Security
Administration will assume that you will continue
to earn above the maximum for the remainder of
your working days. The adjustment is automatic.

If you are below the ceiling and expect your earnings to rise in line with the national average (4
percent or so), again, all you need to do is put
down what you make currently. Social Security
Administration automatically adjusts for average
wage growth.

If you expect future earnings to drop or to rise
faster than 4 percent a year, fill in an amount
that most clearly reflects the changes you anticipate.

Remember, these are merely estimates; you don't
need to be precise. Since you can request this
free estimate as often as you like, you can try
different scenarios.

Adjusting to Inflation

One of the nice things about Social Security is that the amounts that you pay into the
system either through withholding or self-employment taxes are based in "today's dollars." The benefits that you eventually receive will be in "tomorrow's" dollars.

Social Security benefits are indexed to inflation, which means that they rise automatically
in line with the consumer price index for as long as you continue to collect. This may well
be the only piece in your retirement puzzle that offers such a built-in advantage.

The effect of inflation indexing will be to increase the importance of Social Security
relative to your other sources of retirement income over time. Remember, however,
there is a possibility that Congress may trim—or even stop—the cost-of-living hikes
temporarily as a part of the battle against the Federal debt.

Disability Benefits

Social Security also provides the disability coverage—another useful piece in your
retirement plan—that we talked about in Chapter 4. Like private disability insurance,
it is extremely tough to qualify for these payments.

The Social Security Administration considers you disabled only if "you are unable to
do any kind of work for which you are suited and only if your inability to work is also
expected to last for at least a year or to result in death." That would include people with
HIV infection or AIDS, if their ability to continue working has been severely limited.

If you do qualify, however, benefits will continue for as long as your are disabled. A 45-year-old making $40,000 when he becomes disabled in 1996 would be eligible to receive about $1,180 per month in Social Security disability.

Taxes on Social Security

The empty nester who is counting on Social Security as an important and integral part of their retirement plan, should be aware of the drawbacks of the Social Security system as well. In addition to the uncertainty over the future of the Social Security system itself, there is also the impact our tax laws have on Social Security benefits.

In the old days—before 1984—there was no confusion about the taxation of the Social Security benefits. There was no tax, period. Today, there is almost nothing but confusion:

■ For most beneficiaries, benefits remain totally tax-free;

■ For some, however, up to 50 percent of their benefits can be taxed; and

■ For a third group—the most affluent retirees—up to 85 percent of their benefits fall victim to the Internal Revenue Service.

Generally, the higher your income in retirement, the more of your benefits that can be taxed. And that is as matters stand today. Knowing where you stand is important to retirement planning because tax-free benefits go a lot farther than taxable ones will. One dollar of tax-free Social Security benefits, replaces $1.71 of wages nicked by Federal, state and Social Security taxes (28% Federal tax bracket, 6% state taxes). Unfortunately, for more and more retirees, Social Security benefits are no longer totally tax-free.

Your benefits are vulnerable if your "provisional income" exceeds a particular amount based on your tax filing status. Provisional income is a tricky creature. It is your adjusted gross income as reported on your income tax return (that's basically income before subtracting exemptions and deductions), plus 50 percent of your Social Security benefits, plus 10 percent of any tax-free interest income.

If your provisional income is less than $25,000 on a single return or $32,000 on a married filing jointly tax return, you'll be safe. None of your benefits will be taxable.

If provisional income is between $25,000 and $34,000, on a single return or between $32,000 and $44,000 on a joint return, however, up to 50 percent of your Social Security benefits can be taxed. The actual amount that is taxed is 50 percent of your benefits or, if less, 50 percent of the amount by which your income exceeds the $25,000 (single return) or $32,000 (joint return) threshold.

If your income is over $34,000 on a single return or over $44,000 on a joint return, a different formula kicks in and requires that between 50 and 85 percent of your benefits be taxed. Although complicated, the formula generally produces the same result: When provisional income exceeds the $34,000 or $44,000 threshold, the full 85 percent of benefits is usually taxed.

If you are married and file a separate tax return, your threshold amount is zero, so it is almost certain that 85 percent of your benefits will be taxed.

Unlike many numbers in the tax laws, these thresholds are not indexed for inflation. By leaving the thresholds fixed, Congress is relying on inflation to push more and more retirees into the group whose benefits are taxed. That means that you have to look at your income in the future—which in 20 years could be double what it is today—if it simply keeps up with inflation—to predict what part of your benefits will be taxed.

Unheralded Social Security Features

Social Security offers a number of other, largely unheralded features that can make any empty nester's retirement planning a little less stressful. For example, few people stop to consider the value of the life and disability income benefits that are included in Social Security. Yet, to the extent that protection allows you to cut back on private insurance, those savings could go towards financing your new lifestyle and towards your retirement.

Consider just a few of the benefits of our Social Security system, benefits that you may overlook in your own retirement planning.

A Bonus for Couples

Once you begin receiving Social Security benefits, your spouse can also receive benefits based on your record, even if they never worked in a job covered by Social Security. A nonworking spouse is eligible to begin receiving benefits at age 62. Benefits at full retirement age will generally be about half what you are receiving—together you get 150 percent of what you would receive on your own.

If your spouse does work, he or she will receive a benefit based on his or her actual earnings or 50 percent of your benefit—whichever is more. If you and your spouse are both 59, and both of you work and will qualify for the maximum Social Security benefits when you retire at age 65 and two months in 2003, you can expect to receive a combined $3,502 per month in benefits. If one spouse receives the maximum and the other's earnings were average, the combined benefits would be about $2,937 per month at age 65.

Survivor's Benefits

"Life insurance" from Social Security? That's right, part of the Social Security taxes that you pay buys survivors insurance. That survivors insurance will provide monthly benefits for a surviving spouse, children and even dependent parents. In some circumstances, even a former spouse can collect.

The number of work credits that you need in order to qualify for benefits depends on your age. If you die at age 50, for instance, you would need to have accumulated 28 credits in order for the survivor benefits to flow.

Because you are likely to earn four credits for each year that you work, you would need to have worked seven years in order to qualify. Not too surprisingly, most people have little trouble qualifying.

The amount of this "life insurance" is, once again, based on your average lifetime earnings. The more that you made, the higher the death benefits, up to a maximum level. Unfortunately for most empty nesters with older children, the benefit amount drops when each child reaches age 16.

The benefit is also cut if a survivor's earnings top a certain level ($8,280 in 1996). Basically, a survivor loses $1 in benefits for each $2 earned above the threshold. Naturally, the benefits for a child who does not work are not affected by a parent's earnings.

The benefits estimate that you receive from the Social Security Administration will show an estimate of the benefits that your family will qualify for in the event of our death. Take this into account when determining how much life insurance you need to buy.

When Should You Collect?

Social Security offers another nifty feature that helps you fit this piece easily into your retirement puzzle. The choice of when to start collecting is yours. Basically, you have three options:

Going for Full Benefits

At your "full retirement age" (see Table 5.1, below), you can begin collecting full benefits from the Social Security system. Full retirement age today is 65. But that will be changing in stages to age 67 for people born between 1938 and 1960 and later. Every empty nester should factor this change into his or her retirement plan.

If you were born in 1950, for example, "normal retirement age" for receiving full Social Security benefits will be 66. If you were born in 1940, full benefits will be available when you are 65$1/2$.

Tapping in Early

The earliest that you can begin collecting monthly Social Security checks is age 62. That will not change even as "normal retirement age" gradually increases. If you start collecting Social Security benefits early, your benefits will be reduced by as much as 30 percent—for life. The exact amount of the reduction depends on how early you begin collecting.

The following table shows how the full retirement age—i.e., the age at which a beneficiary is entitled to unreduced benefits—will be gradually increased.

Year of attainment of age 62	Retirement age
Years through 1999	65
2000	65 + 2 months
2001	65 + 4 months
2002	65 + 6 months
2003	65 + 8 months
2004	65 + 10 months
2005-16	66
2017	66 + 2 months
2018	66 + 4 months
2019	66 + 6 months
2020	66 + 8 months
2021	66 + 10 months
2022 and beyond	67

Note that in conjunction with the increase in the retirement age, the retirement test was eased for persons age 65 or older.

Although beginning to collect Social Security means that you'll get smaller checks, remember that you'll also get more out of them. After all, even at reduced levels, Social Security benefits collected between ages 62 and full retirement age will give you a head start over someone who waits.

In fact, as matters now stand, it will take a dozen years of fatter checks for those who elect "normal retirement" to catch up with the total payments made to the early retiree. If you invest the early payments and count those earnings, the break-even point is farther away.

In considering when you'll want to start claiming Social Security, don't lose sight of the big picture. How will your Social Security benefits fit into your overall retirement plan? Money that you would make by continuing to work past the first year that you qualify for Social Security would probably far exceed the benefits you would receive over that period. And, working longer would qualify you for higher Social Security benefits and a bigger payment from pension or profit-sharing plans from your employer.

Holding Out for More

As the result of changes taking effect in the coming years, there could be a bonus for future retirees, not to mention providing an interesting twist in every empty nester's planning for retirement. Quite simply, if you delay applying for benefits beyond full retirement age, you'll receive significantly larger monthly checks when you ultimately decide to call it quits.

In order to encourage us to stay in the work force in the years ahead, Uncle Sam will slowly boost the bonuses offered to people who agree to hold off claiming their Social Security benefits. Up until 1990, the bonus for delaying benefits beyond age 65 was a somewhat meager 3.5 percent increase for each year retirement was delayed.

That bonus is now being increased, in steps, all the way up to an attractive 8 percent per year for anyone born in 1943 or later. And that's a compounded 8 percent—that is, each year's 8 percent bonus is figured on the base benefit plus any bonuses already earned. And that's on top of the normal cost-of-living increases.

In effect, the government is offering you a guaranteed 8 percent, partially tax-free return if you agree to leave your Social Security untouched for a few extra years. Even better, if you keep working, the wage base on which your benefits are calculated will also go up, leading to an even bigger sum.

By delaying for three years, as one example, empty nesters born in 1946 will be able to increase the size of their Social Security benefits by a compounded 26 percent, for life, calculated on a higher wage base. Inflation adjustments would be additional. This larger starting benefit ensures that those cost-of-living increases will be larger, too.

How does this late-retirement bonus figure into your plan? Mainly:

■ As retirement nears, if your nest egg and other postretirement income sources aren't measuring up to your expectations, hanging in a little longer could greatly boost your postretirement cash flow. Not only will your Social Security checks be a little bigger, but you'll also have a bit more time to save or invest on your own. A matter of just another year or two could make all the difference in the world.

■ Or you can retire as planned but simply delay your application for Social Security. Your wage base will not rise, but you'll still get the bonus each year that you delay. And remember, the bonus becomes part of the benefits that you will receive for life. If your other income sources are adequate for your retirement needs or investment returns elsewhere simply can't measure up to the partly tax-free 8 percent that Social Security is offering, this may be a good strategy. The trade-off? A short-term delay in exchange for more income long-term.

Social Security, Changes or No Changes

Despite all of the gloom-and-doom talk about the Social Security system's future, it will continue to play a role in every empty nester's retirement—perhaps even a major role.

In reality, the Social Security Administration projects that today's average 46-year-old will receive higher benefits (in today's dollars) than the average 65-year-old currently receives. Tomorrow's average retiree will get back what he or she paid into the system within about 10 years of retirement, tops.

That's true even though higher tax rates and a steadily rising wage base (the maximum amount of income that is taxed each year) mean today's workers are pouring far more into the system then today's retirees did. From a cost-benefits perspective, today's retirees—including, perhaps, your parents—are getting a better deal from Social Security than tomorrow's beneficiaries will.

Of course, that does not mean Social Security is a bad deal for you nor does it diminish the key role that it will play in your financially secure retirement. Yes, you'll pay in more than your parents did, but you'll get more in benefits, too.

It would be foolish to assume that the system won't change between now and the time when you collect your first benefit check. You can count on Social Security to be the focus of a hot political debate. Its very size makes that inevitable.

There may be talk in Washington, D.C., about tinkering with benefits—limiting the cost of living adjustment, for example. But politically, Social Security is a sacred cow and changes won't come easily. The most profound changes of the past 10 years have been increased taxes on Social Security benefits.

As the huge baby boom generation moves from paying taxes to collecting benefits, there's no doubt that the system will come under increasing strain. A sluggish economy—leading to fewer workers earning less on which to pay Social Security taxes—would add to the strain.

However, you do yourself a disservice—and put unnecessary strain on your retirement planning—if you assume that the system will go broke and the government will renege on its promise. That will not happen. You can count on Social Security's filling an important part of your retirement income need.

Naturally, it won't replace all of your income; it was never meant to. But if your preretirement income is at or below the Social Security wage base, a replacement of 27 percent to 42 percent of it is a valuable piece of your retirement puzzle. Sure, you will need other major retirement-income sources to make up the difference—that is what this guide is for.

Chapter 6

COPING WITH A RETURN MIGRATION

Thomas Wolfe may have written that "you can't go home again," but try telling that to children—or aging parents—who want to invade your empty nest. Saying no may be impossible when many of the 20- and 30-something crowd are "boomeranging" each year.

Many experts advise that any return migration should occur only if the parties involved can agree to some general rules. Among the points that should be considered

- ROOM AND BOARD. Returning children should offer to fork over some of their take-home pay for room and board. If they don't have a job, additional household work could substitute or plans made to pay when their cash flows again. Many empty nesters refuse money from live-in adult children because they wish them to remain unaware of their financial needs.

- LEAVING. A target departure date should be set before anyone moves back into the empty nest. Although the date may need to be modified, every effort, on both sides, should be made to meet that departure goal. A deadline will frequently motivate the returning flock to get a job or save money.

- RELATIONSHIPS. When adult children move back in with parents, there is a tendency for everyone to revert to their earlier family roles. No one should allow this return migration to slip into a long-range situation in which the children become emotionally or financially dependent on their parents.

The best way to avoid this is to force a budget, similar to that used by the empty nesters on the children. As parents, you want them to save money, not enjoy a free ride.

Save Regularly for Both Your Goals—and the Unexpected

The best method of preparing for the unexpected is to understand the role that your retirement plan will play in your lifestyle—and its ability to cope with such things as financial disasters or a return migration.

We've explored the difference between saving and investing. But let's take a look at how a regular savings plan can create a "reserve" that is so essential to surviving the unexpected. Whatever amount of money that you can set aside or save will grow over time through something called compounding.

The Benefits of Saving

Naturally, reaching your goals will be possible only if you become committed to making investments in regular amounts every year, quarter or month instead of the occasional contribution. As pointed out already, developing a financial plan will enable you to determine the amount that ought to be set aside regularly. But you must make the commitment to save and put the money to work on schedule if you are going to reach your goals.

The first step in financial planning is to understand the basics of savings. The next is to provide an emergency fund or nest egg should the "flock" return to the nest. Only after the financial plan has been created and regular savings begun, can you begin to think about investing and, hopefully, enjoying your empty nester lifestyle.

HOW REGULAR SAVINGS WILL GROW

You invest At this annual rate of growth $200 per month for:

Years	5%	8%	10%	12%
5	13,660	14,800	15,620	16,500
10	31,180	36,840	41,320	46,460
15	53,680	69,660	83,580	100,920
20	82,560	118,580	153,140	199,820
25	119,600	196,480	267,580	379,520

Banking Your Liquid Wealth

It is important to keep some of your money readily available (liquid, as the experts term it) for a number of reasons. With liquid assets, you won't have to tap your long-term investments whenever you need money. Cash reserves will also enable you to take advantage of investment opportunities when they come along. Or more to the point, liquid funds help lessen the disruption of your lifestyle and your retirement plans that can result from demands by your family.

Liquid wealth includes bank accounts, certificates of deposit and money funds. Some people include as liquid wealth the cash value of their life insurance and the credit available on their credit cards and home equity loans, because these are all money sources that can be quickly and easily tapped in an emergency. Remember, however, with interest, these can be expensive sources of cash.

The Four Types of Bank Accounts

Most bank accounts fall into four categories:

- Regular checking accounts which charge a monthly fee or a certain amount per check, both of which may be reduced or eliminated if you keep balances above a certain figure.

- Interest checking accounts require a higher minimum balance and vary as to interest rates and fees.

- Regular savings accounts allow limited withdrawals and generally pay a low rate of interest.

- Super NOW accounts, sometimes called money market accounts, pay higher rates of interest. They typically allow a limited number of checks and other withdrawals and require higher minimum balances than other accounts.

Which Checking Account is Best for You?

If you maintain a small balance or spend it down to practically nothing each month, a no-interest checking account may be best. For a higher balance, choose an interest-bearing checking account. Better yet, find a bank that links your checking and savings accounts, so money kept in a higher interest savings account counts toward the minimum balance for interest checking. If you occasionally overdraw your account, seek a bank account with overdraft protection (a line of credit that is automatically tapped if you overdraw your account). The interest charged is high, so use overdraft protection sparingly.

The Time Value of Money

Financial planning, as should becoming increasingly more and more evident, is a process of setting goals, determining your financial resources and then taking the steps needed in order to reach those goals. A key element in that process is time.

Understanding the relationship between time and money can help every empty nester develop the appropriate strategy for his or her financial future. And once you have that strategy in place, time will be your most powerful ally in making it a success. The more years that time can be allowed to work for you, the more likely you will be able to reach your goals. That's because where money is concerned, time makes all the difference.

Time works its effect on money through a phenomenon known as compound interest. The compounding of interest is sometimes described as a miracle and it's easy to see why. Interest compounds as earnings from your principal are reinvested and then generate earnings of their own.

Seemingly by magic, money begets more money, doubling, tripling, quadrupling, and so forth as the years roll by. Even a small sum can reach colossal size given enough time. Consider, for instance, the $24 reportedly paid by the Dutch for the island of Manhattan in 1626. That amount, if it had been invested at 7 percent interest, would have grown to $1.7 trillion by now.

Obviously, no one has three or four hundred years to wait while money grows. Fortunately, even during much shorter periods, compound interest packs plenty of power.

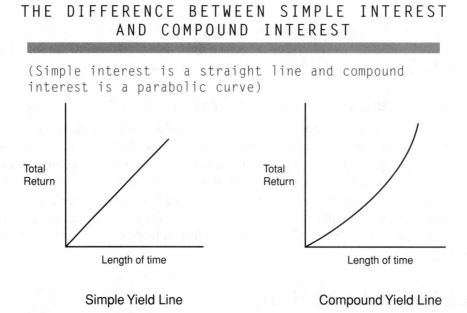

THE DIFFERENCE BETWEEN SIMPLE INTEREST AND COMPOUND INTEREST

(Simple interest is a straight line and compound interest is a parabolic curve)

Total Return

Length of time

Simple Yield Line

Total Return

Length of time

Compound Yield Line

The Rule of 72

You can explore the interplay of time and return with the "Rule of 72." When money doubles over a certain period of time, the product of the number of compounding periods and the rate of return per period will always equal roughly 72. Therefore, if you pick an annual rate of return and divide it into 72, the answer will be a close approximation of the number of years required for your money to double.

At a 7 percent return, for example, your money doubles in roughly 10 years (72 divided by 7). At 9 percent, it takes about 8 years (72 divided by 9) for money to double.

The Future Value of Money

A dollar received today is worth more than a dollar received in the future. Why? Today's dollar can be invested and earn a return. For example, a dollar in your possession today will be worth $1.23 three years from now assuming a 7 percent annual investment return and no taxes or inflation.

Conversely, a dollar to be received three years from now is worth less than a dollar received today. Using the same assumptions, a dollar received in three years has a present value of only 82 cents. Putting it another way, the 82 cents, if invested today, would grow to $1 in three years.

In this fashion, the mathematics of compound interest enables you to project the impact of time on money, such as the money that you expect to save and spend in the years ahead.

If you are planning for retirement, for instance, you can use the mathematics of compound interest to estimate your living costs over the period of years when you expect to be retired. Likewise, you can use it to figure how much to save each year to build a certain size nest egg by retirement—and to estimate how long that money will last.

Risk Management

Not all events in life are predictable. Some things, such as disability or premature death, may be highly unlikely. But they nonetheless may pose a meaningful risk to your financial well-being. As you've already seen, an important part of financial planning involves taking steps to protect yourself—and your family—from risk.

So it is with a return migration to the empty nest. While it is a good idea to have readily available cash or savings to handle unexpected events such as this, insurance is obviously called for. How can you insure against the family returning to the fold or elderly family members needing to move in?

A good solution is to help the family to avoid those situations that might make a move into your empty nest a necessity. If you can accomplish this as an overall part of building your retirement nest egg, so much the better.

Can You Trust in a Trust to Head off the Unforseen?

A trust is a form of property ownership that is used quite commonly in estate planning (see Chapter 20). Trusts are arrangements under which you transfer title to property to a trustee (who can be yourself) with instructions on what to do with it, such as pay the income or principal to a beneficiary or accumulate the income for payment at some future date.

Trusts provide a great deal of flexibility in planning to manage estate taxes and pass property to your heirs. They are also useful in helping family members today rather than wait until after you are dead.

Trusts come in two basic types: (1) irrevocable, meaning that you can't amend, revoke or change the trust in any way, and (2) revocable, meaning it can be amended or even revoked entirely. You might use an irrevocable trust to remove property and any future appreciation from an estate, but you must be willing to give up complete control of the property.

If you retain certain powers in the trust, such as the trust income or a right to change a beneficiary, the trust property will be included in your estate because you didn't give up complete control of the trust assets. Also keep in mind that because you give up control over the property that you give to the trust, you have made a gift for which there may be gift tax consequences.

As we'll see later (Chapter 20), irrevocable trusts are commonly used to remove life insurance from the value of the deceased's gross estate since an insurance policy (especially a term insurance policy without cash value) doesn't do you much good during your life.

The other main type of trust, the revocable trust, is also known as a living trust. This trust can be canceled or revoked so you have the power to get back any assets that you transfer to it. For most purposes, you retain control over the property; you've simply changed title to it from yourself to the trust.

Revocable trusts don't help remove assets from your estate since you still retain control over the property that you transfer to them. But those revocable trusts are valuable tools for avoiding probate since assets that pass under the trust agreement aren't controlled by your will and, thus, don't go through the probate process.

TYPES OF TRUSTS

REVOCABLE	IRREVOCABLE
Can be revoked/amended	Cannot be revoked
Frequently used to avoid probate on trust assets	Often used to remove insurance from both spouse's estates
During life, income taxed to grantor	Income usually taxed to beneficiaries or trust
After death, income taxed to beneficiaries or trust	Usually excluded from grantor's estate
Trust assets included in grantor's estate	
No gift tax	May be gift tax

NOTE: CRUMMEY TRUSTS

There is another type of trust that can also be useful to empty nesters. Called a "Crummey Trust" after the court decision that recognized it, this trust basically allows the distribution of principal and income at the trustee's discretion but does not require the mandatory termination of the trust when the child reaches 21. Instead, the trust documents may allow for the distribution of the principal in stages.

The requirement, however, is that the trustee must notify the beneficiary child annually of his or her right to withdraw over a reasonable period—usually 30 to 60 days—any gifts made to the trust during the year.

Whether a child actually withdraws anything from the trust, that child will be taxed each year on the amount of the trust income that could have been withdrawn.

```
              Since Crummey Trusts are extremely complicated and
              because, under some circumstances, they may actu-
              ally increase the overall tax liability of a child
              older than 14, consult a tax adviser before
              attempting to create one.
```

Giving Directly: Lifetime Gifts

Under our income tax rules, the annual gift tax exclusion allows you to give up to $10,000 per year to any number of people ($20,000 per year for married couples who file a split gift election). Those same rules also allow for direct payments of tuition to educational institutions and of medical expenses paid directly to a medical provider.

While gifts to children and even to grandchildren are a convenient way for affluent families to reduce the size of their taxable estate during their lifetimes, you should be cautioned against being so generous that you end up jeopardizing your own financial well-being. After all, at this stage, you should be in the process of accumulating assets to support you during retirement—and insuring that some of those assets are liquid enough to cope with the financial strain of a return migration.

```
              NOTE: The common practice of the elderly of giving
              money to relatives so that they can qualify for
              Medicaid in the event that they have to go to a
              nursing home is full of pitfalls. The biggest
              problem is that they may not get the money back if
              and when they later need it.
```

Below-Market Interest Loans

Since you are attempting to accumulate assets for retirement, the idea of "lending" money to children or other family members on a temporary basis might appeal to you. You should be aware, however, that the Internal Revenue Service takes a close look at all transactions between family members. They can even restructure those transactions that impact significantly on the tax bills of the parties involved.

Imputed Interest on Below-Market or Interest-Free Loans

Under our tax laws, loans that carry little or no interest are generally recharacterized by the Internal Revenue Service as arm's length transactions in which the lender is treated as having made a loan to the borrower bearing the statutory Federal rate of interest.

In other words, if you offer to loan your children money in an effort to help them remain outside the now empty nest, that loan must be treated in the same manner as a loan to a non-family member. If that loan calls for no interest payments or interest payments at a very low rate, the ever-vigilant IRS can and will restructure the transaction—as soon as they discover it. That means that you, as the lender, will be treated as having received taxable interest income that was never paid. Or, with a worst case scenario, that loan could be treated as a gift—with gift taxes due. And all simply because you failed to treat the transaction as you would a legitimate arm's length transaction.

Concurrently, there is deemed to have been a transfer in the form of a gift, dividend, contribution to capital, compensation or other manner of payment (depending upon the nature of the loan) from the lender to the borrower which, in turn, is retransferred by the borrower to the lender to satisfy the accruing interest.

This rule applies to (1) gift loans, (2) corporation-shareholder loans, (3) compensation loans between employer and employee or between independent contractor and client, (4) tax avoidance loans, (5) any below-market interest loan in which the interest arrangement has a significant effect on either the lender's or the borrower's tax liability, and (6) loans to any qualified continuing care facility not exempt.

In the case of a demand loan or a gift loan, the imputed interest amount is deemed to be transferred from the lender to the borrower on the last day of the calendar year of the loan. As for a term loan (other than a gift loan), there is an imputed transfer from the lender to the borrower, in an amount equal to the excess of the amount loaned over the present value of all payments required under the loan, which is deemed to have taken place on the date the loan was made.

Exceptions: A $10,000 de minimis exception applies to gift loans between individuals if the loan is not directly attributable to the purchase or carrying of income-producing assets. There is also a $10,000 de minimis exception for compensation-related or corporation-shareholder loans that do not have tax avoidance as a principal purpose.

Further, in the case of gift loans between individuals, when the total amount outstanding does not exceed $100,000, the amount deemed transferred from the borrower to the lender at the end of the year will be imputed to the lender only to the extent of the borrower's annual net investment income. If such income is less than $10,000, no imputed interest is deemed transferred to the lender.

A Helping Hand from the Tax Rules

If you can't loan your children or other family members the money that they need to stay away from your empty nest, the tax rules may provide some financial relief. If you perform your good deed by allowing those who have flown the nest to return or those other family members who may really need your help, there is help for you in our tax laws. Consider the basic income tax exemption.

Tax Exemptions

The amount of a personal exemption (for both empty nester and spouse) as well as for a dependency exemption (for the empty nester's dependents) was $2,550 in 1996. This amount is adjusted annually for inflation. Thus, for 1997, the exemption amount should be $2,650.

There are five tests that must be met before any empty nester may take advantage of the dependency exemption:

1) The claimed dependent must have less than $2,550 of gross income for the year. This gross income test does not apply if the dependent is a child of the empty nester and either is under age 19 at the end of the calendar year or is a full-time student under age 24 at the end of the calendar year;

2) Over half of the dependent's total support for that calendar year must have been furnished by the empty nester;

3) The dependent must fall within one of the following relationships:

   a) Son or daughter, grandchild, stepchild or adopted child

   b) Brother or sister;

   c) Brother or sister by the half blood;

   d) Stepbrother or stepsister;

   e) Mother or father, ancestors of either;

   f) Stepfather or stepmother;

   g) Son or daughter of taxpayer's brothers or sisters;

   h) Brother or sister of taxpayer's father or mother

   i) Son-in-law, daughter-in-law, father-in-law, mother-in-law, brother-in-law or sister-in-law (the widower of the taxpayer's deceased wife's brother is not considered a sister-in-law); or

   j) A person (other than the taxpayer's spouse) who during the taxpayer's entire tax year, lives in the taxpayer's home and is a member of the taxpayer's household (but not if the relationship between the person and the taxpayer is in violation of local law).

4) The dependent must not have filed a joint tax return with his or her spouse; and

5) The dependent must be a citizen, natural or resident of the United States, a resident of Canada or Mexico at some time during the calendar year, or an alien child adopted by and living with a U.S. citizen or natural as a member of his or her household for the entire tax year.

Supporting the Dependent

In order to claim the dependency exemption on their income tax return, an empty nester must furnish more than one-half of the total support provided during the calendar year. "Total" support is determined on a yearly basis.

A DEPENDENT'S INCOME. Generally, in order to claim a person as a dependent, that person may not have gross income of $2,550 or more for the year. In fixing the $2,550 income ceiling, any income excludable from the claimed dependent's gross income (such as exempt interest, disability or Social Security) is disregarded. This income however, at least if used to any extent for the support of the dependent, must be taken into account to determine whether the empty nester has furnished more than one-half of the claimed dependent's support.

THE EXEMPTION FOR A MARRIED CHILD. Generally, a parent may claim a married child as a dependent only if the child does not file a joint income tax return and otherwise qualifies as a dependent. If the support test is met, a parent may claim a married child and his or her spouse as dependents. This is the case even though they file a joint return—if neither is required to file a return for the year (the filing merely being for the purpose of claiming a refund).

THE CHILD AND DEPENDENT CARE TAX CREDIT. A nonrefundable income tax credit is allowed for a portion of any qualifying child or dependent care expenses paid for the purpose of allowing the empty nester to be gainfully employed. The credit is computed on Form 2441 (Child and Dependent Care Expenses) or Schedule 2 of Form 1040A, whichever is applicable.

In order to be eligible for the credit, the empty nester must actually maintain a household for one of the following individuals:

1) A dependent under age 13 for whom a dependency exemption may be claimed;

2) Any other person who is physically or mentally incapable of caring for himself. In this case, the empty nester must either: (1) be able to claim the person as a dependent or (2) be able to claim the person except for the fact that the person had income exceeding the exemption amount;

3) The taxpayer's spouse is physically or mentally incapable of self-care;

4) Certain dependent children of disabled parents.

Qualifying expenses include expenses paid for household services and for the care of a qualifying individual. Services outside the home qualify if they include the care of a qualified child or a disabled spouse or dependent who regularly spends at least eight hours a day in the empty nester's home.

Payments to a relative may also qualify for the credit unless the empty nester claims a dependency exemption for the relative or if the relative is the empty nester's child and is under the age of 19. However, no credit is allowed for expenses incurred to send a child or other dependent to an overnight camp.

AMOUNT OF CREDIT. The maximum amount of employment-related expenses to which the credit may be applied is $2,400 if one qualifying child or dependent is involved or $4,800 of two or more are involved less excludable employer dependent care assistance program payments.

The actual credit is worth 30 to 20 percent of employment-related expenses for empty nesters with adjusted gross income of $10,000 or less. For those empty nesters with adjusted gross income over $10,000, the credit is reduced by one percentage point for each $2,000 of adjusted gross income (or fraction thereof) over $10,000. For empty nesters with AGIs (Adjusted Gross Incomes) of over $28,000, the credit is 20 percent.

Qualifying employment-related expenses are considered in determining the credit only to the extent of earned income—wages, salary, remuneration for personal services, net self-employment income, etc. For married empty nesters, expenses are limited to the earned income of the lower-income spouse. Generally, if one spouse is not working, no credit is allowed.

If the nonworking spouse is physically or mentally incapable of caring for himself or is a full-time student at an educational organization for at least five calendar months during the year, the tax law assumes an earned income—for each month of disability or school attendance—of $200 if there is one qualifying child or dependent or of $400 if there are two or more.

> EXAMPLE: A widower pays a housekeeper $5,000 to take care of his house and 10-year-old daughter while he is working. For 1996, his adjusted gross income was $25,000. Since there is only one qualifying child, the maximum credit he can claim is $528 (22% of $2,400).

Generally, a married taxpayer must file a joint return in order to claim this credit. However, a married person living apart from his or her spouse is usually considered unmarried for this purpose, except that the spouse must not have been a member of the household during the last six months of the tax year.

Also, a divorced or legally separated taxpayer having custody of a disabled or under-age-13 child is entitled to the credit even though he or she has released the right to a dependency exemption for the child or is not entitled to the exemption under the terms of a pre-1985 decree or settlement agreement.

Tax Credits for Elderly or Permanently and Totally Disabled

A unique 15 percent tax credit for the elderly or the permanently and totally disabled applies to citizens or residents who are (1) 65 years of age before the close of the tax year or (2) under age 65, are retired on disability and were permanently and totally disabled when they retired.

Again, married taxpayers must file a joint return in order to claim the credit, unless the spouses live apart throughout the tax year. The credit is computed on Schedule R of Form 1040. For individuals age 65 or older, the initial amount of allowable credit varies with their tax filing status, as follows:

Single individual	$5,000
Married individual, joint return, one spouse is a qualified individual	$5,000
Married individual, joint return, both spouses are qualified individuals	$7,500
Married individual, separate return	$3,750

This initial amount is then reduced by amounts received as pension, annuity or disability benefits that are excludable from gross income and are payable under the Social Security Act (Title II), the Railroad Retirement Act of 1974 or a Veterans Administration program or that are excludable under a nontax law provision. No reduction is made for pensions, annuity, or disability benefits for personal injuries or sickness.

The maximum amount determined above is then further reduced by one-half of the excess of the adjusted gross income (AGI) over the following levels, based, once again, on filing status:

Single taxpayer	$ 7,500
Married taxpayer, combined AGI on joint return	$10,000
Married, individual filing separately	$5,000

For permanently and totally disabled individuals under the age of 65, the applicable initial amount noted above may not exceed the amount of disability income. In determining this initial amount, special rules apply to a married couple filing a joint return when both spouses qualify for the credit and at least one of them is under the age of 65.

Disability income for the purposes of this credit means the total amount that can be included in an individual's gross income for the tax year to the extent the amount constitutes wages (or payments in lieu of wages) for periods during which the individual is absent from work due to permanent and total disability.

An individual is considered permanently and totally disabled for credit purposes if he is unable to engage in any substantial qualified activity by reason of any medically determinable physical or mental impairment that can be expected to result in death or to last for a continuous period of not less than 12 months.

Coping with the Return Migration

As seen, the best way to cope with a return migration is to attempt to provide a cushion against the unexpected. If legitimate loans or outright gifts don't work, perhaps establishing a trust that will pay the family members an income, without allowing them to gain control of your assets, might be in order.

If all else fails, our tax rules provide a number of tax breaks that every empty nester should be aware of—just in case.

From learning how to cope with the unexpected we next go to something everyone enjoys, their hobbies. And, best of all, how to enjoy those hobbies, create a "shelter" from income taxes and allow Uncle Sam, in the form of our tax rules, to foot the bill for part of the cost of those enjoyable activities.

Chapter 7

MAKING THE MOST OF HOBBIES

In the past, many promoters "hyped" investments in such exotic fields as oil drilling and exploration, rail car leasing and, lately, high-definition television. All have been touted as programs that could produce income tax deductions and/or credits that would offset otherwise taxable income.

Usually, an investment in any of these programs would generate two or more dollars of tax write-offs or deductions for every dollar invested. This was a pure and simple tax shelter, a device that has been largely restricted by changes to our income tax laws and crackdowns by the Internal Revenue Service.

The proper definition of a "tax shelter" is any partnership or other entity, any investment plan or arrangement if the principal purpose of such partnership, entity, plan, or arrangement is to avoid or evade Federal income taxes. Naturally, to evade income taxes is illegal, to avoid paying taxes is extremely tough but often legal.

Under our present tax rules, any item of income, gain or loss deduction is a "tax shelter item" if that item is directly or indirectly attributable to the principal purpose of the tax shelter. A tax shelter is an investment with a greater than 2:1 ratio of deduction plus 350 percent of the credits to the amount invested.

By any definition, however, tax shelters have gained a bad reputation. Fortunately, it still remains perfectly legal to use any legitimate method in order to "avoid" income taxes. Suppose, then, that there was a perfectly legal method of reducing your current tax bill while, at the same time, enjoying a hobby or other activity. You would, in essence, have your own do-it-yourself tax shelter.

It is true! Uncle Sam, in the form of our income tax laws, will actually help underwrite a portion of the costs that you incur while enjoying any activity which has the potential to make money. This unique loophole in our tax rules stems largely from the hobby business rules of our tax laws.

Hobby Businesses and the Tax Law

According to our tax laws, the income generated by any activity or hobby is taxable. A surprising number of empty nesters simply ignore any income or money that has been generated from those hobby-related activities; others use a portion of the expenses of that hobby activity to offset or reduce that "hobby" income. A few astute empty nesters go one step further by utilizing our tax rules to create a tax business whose tax deductible losses can be used to offset or reduce income from other sources. In other words, their very own tax shelter.

Unfortunately, the ever-vigilant Internal Revenue Service always has the last word, frequently discovering overlooked income, disallowing tax deductions and simply shooting down many of those tax "businesses" created by naive empty nesters.

Our lawmakers have also increased the tax bills of many empty nesters by imposing limits on the tax deductions for hobbyists. Similar restrictions have been created by adding rules about passive losses, that is those situations where the empty nester merely invests in an activity rather than participates. Those same lawmakers have also frequently attempted to include income and deductions from those activities in the much-dreaded "alternative minimum tax" computations.

Fortunately, our tax rules are not as overwhelming—or as negative—as they at first might appear. After all, our lawmakers merely want to ensure that everyone pays tax on all income received. Thus, the empty nester who receives any money at all from a hobby-related activity can simply report it as "miscellaneous" income on their Form 1040 personal income tax return and pay any tax due.

Of course, all "hobby" income may legitimately be offset or reduced using the expenses of operating or conducting that activity. The tax rules allow only expenses up to the amount of hobby income to be utilized in order to reduce or eliminate the amount of activity income that will be taxed.

It is almost inevitable that any income derived from a hobby-related activity is going to be reported and taxed. Thus, offsetting or reducing it with the expenses of that activity makes a great deal of sense. Many empty nesters have gone one step further by operating the activity as a tax "business." As a business, the losses, the amount by which expenses exceed income, can be used to reduce income from other sources such as wages, salaries and investments.

In other words, a surprising number of empty nesters have discovered that they can own a sailboat in the Caribbean, a farm, an airplane-related activity, a horse or dog racing, breeding or training activity or many other enjoyable enterprises, enjoy those activities and reap income or tax deductions from them. In other words, if they profit, they generate additional income with which to enjoy their empty nester lifestyle—and tax deductions to cut the tax bill from that activity. If, on the other hand, those activities suffer losses, qualifying it as a tax "business" will enable the empty nester to enjoy the activity and benefit from its losses as they offset, reduce or eliminate income from such things as jobs and investments.

Proving a Tax "Business" Exists

The well-known three consecutive profit years out of five (two out of seven with horse-related activities) is not a guarantee that the activity will be automatically accepted by the IRS as a tax business. Rather, those profit years merely pass the burden of proof that the activity is a hobby to the IRS.

In other words, with profitable years, the IRS has the burden of proving that the activity is a "hobby." Without profit years, the hobbyist must prove that a business exists; with profit years, the IRS must prove that the activity is a hobby.

Despite year after year of continued losses, many empty nesters have been quite successful in proving that their activities are a business. After all, all that is required is the "intent" to make a profit, not actual profits. That the activity is a business and that it is operated with the intent of making a profit, can be shown by using nine tests established by the courts and now included in our tax rules. Consider those factors:

1) *The manner in which the taxpayer carries on the activity.* The keeping of accurate books and records, maintaining a separate bank account for the activity and, most importantly, making changes to improve that activity's profitability may indicate a profit motive.

2) *The expertise of the taxpayer—or his or her advisers.* Anyone who studies the activity or consults with experts in area may be considered to have a profit motive. However, if the empty nester does not follow the advice of those advisers, the profit motive may not be present.

3) *Time and effort expended.* If a taxpayer spends a considerable amount of time on the activity, the probability of a profit motive increases. Fortunately, a lack of time spent on the activity does not necessarily indicate a lack of profit motive—if the taxpayer hires competent personnel to work in the activity.

4) *Expectation that assets used in the activity may appreciate in value.* A profit motive may be present if the empty nester expects to realize a gain from appreciation on any of the assets used in the activity.

5) *The success of the taxpayer in carrying on other similar or dissimilar activities.* A profit motive may be indicated, according to our lawmakers, if the taxpayer has a history of engaging in activities that show losses early and that later turn profitable.

6) *The activity's history of income or losses.* Losses in the early years of an activity do not necessarily mean that the empty nester does not have a profit motive. Such

losses are quite common in the early life of many businesses. If the losses continue beyond a reasonable period of time, however, a lack of profit motive may be indicated. Of course, if the losses are caused by casualties or other unforeseen events, it doesn't mean a lack of a profit motive.

7) *The amount of occasional profits.* If profits are realized only occasionally, a profit motive may be indicated so long as such profits are large in relation to the losses incurred in other years. Those losses should also be compared to the amount invested in the activity.

8) *The financial status of the taxpayer.* If the empty nester has substantial income from other sources, it is more likely that the activity will be considered a hobby by the IRS. Since a taxpayer might be motivated to use the losses from the activity to reduce taxes on the other income, the less income the taxpayer has from other sources, the more likely it is that the activity will be determined to be engaged in for profit.

9) *Elements of personal pleasure or recreation.* If an activity does not provide a taxpayer with any recreational or personal pleasure, it is more likely to be considered a business. Naturally, no activity will be classified as a hobby merely because the empty nester derives pleasure from it.

In fact, no one of these nine factors alone is conclusive of the empty nester's intent or lack of intent to derive a profit from the hobby-related activity. They are all, however, relevant and useful guidelines for qualifying any activity as a business for income tax purposes.

Although the existence of a profit motive can frequently be proven using the nine factors, many empty nesters—as well as the IRS—prefer to rely on profit years. Anyone can choose to postpone the actual determination of whether an activity is a business or a hobby. This determination can be made up to 60 days after the IRS auditors have disallowed the business loss deduction or it may be made at the time the tax return is filed if the empty nester doesn't mind drawing attention to the return.

As already mentioned, our tax rules clearly state that all income from any source is considered to be taxable unless specifically excluded. This means that all gains from the sale or exchange of property, receipts for services, profit on the sale of any property, capital gains and even rent received for the use of property used in the activity are taxable.

Hobby Business Tax Deductions

Generally, an empty nester, whether conducting his or her tax business as a corporation, an individual or as a partnership (or even as a trust or estate) may deduct from their gross income all of the ordinary and necessary expenses of carrying on that "trade or business." Naturally, no deduction is permitted for any expenditure properly classified as a capital expense.

Whether an expense is ordinary and necessary is based upon the facts surrounding the expense. An expense is necessary if it is appropriate and helpful to the taxpayer's business, according to the IRS. An expense is ordinary if it is one that is common and accepted in the particular business activity.

What is a capital expenditure? An expense that adds to the value or useful life of property is considered to be a capital expense and generally cannot be claimed as a current tax deduction. Capital expenditures include those for buildings, improvements or betterments of a long-term nature, machinery, architect's fees as well as the costs of defending or perfecting title to property.

Expenditures to keep property in an ordinarily efficient operating condition and which do not add to its value or appreciably prolong its useful life are generally deductible as repairs. Repairs include repainting, tuck-pointing, mending leaks, plastering and conditioning gutters on buildings.

Remember, however, the costs of installing a new roof and bricking up windows to strengthen a wall are capital expenditures recoverable only through annual depreciation deductions.

Another area of our tax law, Section 179, permits tax deductions of up to $17,500 per year for newly acquired business property that might otherwise be subject to the slower cost recovery under depreciation.

When it comes to that dreaded alternative minimum tax (AMT), the tax designed to ensure that everyone pays taxes despite loopholes and excessive deductions, you can fully include hobby income in the computation. The only hobby expenses that may be used to reduce the AMT income are those which can be deducted as something other than itemized personal deductions.

Profiting from Hobby Businesses

By now it should be obvious that a hobby-related activity that generates any type of income can be costly to any empty nester's tax bill. There are, admittedly, a number of methods of legitimately reducing the tax bite on that hobby income, but truly significant tax savings result only for those empty nesters whose activities qualify as a "business."

In order to insure maximum utilization of that "business" and minimum tax consequences from the many levies placed on businesses, understanding our tax rules is vital.

That is one of the things advisers are good for—as well as helping qualify a money-losing hobby, part- or spare-time activity as a tax "business."

More Than a Tax Shelter

Operating your own "business" for income tax purposes, means more than sheltering income from the tax collector. It means being entitled to claim all of the legitimate expenses of operating your business as tax deductions. Naturally, you won't be able to deduct the routine living costs as business expenses, but look at just a few categories of expenses and how they can further help reduce your annual tax bill:

HOME OFFICES. Those empty nesters who use their homes for business purposes may be entitled to a home office deduction. Remember, however, that no deduction is allowed for personal, living or family expenses. Thus, no home office expense is allowed if the home office or shop is not used to conduct business.

FIRE AND CASUALTY INSURANCE PREMIUMS. A premium paid for insurance against losses from fire, storm, theft or other casualty is a legitimate tax deductible expense. Naturally, it must be ordinary and necessary to the operation of a trade or business in order to qualify.

ADVERTISING EXPENSES. Advertising expenses are deductible if they are reasonable in amount and bear a reasonable relation to the business operation. The expense may be to develop goodwill rather than to obtain immediate sales.

LEGAL EXPENSES. All legal expenses paid or incurred in connection with a business transaction or primarily for the purpose of preserving existing business reputations and goodwill are tax deductible. It is not necessary that litigation be involved in order for legal expenses to be tax deductible.

TRAVEL EXPENSES. The following expenses paid or incurred while traveling away from home ordinarily are tax deductible: travel, meals and lodging; transportation, plus a reasonable amount for baggage, including samples and display materials; hotel rooms, sample rooms, telephone and fax services and public stenographers; and the costs (including depreciation) of maintaining and operating a car for business purposes.

NOTE: Travel expenses are not allowed for a spouse, dependent or other individual who accompanies the empty nester on a business trip—unless that person is an employee of the person who is paying or reimbursing the expenses, the travel of

> such a person serves a legitimate bona fide busi-
> ness purpose and the expenses of such persons are
> otherwise tax deductible.

DEPRECIATION. Depreciation is simply the recovery of the cost of capital assets over a period of time which our lawmakers have determined represents the "useful life" of that asset. In order to encourage investment in business assets, that depreciation allowance has been augmented with something called "Section 179" which permits a business to immediately expense or write-off up to $17,500 of the cost of newly acquired business assets in the year in which they are placed in service. If more assets are placed in service during that year, their cost must be depreciated.

Don't Ignore "Listed" Property

The availability of depreciation deductions for so-called "listed property" is restricted. This term embraces automobiles and other forms of transportation if the property's nature lends itself to personal use (airplanes, trucks, boats, etc.), entertainment, recreational and amusement property; computers and peripheral equipment; cellular telephone and similar telecommunications equipment; and any other property specified under the rules.

Unless this so-called "listed" property is used predominantly for business (i.e., used more than 50 percent for business), depreciation (MACRS—Modified Asset Cost Recovery System) deductions for that property must be determined using an alternative MACRS method.

If the property satisfies the business use test in the year in which it is placed in service but fails to meet that test in a later year, depreciation deductions taken previously are subject to recapture or payback in that later year. This rule also applies to any portion of the cost of purchased "listed property" that an empty nester elects to expense under Code Section 179.

In other words, if the more-than-50-percent-business-use test is not satisfied in the year that the property is placed in service, the property will not qualify for the expensing election. If the more-than-50-percent test is initially satisfied but is not met in a later tax year, the deduction taken under Code Section 179 election will be treated as if it were a depreciation deduction for purposes of depreciation recapture.

Automobiles, More "Listed" Property

Even though an automobile may be used more than 50 percent for business purposes, there are further limits on the annual depreciation that may be claimed. It was the intent of our lawmakers to prevent business owners, particularly those running small businesses producing mainly tax write-offs, from using expensive "luxury" cars as business assets.

The maximum MACRS depreciation deduction (including the Code Section 179 expensing deductions) that may be claimed for any automobile placed in service in 1995 or 1996 is $3,060 for the first recovery year, $4,700 for the second year, $2,850 for the third year and $1,675 for each succeeding year in the recovery period.

If after the normal recovery period for automobiles, the empty nester continues to use the car in his or her trade or business, the remaining basis or book value may be written-off at a maximum annual rate provided for the fifth and succeeding recovery years, whichever amount applies. This rule permits deductions beyond the normal recovery period.

Naturally, the above maximum ceiling figures are based on 100 percent business use of the automobile. If business use is less than 100 percent, the maximum amount must be reduced to reflect the actual business use percentage.

Starting Your Own Business

Starting a business might begin as a way to profit from an existing hobby or from a special interest of the empty nester. Whether that business activity succeeds, however, depends largely on common sense and what the empty nester views as success. Success, after all, can be profits or simply tax losses to offset income from other sources.

As most empty nesters are already aware, the income from any activity is taxable. That income, of course, may be reduced by the expenses of the activity in order to eliminate a tax bill. However, it is only a "business" that can go one step further by using the amount by which the activity's expenses exceed its income (losses) to offset taxable income from other sources. Thus, when starting any business, close attention should be paid to convincing the Internal Revenue Service that a tax business exists— especially if tax deductions rather than profits are the goal.

Not too surprisingly, many empty nesters are more interested in convincing the Internal Revenue Service that the activity is operated with "an intent to show a profit" than actual profits. A key factor in convincing the IRS is maintaining books and records for the activity. But records usually only document business activities while bookkeeping systems measure the income and expenses.

Common sense dictates the establishment of a goal and charting a course of action to achieve that goal. The tool most often used is a business plan. That business plan will also guide the empty nester to whatever goal is desired, help convince the IRS that a business exists for income tax purposes, and, with a little modification, even help attract the financing or capital needed to reach that desired goal.

During the preparation of a business plan, the average empty nester will discover many areas in which he or she lacks necessary skills and knowledge. Since one of the criteria the IRS has adopted for determining the existence of a business is the skill of the principal—or his or her advisers—the discovery of a lack of skill or knowledge exposed during the preparation of the business plan should result in a search for qualified advisers.

Common sense dictates that after the empty nester has determined just what types of experts will benefit his or her hobby operation and help it grow, the needed individuals can usually be found among acquaintances, business associates and friends or by asking them for recommendations. Every empty nester should keep in mind that an insurance broker, lawyer or accountant who is familiar with your particular type of activity may not be easy to find. But is that extra knowledge really essential?

Another pitfall to be avoided with experts is too much service. Just as the empty nester will usually pay extra for a lawyer specializing in a particular field (or pay more for an inexperienced lawyer or accountant who must research questions unique to the operation), there is such a thing as too much service.

Most small business start-ups do not need, nor can they really afford, the full services of an accountant. A hand in setting up the proper books and records with, perhaps, the preparation of income tax forms is all that is usually required by most small business start-ups. Similarly, beyond a few basic legal services and initial start-up or compliance advice, few small business owners have the need to pay a lawyer an annual retainer.

Many empty nesters operate their businesses as sole proprietorships, merely attaching a Schedule C to their personal income tax returns. Others band together with friends or relatives to form a separate tax entity known as a partnership. While the partnership passes all of its income and deductions to the individual partners, it is required to file an informational tax return explaining the distribution of that income and tax benefits.

Facing high personal tax rates, many empty nesters choose the corporate form of doing business. The corporation, after all, is a separate, taxpaying entity that can legitimately offer a number of fringe benefits to its owners/shareholders. However, since it is unlikely that a start-up business will be able to afford those benefits initially, perhaps a pass-along entity called an "S" corporation might be more appropriate.

While offering the mostly illusional limited liability of a regular or "C" corporation, the S corporation passes along the inevitable losses to the shareholder for use in reducing their individual tax liability.

When discussing the business plan and operating entity with the new operation's advisers, thought must be given to financing the fledgling enterprise. Bankers and other investors are more likely to invest or lend to corporations where the risk of running up against local usury laws is greatly reduced. Naturally, few small enterprises will obtain any financing without the owner/shareholder's personal guarantee.

Unfortunately, today few small start-up businesses qualify for conventional financing (with or without the personal guaranty of the owner/shareholder), even if a sympathetic banker is consulted during the search for expert advisers. It is here that our basic business plan again proves its value.

Most empty nesters will walk into a bank and apply for a loan with the first clerk they encounter. A successful loan applicant uses his or her basic business plan in the form of a "loan proposal." Employing this tool, shopping for a compatible banking executive or branch manager and taking into consideration which of the many services the banks sell and which might benefit the new business, the result will often be an extra "expert" to help guide the operation and the necessary funds to do the job.

By using a loan package, all information required by the loan application is presented only it is presented in a manner favorable to the new business. By employing a loan package or proposal, the empty nester can attempt to explain any potentially damaging facts or figures while, at the same time, educating the banker about the industry or the uniqueness of the start-up operation.

So that the loan package is not wasted, it can also be used, in fact often best-used, to attract investors, venture capitalists and even others who wish to invest in, become involved with or sell to the new enterprise. That's right, suppliers often extend credit in order to win business, particularly future business, from their prospects.

Other financing sources include banks (don't forget the many invaluable services offered such as checking accounts, payroll services and credit checks along with short-term loans); finance companies specialize in intermediate term loans in moderate amounts; government agencies and related organizations usually limit themselves to attracting ventures that will guarantee employment or require capital for plants and equipment; underwriters specialize in selling stock, another form of raising capital for the new operation. Funding is often available from family members and friends. Venture capital investment is generally limited to high technology start-ups.

At the same time that the essentials are being worked out, less tangible features shouldn't be ignored. In order to be considered as a tax business, for example, the IRS requires every empty nester to actually hold themselves out to be in business. The business plan that contains a section on promoting the activity, its products or services will both satisfy the IRS and take the empty nester a step closer to success.

The IRS looks favorably on anyone who quits his or her job to depend upon the start-up activity for his or her livelihood. Obviously, this is not realistic for many of us. A good substitute is the amount of time devoted to the activity—or the time devoted by employees or those experts. An empty nester who has enjoyed success in another field is viewed by the IRS as also having a good chance to succeed in the present endeavor, success that can almost be guaranteed by a good business plan.

Profits in relation to the amount of time and money invested in the operation are what the IRS wants to see. That old two-out-of-five (two out of seven for horse breeding, racing and training activities) test merely means only that the burden of proving the existence of a profit motive is lifted from the empty nester's shoulders. With profits, it is up to the IRS to try to prove the activity is a hobby.

That business plan to establish a goal and chart a path to it, backed up with the proper records and books to keep the new operation on course and, perhaps, indicate another path or a shortcut, increases the chances of success—and satisfies the IRS.

If the IRS is satisfied that a business exists, the ultimate reward is a helping hand from Uncle Sam in the form of a reduced tax bill. However, it takes common sense to start a business, particularly a hobby-related business that is either a legitimate tax shelter— or one that provides funds and benefits to enhance your retirement plans.

Chapter 8

TAX BREAKS FOR A SECOND INCOME

It may come as a surprise to many empty nesters, but there are people who actually enjoy filling their spare time with work. There are those who enjoy hobbies and have taken their newfound free time to convert those activities into tax "businesses" for additional income or merely tax write-offs.

Others have gotten into the habit of working long hours, overtime or even two jobs merely in order to meet their family obligations. Now that the nest is empty and those obligations reduced, they work simply because they enjoy it. It is also a good way to add to your retirement nest egg.

Boosting Your Income

Even if you devise and follow the perfect budget, you may still need (or want) more money—or just something to fill your newly discovered spare time. In addition to lobbying for a raise from your employer or finding a higher paying job, you can increase your income through a little creative moonlighting.

The best way to increase your income, however, is to take maximum advantage of all of the expenses that you pay to perform that job for your employer. Claiming an income tax deduction for those job-related expenses that your employer reimburses you for—and includes on your annual W-2 statement—is one way of reducing your tax bill. Claiming job-related expenses that your employer doesn't foot the bill for, produces even more potential tax deductions.

Deducting the Costs of Being an Employee

The performance of services as an employee is considered to be a trade or business for income tax purposes; thus, employee business expenses are generally tax deductible. Reimbursed employee business expenses are deductible from gross income (right off the top, in other words).

As a practical matter, however, most employees do not claim the deduction on their returns because employers have been instructed by the IRS not to report the reimbursed amount as part of their employee's gross income.

WHY DO YOU WORK?

One way to examine the value of your present work experience is to identify the "goodies," that is, the things that have kept you at your job all these years. Here is what 3,000 survey respondents said kept them at their jobs:

✗ Feeling challenged by my work.

✗ Liking the people I work with.

✗ The opportunity to learn.

✗ Traveling for the company.

✗ Working as a team member.

✗ Helping the company grow.

✗ Being part of a respected company.

✗ The income and benefits.

✗ Influencing the company's direction and success.

Source: AARP, 1993

Generally, unreimbursed employee business expenses are deductible only as miscellaneous itemized deductions and even that deduction is subject to both the 2 percent floor imposed on all personal deductions, as well as the 50 percent limit for meal and entertainment expenses.

Reimbursed Job-Related Expenses

The tax treatment of an employee's business expenses depends upon whether the employer's reimbursement or expense allowance arrangement is an accountable or nonaccountable plan. Expenses that are reimbursed under an accountable plan are not reported as income on an employee's Form W-2; hence, employees need not account for them on their income tax returns.

In this situation, the percentage limit on the deduction for meals and entertainment applies to the employer. That means, that the employer may legitimately pay the empty nester the full amount spent for meals and entertainment while limited in the amount that they may claim as a business expense deduction.

On the other hand, any amounts considered paid under a nonaccountable plan must be included in the employee's income.

If deductible business expenses exceed charges and reimbursements considered paid under an accountable plan, and if these expenses are substantiated, then the excess expenses are deductible as miscellaneous itemized deductions, subject, once again, to the 2 percent floor and the 50 percent limit for meals and entertainment.

Commuting Expenses

Commuting expenses between an empty nester's residence and a business location within the area of the empty nester's home generally are not tax deductible. However, a tax deduction is allowed for those expenses that are incurred in excess of ordinary commuting expenses if the empty nester must transport job-related tools and materials. An individual who works at two or more different places in a day may deduct the costs of getting from one place to another.

There is an exception to the general rule that commuting expenses are not tax deductible. If any taxpayer has at least one regular place of business away from home, then, and only then, will daily transportation expenses for commuting between that individual's residence and a temporary work location be permitted as a tax deduction. A temporary place of business for this purpose is a location at which the empty nester performs services on an irregular or short-term basis.

Travel from a Home Office

Empty nesters who use their homes as their principal place of business are permitted to deduct transportation expenses that would otherwise be classified as nondeductible commuting costs. A recent Tax Court decision permitted one individual to deduct daily transportation costs incurred in traveling between his home and numerous temporary work sites because the home was the individual's "regular place of business." However, the IRS has ruled that it will not follow the Tax Court's decision in a similar situation unless the residence is also the taxpayer's principal place of business.

In addition to claiming a reimbursement from your employer for job-related expenses or deducting those expenses on your own income tax return, empty nesters may create additional tax deductions from self-employment.

Going the Self-Employment Route

As we explored earlier (Chapter 7), almost any hobby can turn into a tax-sheltered business. So, too, any skill can be turned into a moneymaker. Then, as a self-employed individual, you can set up your own self-employment retirement plan—either a Keogh or SEP (Simplified Employee Pension Plan).

Self-employment income can be used to fund your retirement plan—and create a tax deduction—as well as deductions for many other items that you can only dream about as an employee. Even better, you can do this even if you have a retirement plan where you work.

The money that you put into a Keogh or into a SEP is tax deductible going in and grows on a tax-deferred basis until you take it out. That's right, contributions to a retirement plan by a self-employed empty nester are tax deductible. Earnings from the money invested in that retirement plan are also tax free. The only time taxes are paid, in fact, results from an early withdrawal or after you have retired (and your tax bracket is lower).

Home Offices for Employees—and the Self-Employed

A home office deduction is allowed to the extent attributable to a portion of the empty nester's residence. Naturally, in order for any home office or shop expenses to be deductible, the space must be utilized exclusively and on a regular basis as the principal place of business for the empty nester's trade or business.

The deduction, here, is limited to the gross income that is derived from the taxpayer's trade or business reduced by (1) all expenses that are allowable regardless of qualified use (e.g., real estate taxes and mortgage interest) and (2) deductible expenses that are not attributable to the actual use of the home (e.g., postage, professional fees, supplies, etc.). The home office expenses not deductible by virtue of this limitation may be carried forward to future years.

Employees

In addition to those who operate their businesses from home, employees are also allowed to deduct the expenses of maintaining an office at home. Of course, in addition to meeting the exclusive use test and being used on a regular basis, home offices maintained by employees must also be for the convenience of their employers.

> NOTE: Many employees and even some people who are
> employees of their own businesses have, in the
> past, attempted to circumvent our tax rules by
> renting the home office to their employer or busi-
> ness. It should be noted that the IRS discovered

```
this ruse quite some time ago and it rarely
escapes their attention. It just won't work as
even the courts agree.
```

Self-employed empty nesters and those who operate their own businesses are permitted to depreciate the cost of any capital assets that they acquire for use in the business. Capital assets range from a garage converted into an office all the way down to the computer system used in the activity. Generally, a capital asset has a useful life in excess of one year; immediately deductible business expenses, on the other hand, usually have shorter periods of usefulness to the self-employed individual or his or her business.

The self-employed empty nester will find what many small business owners long ago discovered: Uncle Sam wants you to buy equipment. To encourage spending on equipment, our depreciation rules permit larger write-offs in the early years when out-of-pocket costs are usually higher. There is even a special write-off or expensing election for newly acquired equipment that can be claimed in the year when it is first placed in service.

In general, a taxpayer can immediately expense up to $17,500 of equipment acquisitions in a particular year. The amount that may be expensed must be reduced, dollar for dollar, to the extent that the cost of the equipment exceeds $200,000.

Self-Employment Taxes

It should be noted that there is a downside to both owning your own "tax business" and being self-employed. That downside is largely represented by more taxes. Yes, Uncle Sam not only wants taxes on any money made by the self-employed but also payroll taxes such as those footed by your employer.

The combined rate of tax on self-employment income was 15.3 percent for 1996. This rate consists of a 12.4 percent component for old-age, survivors and disability insurance (OASDI) and a 2.9 percent component for hospital insurance (Medicare).

The self-employment tax, which is computed on Schedule SE of Form 1040, is treated as part of the income tax and must also be taken into account for purposes of the estimated tax. A married couple filing a joint return must file separate Schedules SE where each spouse is self-employed. It should be noted that one-half of the empty nester's self-employment tax is deductible in arriving at adjusted gross income.

Who Must Pay?

Any individual who is self-employed is subject to the self-employment tax, the purpose of which is to provide Social Security benefits. The tax is assessed on the individual's self-employment income. If net earnings from self-employment are less than $400, no self-employment tax is payable.

NOTE: Self-employed people may deduct the expense of business meals and entertainment before they determine their self-employment income—so long as they abide by the meals and entertainment limits.

Hiring Your Kids

Hiring the kids can help any self-employed empty nester to trim their tax bills in any of several ways. For starters, you may deduct your kids' salaries on your Schedule C to reduce your business profits. This, in turn, reduces the amount of income tax that you pay on your business's net earnings, which are likely to be taxed at a rate of 28 percent or more.

Reducing your earnings may also reduce the amount of self-employment tax, including Medicare health insurance (HI) payroll tax, you'll owe on your self-employment earnings. Remember, however, the self-employment earnings reductions will not be dollar-for-dollar, since as a self-employed individual you may effectively deduct a portion of your self-employment tax in determining both your net earnings subject to self-employment tax and your adjusted gross income (AGI).

Most empty nesters pay taxes through payroll withholding. Thus, they never see the money employers send to the IRS on their behalf. Taxpayers who are self-employed or who have substantial nonwage income—dividends, for example—usually must make estimated tax payments four times a year.

Under our income tax rules, it makes no difference whether you make the payments yourself or rely on your employer to withhold them for you. Naturally, the IRS still holds you responsible for making sure that the taxes that you pay throughout the year are adequate according to the law. Indeed, the IRS penalizes taxpayers who underpay their estimated taxes.

Controlling Taxes: Self-Employed Empty Nesters

On the plus side, business owners and self-employed empty nesters enjoy a great deal of flexibility when it comes to both income and deductions. Utilizing this flexibility permits them to keep their income—and their tax bills—at a manageable level year after year.

A business owner or self-employed empty nester with substantial income in one year might want as many income tax deductions as possible to help offset that income and reduce the tax bill. A self-employed empty nester with little or no income would, of course, try to legally postpone as many deductions as legally possible until such time as their is taxable income that would benefit from those write-offs.

A PERK FOR THE SELF-EMPLOYED

Here is some good news about paying health insurance premiums on your own. If you are self-employed you can now take a tax deduction for 30 percent of what you pay in health insurance.

Politicians played Ping-Pong with the deduction (previously 25%) for the self-employed, allowing it to expire five times between 1986 and 1995. Finally, with a law passed in 1995, the deduction was increased to 30 percent and made permanent.

But there's a hitch. Your business must show a profit before you qualify to take the deduction. And, you can't claim it if you are eligible for coverage under another employer-sponsored plan, including a plan that your spouse may have.

Consider these suggestions for smoothing out your own income and deductions resulting from self-employment:

■ If you are self-employed and you usually bill your clients or customers during the month, don't bill them until the end of December, so that they won't pay you until January for your products or services.

■ If you are expecting a large check in the mail that you cannot delay, consider taking a trip during the last few days of the year. If you are not at home to receive the check, you won't be taxed on it until next year—at least according to some experts.

■ Even if you are at home, a check mailed to you on December 31 will not reach you until the following year and so need not be included in your gross income until then.

■ If you receive a Form 1099 reporting income which you did not receive until the following year, you should include the full amount reported to you on the Form 1099 as gross income on your tax return and include the amount of the delayed payment as a tax deduction under the heading "returns and allowances" on your tax return.

■ Naturally, you'll save appropriate records, such as the postmarked envelope in which the payment arrived and records of your trip if you are not at home to receive the payment, in case the IRS questions the deductions or failure to report income.

The other side of the coin benefits from these strategies:

ACCELERATED DEDUCTIONS. To accelerate deductions for your cash-basis business, pay as many expenses as you can by the end of the year. Order and pay for office supplies that you will be using early in the year and prepay for business publications, dues and licenses for the coming year.

DON'T FORGET THOSE RETIREMENT PLANS. Save income taxes by setting up a retirement plan for you and your employees. A corporation may set up a pension or a profit-sharing plan.

If your business is not incorporated, you may set up a Keogh plan or SEP (Simplified Employee Pension Plan), with fewer reporting requirements. In general, you may contribute up to 15 percent of your net business income, up to a maximum of $30,000 per year, to a retirement plan.

Your contributions to the plan are, of course, tax deductible in the year that you make them and you will not have to pay tax on the contributions or plan earnings until you withdraw them. You have until the due date of your tax return, with extensions, to set up and contribute to a SEP.

A pension plan, profit-sharing plan or Keogh plan must be set up by year-end, but you have the extended period to make your contribution.

Social Security, Your Financial Plans and Self-Employment

Those Social Security quarters of coverage we learned about in Chapter 5 may, may be based on self-employment income derived in taxable years beginning after 1952. There are special rules to be followed in the allocation of self-employment income to calendar quarters.

The self-employed empty nester's net earnings from covered self-employment must amount to at least $400 for the taxable year. However, a self-employed farmer with actual net earnings of less than $400 may still be credited with quarters of coverage if his or her gross earnings amounted to at least $600 and the "optional method" of reporting his farm earnings is used; similarly, self-employed persons can elect to report two-thirds of their gross income from nonfarm self-employment, but not more than $1,600. In the case of nonfarm self-employment, there is a regularity-of-coverage requirement and the option cannot be used more than five times by any individual.

Starting a Business

This idea of staring a business as opposed to making the most of your present income and its tax deductions or earning a second income or income from self-employment is a good one. We've already delved into the tax rules governing a hobby that you might wish to operate as a "tax business." But, what about actually starting a business of your own.

The idea of starting a business after retirement has a lot of appeal for many empty nesters. You can be your own boss and set your own hours. But please remember: Don't start your business at the expense of your nest egg.

It's easy and tempting to sink a lot of money into getting a new business off the ground. The "big break" seems to always be just around the corner, if only you had a few dollars to get there.

A good rule of thumb when starting a business is to earmark an affordable amount to bankroll your business—no more than you can afford to lose. And be sure that the other elements of your financial/retirement plan are firmly in place before putting any money at risk.

In fact, one of the reasons using your hobby as a basis for additional income or tax write-offs was the low amount of money that you, personally, would have to part with initially. The wheelers and dealers long ago discovered the sense of using other people's money to start and finance their businesses.

Despite the low interest rates available today, money is tight especially for anyone attempting to start a new business. Fortunately, there are hundreds of books about finding money for this purpose and the U.S. Government's Small Business Administration is more than willing to help in that search for someone else's money.

Often starting your own business can be as simple as holding yourself out as a consultant. Or, you may offer your services to a number of potential employers. You are, in essence, starting your own business by being a self-employed, independent contractor. But beware!

Independent Contractors

It is only natural that many of those who provide services to a business prefer to be labeled—and treated for income tax purposes—as independent contractors. After all, as an independent contractor, the empty nester gets more tax breaks or deductions than an employee. Of course, on the downside, an independent contractor may end up paying more in Social Security and Medicare taxes.

From an employer's perspective, every business can reduce its already overwhelming paperwork burden and, in many cases, payroll expenses, by labeling workers as independent contractors. However, blindly treating everyone who performs services for a business as an independent contractor can prove quite expensive to both the business and the planner.

When independent contractors are used, the business can save on employer-paid employment taxes such as FICA (Federal Insurance Contributions Act or Social Security), FUTA (Federal Unemployment Tax Act) taxes and state unemployment compensation taxes. Workers' Compensation contributions may also be reduced or eliminated through the use of independent contractors.

But would you, as an empty nester, benefit from independent contractor status?

Who is an Independent Contractor?

The general rule is that an individual is an independent contractor if the person for whom he or she is rendering services has the right to control or direct only the result of the work and not the means and methods of accomplishing the result.

People such as contractors, subcontractors, public stenographers, auctioneers and so on who follow an independent trade, business or profession in which they offer their services to the general public are generally independent contractors. However, whether such people are actually independent contractors or employees depends on the facts and circumstances in each case.

Direct sellers and licensed real estate agents are two general exceptions to the employee classification and are considered independent contractors if certain qualification requirements are met. Generally, to qualify under the exceptions, substantially all payments for the services of the workers must be directly related to sales or other output (rather than number of hours worked) and the services must be performed under a written contract providing that they will not be treated as employees.

Employee or Independent Contractor

The IRS utilizes a 20-factor test (i.e., "common-law rules") as an aid in determining whether a taxpayer has sufficient control over a worker to establish an employer-employee relationship or if the worker is an independent contractor.

The 20 common-law factors have been developed based on a examination of court cases and rulings considering whether a worker is an employee. The degree of importance of each factor varies depending on the occupation and the factual context in which the worker's services are performed.

Examples from some of the 20 common-law factors indicating a sufficient level of control over the worker to establish an employer-employee relationship are

INSTRUCTIONS. A worker who is required to comply with the taxpayer's instructions about when, where and how he or she is to work is ordinarily an employee.

TRAINING. Training a worker to perform services in a particular method or manner is a factor indicating control.

SET HOURS OF WORK. The establishment of set hours of work is a factor indicating control.

DOING WORK ON TAXPAYER'S PREMISES. Work performed on the taxpayer's premises suggests to the IRS control over the worker, especially if the work could be done elsewhere.

PAYMENT BY HOUR, WEEK OR MONTH. Payment by the hour, week or month generally points to an employee-employer relationship.

Examples of some of the 20 common-law factors indicating a lack of sufficient level of control over the worker to establish an independent contractor status are:

HIRING, SUPERVISING AND PAYING ASSISTANTS. If a worker hires, supervises and pays other assistants pursuant to a contract under which the worker is responsible only for the attainment of a result, this indicates independent contractor status.

SIGNIFICANT INVESTMENT. If the worker invests in facilities (e.g., office space from an unrelated third party) used by the worker in performing services and such facilities are not typically maintained by employees, this indicates independent contractor status.

REALIZATION OF PROFIT OR LOSS. A worker who can realize a profit or suffer a loss as a result of the worker's services is generally an independent contractor.

WORKING FOR MORE THAN ONE FIRM AT A TIME. If a worker performs more than de minimis services for a number of unrelated persons or firms at the same time, this is a factor generally indicating independent contractor status.

MAKING SERVICES AVAILABLE TO GENERAL PUBLIC. The fact that a worker makes his or her services available to the general public on a regular and consistent basis indicates an independent contractor relationship.

Don't Ignore Fringe Benefits for Self-Employed, Independent Contractors and Small Business Owners

HEALTH INSURANCE PREMIUMS. Accident and health insurance premiums paid by an S corporation for a more than 2 percent shareholder are deductible by the corporation and are included in the shareholder's gross income. Thirty percent of the amount included in income generally may be deducted by the shareholder employee.

DISABILITY PAYMENTS. Self-employed persons may deduct from gross income 30 percent of amounts paid during the tax year for health insurance for themselves, spouses and dependents. The deduction is limited to the taxpayer's earned income derived from the trade or business for which the insurance plan was established.

> NOTE: For tax years after 1996, the self-employed health insurance deduction will increase to 40 percent in 1997, 45 percent in years 1998-2002, 50 percent in 2003, 60 percent in 2004, 70 percent in 2005 and to 80 percent in 2006 and later years.

A CONTRIBUTION IS NOT A BUSINESS EXPENSE. A contribution to a qualified plan for the benefit of a self-employed individual is not a business expense of that individual. Thus, it is not deductible on Schedule C of Form 1040 or Page 1 of Form 1065 (partnership) and therefore, is not deductible in calculating self-employment tax.

In the case of a sole proprietorship, such a contribution may only be claimed as an adjustment to income on page 1 of Form 1040. In the case of a partnership, it is shown on Schedule K-1 of Form 1065 and carried to page 1 of Form 1040 as an adjustment to income.

Which Path to Tax Deductions or More Income?

Every empty nester has a number of paths that they can take from empty nest to retirement—or beyond. Merely utilizing an already existing and enjoyable hobby activity as a tax business to generate tax deductions or income is one enjoyable option.

Reaping as many income tax deductions as possible from your status as an employee means more after-tax money available for your retirement nest egg. Or perhaps you'll choose to earn additional income from a second job or from self-employment.

Starting a business will initially be a drain on your finances unless you tap other people's money, but the accompanying variety of available tax deductions may make this path worthwhile. Or maybe simply operating as an independent contractor will produce the tax deductions and income needed to meet your retirement plan.

There is also another option that can produce both tax deductions and income: your collectibles.

Chapter 9

PROFITING FROM COLLECTIBLES

Although it already has been pointed out, it bears repeating that now, with the nest empty, is a good time to utilize your newly discovered spare time in order to enjoy heretofore neglected hobby activities or even to find a second job or change careers. Additional income and/or tax breaks are an added bonus as has been demonstrated. Now it is time to think about collectibles.

That's right, the stamps that you collected as a child, your long-forgotten coin collection or even that barbed wire collection of cousin Jake, can all provide income, tax breaks and enjoyment to an empty nester.

Collectibles can best be defined as rare objects collected by investors. Examples are stamps, coins, Oriental rugs, antiques, baseball cards and photographs. Notice the fact that they are all "investments."

Collectibles typically rise in value during inflationary periods although they are far too risky to be valid investments for IRAs or self-directed Keogh plans. In fact, among the drawbacks of collectibles are the need for high security and expensive insurance, their poor liquidity, the lack of income and even the possibility of forgeries.

Fortunately, collectibles enjoy just as many tax benefits as do the other investments that you will be using to ensure a financially secure retirement. Enjoyment, increasing values and, most importantly, tax benefits are all possible with collectibles. Wherever the area of your interest lies, collectibles provide an excellent place to illustrate how our tax laws impact on all of the investments that you will be making as part of your retirement plan.

Off-the-Wall Collectibles Are Also Valuable

In recent years, the collectibles field has attracted a number of specialties that hardly seem to justify the title "collectible." Who, after all, would find beauty and value in barbed wire? To most of us, old bottles are merely something our parents used before plastic containers became so popular. Surprisingly, however, these and many other types of collectibles have won a great deal of popularity in the last decade and offer just as many tax benefits, profit potential and enjoyment as the more mainstream collectibles such as antiques, art and thimble collections.

Regardless of where your own areas of interest lie, chances are there is an established market for your collectibles; books describing the best way to collect, preserve and sell those collectibles; and a number of magazines that devote their pages to exploring how others profit from similar collectibles.

Acquiring Collectibles

Collectibles are normally acquired through dealers, at auctions or directly from their previous owners. How a collectible is acquired is as important for tax purposes as the price at which it is acquired.

COMPUTING GAIN OR LOSS

The basis for computing gain or loss on property acquired in most common types of transactions is outlined below. This basis, after adjustments, is subtracted from the amount realized in order to determine the actual amount of gain or loss that results from a sale or exchange.

Type of Transaction	Basis For Gain or Loss
Bargain purchases	
Arm's length	Cost
Employee's	Cost, plus amount taxable as compensation for services
Relative or friend	Cost, unless say it is gift
Bequests	For property acquired from a decedent, basis is generally its fair market value at the date of the decedent's death
Cash purchase	Cost

Type of Transaction	Basis For Gain or Loss
Gift Property	Donor's basis, increased by gift tax in some cases. Basis for loss limited to lesser of donor's basis or fair market value at time of gift.
Purchase for more than value	Cost—but excess may be a gift.

Under our income tax rules, the basis or book value of all property is usually its cost. Where collectibles or other property is acquired in a fully taxable exchange, the cost of the property acquired is the fair market value of the property given up. Since, in an arm's length transaction, both pieces of property are considered to be equal in value, the basis for the acquired property can be expressed as its fair market value.

When it comes time to sell the property, gain or loss must be computed. For computing taxable gain or loss on the sale of collectibles or other property, the cost or other basis must be adjusted for any expenditures, receipt, loss or other items properly chargeable to the capital asset.

This means that to that basic cost of the collectible, the collector or investor must add all expenditures made to preserve, protect, maintain or improve that collectible. As the tax rules put it, this "necessitates an addition for improvements and betterments made to the property since its acquisition."

To that adjusted value (your cost plus improvements and carrying charges), other capital charges are added to determine the collectible's cost (for example, brokers' commissions, lawyers' fees, etc.).

> NOTE: Generally, expenditures incurred in defending or perfecting title to property are also a part of the cost of the property.

Collectibles and Property Acquired by Gift

If Aunt Millie left you her collection of teaspoons, while it remains in your hands, the regulations tell you how it must be treated for income tax purposes. For example, if collectibles or other property was acquired by gift, your basis or book value would be the same as it was in the hands of the donor (or the last preceding owner by whom it was acquired by gift).

The figures used for determining a loss on a gift of property is its basis (or book value), adjusted for the period prior to the date of the gift, or the fair market value of the property at the time of the gift, whichever is less.

Obviously, in some cases, there is neither a gain nor loss on the sale of property that has been received by gift. This usually results when the selling price is less than the basis for gain and more than the basis for loss.

In the case of a gift made after 1976 on which the gift tax has been paid, the basis of the property is increased by the amount of gift tax attributable to the net appreciation in value of the gift. The net appreciation for this purpose is the amount by which the fair market value of the gift exceeds the donor's adjusted basis immediately before the gift.

Contributing Collectibles and Other Property

Aunt Millie's spoon collection may help you solve another problem you're likely to encounter: a request for contributions. Why not kill two birds with one gift by donating the spoon collection Aunt Millie left you, and which you have no interest in, to charity. You'll have put that collection to good use, satisfied your charitable obligations and saved your cash for your retirement investments. And don't forget the added benefit provided by our tax rules.

As most of us are already aware, when it comes to cash contributions, the empty nester need only enter the total amount contributed on Form 1040, Schedule A—but written records are required to substantiate the deduction.

For non-cash contributions over $500, the empty nester must complete Section A, Form 8283, giving details of the donation, and attach it to their tax return. If the non-cash contribution exceeds $5,000, the empty nester must obtain an appraisal for the contribution, complete Section B of Form 8283, giving details of the donation, and attach Section B to the annual tax return.

What could be easier?

> NOTE: Appraisal fees incurred by an individual in determining the fair market value of donated property are not to be treated as part of the charitable contribution but may be claimed as a miscellaneous deduction on Schedule A of Form 1040.

Appraisals for Non-Cash Contributions

Individuals who make a contribution of property (other than money or publicly traded securities) valued in excess of $5,000, must substantiate each contribution with a qualified appraisal of the value of that property. An appraisal summary, made on Section B, Form 8023, must be attached to the tax return on which the deduction is first claimed.

The appraisal requirement is also triggered if an empty nester donates a number of similar items (whether or not to the same donee), such as stamps or coins, with a total value in excess of $5,000.

There is no appraisal requirement for publicly traded securities for which market quotations are readily available on an established securities market.

Substantiation is required for both cash and non-cash contributions of $250 or more for all contributions made after January 1, 1994.

Valuation Rules: Fair Market Value

Fair market value is the standard for determining the value of property acquired by a corporation for its stock, the value of a decedent's property at date of death, and is also used for determining whether and to what extent property received in an exchange is the equivalent of cash.

The IRS has recognized a judicial definition of fair market value as being the price which property will bring when offered for sale by a willing seller to a willing buyer, neither being obliged to buy or sell. Only in rare and extraordinary cases does property have no determinable fair market value.

Gifts of Appreciated Property

One of the primary benefits of collectibles is the fact that they will, in all likelihood, increase in value. This increased value can be a big help when you reach retirement age. You don't, however, have to wait until retirement to benefit.

We've lightly touched on the tax consequences of selling those collectibles or any other assets you might posses. Those sales have tax consequences, usually adverse or limiting. If, however, the collectible or other property is donated to charity, the benefits are largely on the favorable side.

The amount deductible for a charitable contribution of collectibles and other property that has appreciated or increased in value, depends on whether it is ordinary income property or capital gain property—or a combination of both.

Ordinary Income Property

Ordinary income property is property that, if sold at its fair market value on the date of its contribution, would give rise to ordinary income or short-term capital gain. The tax deduction for this type of property is limited to the fair market value of the property less the amount that would be ordinary income.

Under this category would come such property as the inventory of a business, stock in trade, artworks and manuscripts created by the donor, letters, memoranda and capital assets held for less than the required holding period for long-term capital gains treatment.

Capital Gain Property

Capital gain property includes any asset on which a long-term capital gain would have been realized if the empty nester had sold the asset for its fair market value on the date of contribution. As a general rule, gifts of capital gain property are deductible at their fair market value on the date of contribution.

Unfortunately, the empty nester's contribution must be reduced by the potential long-term gain (appreciation) if the gift is tangible personal property put to a use that is unrelated to the purpose or function upon which the organization's exemption is based.

A good example of donating property to an organization is provided by the gift of an automobile given to any charity. Chances are, that car will be used by the charity in the activities for which it is chartered. Donating Aunt Millie's spoon collection to a group such as the Red Cross or Salvation Army would, almost inevitably result in it being sold by the organization. Donating that spoon collection to a tax-exempt historical society would, however, result in a gift that could be used by the recipient organization and satisfy our lawmakers.

A Limit on Giving

Even giving has its limits. Thus, our lawmakers have imposed a limit on how much anyone can donate—and still claim a tax deduction. Generally, the charitable deduction allowed to any individual for any tax year is limited to a percentage of the individual's so-called "contribution base." This percentage is determined by two factors: the type of organization to which the donation is made and the type of property donated.

Any amount in excess of the percentage limitations for the tax year may be carried forward for a period of five years. An individual's contribution base is his or her adjusted gross income (AGI), computed without regard to any net operating loss carryforward.

Individuals also have a limit as to the amount of a charitable deduction allowed for gifts of appreciated property.

Contributions to (but not for the use of) the following types of tax-exempt organizations qualify for the maximum deduction of 50 percent of a taxpayer's contribution base for the taxable year:

1) churches or conventions or associations of churches;

2) educational institutions;

3) hospital or medical research organizations (not including a home health care organization, convalescent home, homes for children or aged or vocational institutions that train handicapped individuals);

4) endowment foundations in connection with a state college or university;

5) a government unit, state, Federal or local, if the contribution is made for exclusively public purposes;

6) an organization normally receiving a substantial part of its support from the public or a governmental unit; and

7) a private operating foundation.

There is a special 30 percent limitation on certain capital gain property contributed by an individual to the 10 types of organizations listed above.

Capital Gain or Loss

Although our present tax rules contain only limited preferential treatment for capital gains, every empty nester must characterize all income as either capital or ordinary as well as differentiate between long-term and short-term capital gains and losses.

Gain or loss from the sale or exchange of a capital asset (including most collectibles) is characterized as either short-term or long-term depending on how long the asset was held by the empty nester. If the empty nester has both long-term and short-term transactions during the year, each type is reported separately and gains and losses from each type are netted separately.

The net long-term capital gain or loss for the year is then combined with the net short-term capital gain or loss for the year to arrive at an overall (net) capital gain or loss. If capital gains exceed capital losses, the overall gain is included with the taxpayer's other income but is subject to a maximum tax rate of 28 percent. If capital losses exceed capital gains, the overall losses are subject to deduction limitations.

```
NOTE: The maximum tax rate on the net capital gain
(i.e., the empty nester's long-term capital gain
less short-term capital loss, if any) of individu-
als, estates and trusts is, as mentioned, 28 per-
cent. However, if taxable income, including net
capital gain, does not exceed the top of the 28
percent tax rate bracket (for example $58,150 for
single individuals and $96,900 for joint filers in
1996), then all long- and short-term capital gains
are axed in the same manner as ordinary income.
```

Neither a Dealer or a Deadbeat Be

A word of warning to the owners of collectibles might be in order: Several chapters back it was explained how hobbies could be conducted as a business instantly creating an excellent do-it-yourself tax shelter. The axiom: "Don't try this at home" applies here.

Unlike securities or property held by investors, securities or property held for sale by a "dealer" to customers in the ordinary course of business are not capital assets.

The tax rules clearly state that the capital gain and loss limitations do not apply to securities of a dealer, except for securities held primarily for investment. Nor do they apply to real estate sales by a dealer in realty, except for property held as an investment. Recently, the IRS has been lumping others into the broad category of "dealer."

A person who buys and sells securities or property for his or her own account is not a dealer. However, a person can be a dealer and still trade for his or her own account.

Because a collector or trader, as distinguished from a dealer in securities, is subject to the capital gains and loss limitations, it is important to distinguish between a "dealer" and a "trader"—in any field.

Clearly stated in the tax regulations it says that a "securities" dealer is comparable to a merchant in that he purchases stock in trade (securities) with the expectation of reselling at a profit. Such profit is based on hopes of merely finding a market of buyers who will purchase the securities from him at prices in excess of their cost.

On the other hand, a "trader" buys and sells securities or collectibles for his or her own account. A trader's expectation of making a profit depends upon circumstances as a rise in value or an advantageous purchase to enable him to sell at a price in excess of cost.

Limits on the Deduction of Investment Interest

The deduction by any noncorporate taxpayer for interest on investment indebtedness (which is reported on Form 4952) is limited to the empty nester's net investment income. In other words, you can't deduct the interest on money borrowed for investment purposes if it exceeds the amount of investment income.

Net investment income is the excess of investment income over investment expenses. The disallowed investment interest can be carried over to a succeeding tax year.

Interest subject to the investment interest limitation is any interest on debt that is properly allocable to property held for investment, be it securities, real estate or collectibles. It does not include qualified residence interest, interest that is properly allocable to a rental real estate activity in which the empty nester actively participates (see the tax rules on passive losses, Chapter 10) or interest that is taken into account in computing income or loss from a passive activity.

For tax years after 1992, the net capital gain resulting from the disposition of investment property is not considered investment income. However, individuals can choose to treat all or any portion of such net capital gain as investment income by paying tax on the elected amounts at their ordinary income rates. Thus, the empty nester loses the benefit of the 28 percent maximum capital gain tax rate with respect to the elected amount.

Embezzlement or Theft Losses

Every empty nester who decides to dabble in collectibles runs the risk of loss from a variety of sources. In addition to insurance, our tax laws can provide some cushion against those collectibles losses or any losses suffered by the empty nester.

A loss from theft or embezzlement is generally tax deductible for the tax year in which the empty nester discovers the loss. Naturally, no tax deduction is available for lost or mislaid articles. The deduction of theft losses is determined in the same way as other casualty losses.

Casualty Losses

Our tax rules limit any loss, at least in the case of nonbusiness property, of individuals to that arising from fire, storm, shipwreck or other casualty or from theft. Each loss is subject to a $100 floor and total losses are tax deductible only to the extent that the total loss amount for the year exceeds 10 percent of your adjusted gross income (AGI).

A loss from a casualty arises from an event due to some sudden, unexpected or unusual cause.

The amount of any casualty loss is the lesser of (1) the difference between that fair market value of the property immediately before the casualty and its fair market value immediately thereafter or (2) the adjusted basis of the property immediately before the casualty.

The amount of any theft loss is (1) the amount of money stolen or the lesser of the value of the property other than money or its adjusted basis.

Again, a personal casualty loss is subject to a $100 floor and to a 10 percent of AGI limitation.

Why Collectibles?

We've attempted to point out that many empty nesters choose to enhance their enjoyment of their newly discovered lifestyle with collectibles. Today, virtually every type of collectible benefits from steadily escalating values and can, in many instances, prove to also be quite good investments.

Collectibles also provide an excellent place to demonstrate the complexities of our tax rules. Determining the price of a collectible is much the same as for any type of investment property. The non-cash gift rules are the same for both appreciated property and collectibles that have increased in value.

Naturally, our lawmakers frown on collectibles as investments mainly because it is so difficult to value them. Thus, collectibles are not allowed for many tax-favored retirement plans. But as an illustration of how some areas of tax laws impact on investments in general and as an enjoyable pastime for an empty nester—with profit potential—collectibles are an area worthy of consideration.

In the next chapter we'll see how investing in an activity without becoming involved can lead to tax problems. So-called "passive activities" have more than their share of tax "Dos" and "Don'ts" as you will discover.

PASSIVE ACTIVITIES

A passive activity is any rental or other activity in which the investor does not materially participate. With certain exceptions, losses generated by passive activities may not be used to offset active income or portfolio income. Instead, losses from passive activities are suspended until passive income is generated.

The Losses from Passive Activities

In Chapter 7 we discovered how the losses from so-called "hobby businesses" could be utilized to offset income from other sources such as wages, investments and the like. However, if you merely invest in an activity that generates losses, you may not be able to deduct those losses on your income tax return.

Special rules limit the amount of loss that any empty nester can claim in a given tax year if those losses are from what our lawmakers call "passive" activities.

What Is a Passive Activity?

In the eyes of our lawmakers and the IRS, a passive activity is considered to be any trade or business activity in which you, the empty nester, invest but aren't a material participant. That means an activity in which you, the empty nester, are not regularly, continuously and substantially involved in the operation of. Even worse, for most of us, this also includes rental activities.

> NOTE: Because limited partners almost never materially participate in managing the trade or business of the partnership, limited partnership investments are almost always passive.

Generally, losses from passive activities may not be deducted from other types of income (for example, wages, interest or dividends). Similarly, tax credits from passive activities are generally limited to the tax allocable to those activities. In determining an empty nester's allocable loss, the so-called "at risk" rules are applied before the passive activity loss.

When our lawmakers passed the law governing passive activities, their intent was to discourage tax shelters. Unfortunately, the rules that resulted went far beyond that simple goal.

The present rules affect nearly every person engaged in a business. If, for instance, you are a shareholder in an S corporation, a shareholder in a closely held or personal service corporation, a self-employed person, a partner in a partnership or even the beneficiary of a trust or an estate, you cannot afford to be ignorant of the potential impact of the passive loss rules.

You are also affected if you own rental real estate or rent out other types of property such as videotapes, hotel rooms or tools. And, as a result you may face burdensome restrictions and paperwork requirements.

Ordinarily, at least to the extent that the total deductions from passive activities exceed the total income from these activities for the tax year, the excess (the passive activity loss) is not allowed as a deduction for that year. A disallowed loss is suspended and carried forward as a deduction for the passive activity in the next succeeding year.

Any unused suspended losses are allowed in full when the empty nester disposes of his or her entire interest in the activity in a fully taxable transaction. Most empty nesters use Form 8582 and Form 8582-CR to calculate their allocable passive losses and credits.

What Income?

Another important point to remember about our passive activity rules is that passive activities produce more than losses. In fact, they can generate two kinds of income.

One is passive income, which is income from a trade or business or even certain rental activities. The other is portfolio income, which includes interest, dividends, annuities, royalties, etc. The rules also state that income from personal services—that is, payments that you receive from services rendered—and retirement plans is considered to be nonpassive income.

Why this confusing difference? Although admittedly somewhat confusing, it should be remembered that passive activity losses may offset only passive activity income. In other words, your losses from passive activities may not be used to reduce other taxable income from nonpassive sources—such as salary or portfolio income.

Passive "Activities"

In order to correctly apply the passive loss rules, empty nesters must determine which of the operations that they may be involved in actually constitute an "activity" under these rules. One or more trade or business activities are treated as a single activity if they constitute an appropriate economic unit for the measurement of gain or loss for passive activity loss (PAL) purposes.

Once activities are grouped together or kept separate, they may not be regrouped by the empty nester in future years unless the original grouping was clearly inappropriate or becomes inappropriate due to a market change in facts and circumstances. Of course, the IRS may disallow and regroup any taxpayer's grouping of activities that does not reflect an appropriate economic unit and that has circumvention of the passive activity rules as a primary purpose.

One or Many Passive Trades or Businesses?

What actually constitutes an "activity" when it comes to your involvement in one or more trades or businesses? The passive activity rules require you to first determine whether your involvement with numerous (or more than one) trades or businesses constitutes a single activity or multiple activities.

Our present tax rules call for the application of a so-called "facts and circumstances" test to identify and segregate businesses into separate activities. In order to determine whether multiple trades or businesses qualify as a single activity or multiple activities, these five factors are given the greatest weight:

- Similarities and differences in the types of businesses.
- The extent of common control of the businesses.
- The extent of common ownership of the businesses.
- The geographical location of the businesses.
- The interdependencies of the businesses.

The interdependencies of the business activities can be based on the extent to which the businesses purchase or sell goods between or among themselves, involve products or services that are normally provided together, have the same customers, have the same employees or are accounted for with a single set of books and records.

Material Participation

As already mentioned, a passive activity is one that involves the conduct of any trade or business in which the taxpayer does not materially participate. Any rental activity is a passive activity whether or not the taxpayer materially participates.

If you pass the material participation test, your trade or business (or your rental activity that fell into one of the exceptions) will not be classified as passive. You materially participate in a rental activity or a trade or business if you are involved in its operations on a "regular, substantial, and continuous basis."

Generally, in order to be considered as materially participating in any activity during the course of a tax year, an individual must satisfy any one of the following tests: (1) he participates for more than 100 hours and this participation is not less than the participation of any other individual; (2) the activity is a so-called "significant participation activity" (see below) and his participation in all such activities exceeds 500 hours; (3) he materially participated in the activity for any 5 years of the 10 years that preceded the year in question; (4) the activity is a "personal service activity" (see below) and he materially participated in the activity for any three years succeeding the tax year in question, or (5) he satisfies a facts and circumstances test that requires him to show that he participated on a regular, continuous and substantial basis.

SIGNIFICANT PARTICIPATION ACTIVITY. A significant participation activity is one in which the empty nester participates more than 100 hours during the tax year but does not materially participate under any of the other five tests set forth above.

PERSONAL SERVICE ACTIVITY. A personal service activity involves the performance of personal services in (1) the fields of health, engineering, architecture, accounting, actuarial services, the performing arts or consulting; or (2) any other trade or business in which capital is not a material income-producing factor.

NOTE: It is not enough to merely satisfy one of the tests in just any one year. The IRS requires you to reevaluate your participation annually. You may be a material participant one year and a passive investor the next.

Passive Activity Interest

In 1986, Congress created a new category of interest expense: interest relating to passive activities. The tax law treats this interest much like investment interest.

For instance, just as you may deduct investment interest only against investment income, you may write-off passive activity interest only against passive activity income.

If you report no passive activity income, you claim no deduction for interest expenses. In other words, the tax law says that if an investment is a passive activity, interest expense on loans associated with that activity isn't subject to the personal or investment interest limits. But, you may write off such passive activity interest only to the extent of your passive activity income. If you report no passive activity income, you may not claim a deduction.

Fortunately, you may carry forward, indefinitely, your passive activity interest. It can be used to offset passive income in future years. And in the year that you dispose of your passive activity, you may deduct all passive activity interest that you haven't been able to deduct before. In essence, passive activity interest is treated much the same as passive losses.

What does this mean? If you borrow money to purchase a passive activity, the interest expense is passive activity interest expense and is offset against your income or loss from the activity to determine your net passive income or loss from the activity.

The one exception to this rule is a passive activity that reports portfolio income, such as a real estate partnership that earns interest income on its excess cash reserves. In this case, you must classify a portion of your interest expense (to the extent of your portfolio income) as investment interest (in which case it is subject to the investment interest limits).

Also like investment interest, you may carry passive activity interest expenses forward indefinitely. That is, you may use the interest that you are required to carry forward— the interest that you are unable to claim—to offset passive income in future years.

But there is one difference between investment interest and passive activity interest. In the year that you dispose of a passive investment, the tax law lets you deduct any remaining undeducted passive activity interest related to the activity. This break does not apply to investment interest.

Treatment of Current Losses

A loss arising from a passive activity is deductible against the net income of another passive activity—at least most of the time. Losses that are not deductible for a particular tax year because there is insufficient passive activity income to offset them (suspended losses) are carried forward indefinitely and are allowed as deductions against passive income in subsequent years.

Unused suspended losses are allowed in full upon a fully taxable disposition of the taxpayer's entire interest in the activity. But what if you don't have profits from your passive activities?

Without passive activity profits you may, as already explained, carry any losses forward for use in future years. But you must keep track of those suspended losses from each of your passive activities from year to year.

Consider this simple scenario:

The year is 1996 and you have invested in three limited partnerships—A, B and C. All these partnerships are passive investments and, under the tests outlined earlier, all are considered separate activities.

Partnerships A and B each generate $10,000 in losses this year. Partnership C, however, rewards you with a $5,000 profit. In total, you lost $15,000 on passive investments— that is, a $10,000 loss plus another $10,000 loss (or $20,000) minus the $5,000 profit.

The passive loss rules won't allow you to deduct your $15,000 net loss on your current income tax return. So you carry forward the suspended loss to future years.

The losses from partnerships A and B are used pro rata—meaning in proportion against C's $5,000 passive income, resulting in $7,500 of suspended loss you can carry forward for each partnership, A and B.

To do the actual calculations, multiply the suspended loss of $15,000 by the ratio of each partnership's loss to their total losses.

Partnership A's suspended loss is $7,500—that is, $10,000 (A's loss) divided by $20,000 (A's loss plus B's loss), or 0.5 times $15,000.

Now the year is 1997. Partnership A earns a $20,000 profit. Partnership B, once again, generates a $10,000 loss, and Partnership C again posts a $5,000 profit. You have a net $15,000 profit for the year ($20,000 from A plus $5,000 from C minus $10,000 from B).

You carry forward your total $15,000 loss for 1996 from partnerships A and B and will apply it against 1997's $15,000 profit. The result, you have reduced your income from passive investments in 1996 to zero.

Even better, as mentioned, you may carry over these suspended passive investment losses indefinitely, using them to offset as much passive income as possible in each future year.

What's more, when you sell a passive investment, the tax law allows you to use (deduct currently) all suspended losses from the activity you sold right away. You use these losses not only to offset your passive income but then any other income, including earned income, or wages, and portfolio income as well.

You add suspended losses from an activity that you dispose of this year to any current losses from the same activity and any losses that you recognize at the time that you dispose of the activity. All of these losses will be allowed in full, first as an offset against any net income or gain from all your other passive activities, then as an offset against any income including wages and portfolio income.

NOTE: What if selling a passive activity results
in a loss and the passive activity was a capital
asset? In this case, the loss on the sale is
treated both as a passive loss for the purposes of
the passive loss rules, including your passive
loss limitation for the year, and as a capital
loss subject to the capital loss rules, including
determining the allowable capital loss deductions
for the year.

Playing the Passive Loss Game

If you have substantial passive losses from old tax shelter investments, you might consider investing in so-called "passive income generators" (PIGs). A PIG may generate a positive cash flow as well as taxable passive income.

Among the more common types of PIGs are limited partnerships that operate ongoing, profitable businesses—a ski resort, a golf course or conference center for example. The benefit of these investments is that the income that they generate is passive. Thus, you may use your passive losses, current or carried over from earlier tax years, to offset this passive income.

How do you know which, if any, PIGs might make sense in your circumstances? First, remember that many PIGs are syndicated—that is, they are offered to the public through public offerings—and are actively marketed by brokers. However, special rules may limit the benefits from many of these syndicated offerings.

Once you've decided that a passive income generator may help you at tax time, you should compare a specific PIG to other investments and consider the investment merits of the PIG exclusive of any tax benefits.

In fact, using the same methods, you should compare rates of return. Also take a look at how the deal and the promoter stack up against others in the same industry. Make sure to include in your analysis any fees that might be involved in buying or selling both investments.

Another Strategy

Although the passive loss restrictions and rules were created to prevent anyone from taking advantage of the tax rules through the use of abusive tax shelters, there remain a number of perfectly legitimate methods of reducing the impact of the passive loss restrictions. Another useful strategy that you might consider applies if you own a profitable corporation that isn't organized as a personal service corporation or as an S corporation.

Simply transfer ownership of investments that generate passive losses to your corporation. Why? The tax law allows a corporation to use passive losses to offset its regular business income and it makes no difference if the corporation is closely-held or not.

> NOTE: This strategy doesn't really make sense if your passive investments generate income (not losses) currently or will do so in the foreseeable future. That's because the income that a corporation earns is taxed twice—once at the corporate level and then again when the income is passed along to you in the form of dividends.

Remember, you add together income and losses from all of your passive investments. So, if you find yourself locked into some older investments that you expect will generate passive losses, follow the obvious strategy and invest in vehicles that generate passive income. You may then use that income to offset your losses.

Active Participation in Real Estate Activities

It should be noted that you can also qualify for a special exception designed to help the "moderate-income" taxpayer avoid the passive loss rules and restrictions. This exception allows empty nesters to deduct rental real estate losses of up to $25,000 from their regular income.

To qualify for this so-called "loophole," empty nesters must meet three conditions: They must meet certain income guidelines, they must actively participate in the operation of rental property, and they must own at least 10 percent of the real estate.

As long as your adjusted gross income (AGI) is $100,000 or less—figured before you subtract any rental or passive losses—you may deduct from your ordinary income up to $25,000 in rental losses from residential or commercial rental property.

Unfortunately, under this "loophole" you will lose part of your loss deduction if your income falls between $100,000 and $150,000. You're not entitled to any deduction, under this exception, if your AGI tops $150,000.

What if your AGI is between $100,000 and $150,000? You must reduce the $25,000 limit by 50 percent of the amount by which your AGI exceeds $100,000.

Still on a down note, you should know that this $25,000 limit applies in the aggregate to all of your rental property. No matter how many rental buildings you own, the loss that you can claim cannot exceed the $25,000 total. There are no exceptions to these rules unless you qualify as a real estate professional. (See Chapter 3.)

Another Angle on Gifts

When you give away an interest in any passive activity to a relative or friend you lose your right, forever, to claim or deduct suspended losses allocated to that interest. Instead, the recipient of your generosity must add these suspended losses to his or her basis—which is otherwise determined by your basis or book value—in the investment.

What if, later on, the recipient sells the investment at a loss? Then, for purposes of determining the donee's loss, his or her basis is limited to the fair market value of the interest on the date that you made the gift.

If the fair market value at the time of the gift is less than the donee's basis (including the suspended losses), part or all of the suspended loss will be lost forever as a tax deduction.

If, however, the donee sells the investment at a gain, the fair market value of the interest on the date you made the gift is ignored. In this case, the donee's gain will be figured using the donee's basis, which is determined by reference to the donor's basis and the donor's suspended losses.

Passive Activities, Income and Losses as a Stumbling Block

Our lawmakers have succeeded in putting severe limits on the amounts that can be claimed as losses from so-called "passive activities." Fortunately, the investments that we've covered thus far, such as hobby businesses, not only require your participation, they are extensions of activities that you are already involved in or enjoy.

Even if you've felt the need in the past to "shelter" your income using devices such as limited partnerships, there are a number of legitimate means of utilizing past losses and skirting the restrictions.

For most empty nesters, however, passive investments should be avoided if at all possible. They have become a target for lawmakers bent on ridding our society of all "tax shelters" at any cost. Fortunately, if they can't be completely avoided, strategies exist for minimizing the impact of the passive activity loss rules.

Next, we'll start exploring the more conventional types of investments that empty nesters should consider. While perhaps not as enjoyable as hobby businesses and collectibles, these basics can be fun. More importantly, from basic savings to more exotic investment vehicles, strategies and techniques, savings and investments can ensure that your enjoyment continues even after retirement.

Chapter 11

SAVINGS OPTIONS

The founder of McDonald's, the late Ray Kroc, reportedly bragged about his business: "We work on the KISS system. KISS is short for Keep It Simple, Stupid."

Empty nesters should apply this advice from the founder of McDonald's when it comes to saving. The simpler it is, the more likely that you will stash money away in your retirement nest egg.

When it comes to creating or adding to that retirement nest egg, what could be simpler? You put money away now for retirement later. Consider a number of mistakes many of us make when managing our money:

- Lack of involvement. Only one family member is involved in money decisions, or worse, no one is in charge.

- No budget. If you don't have a plan for the coming year, your spending will be constrained only by income and credit card limits.

- No cash reserves. Keep money available to fund a family emergency or an investment opportunity.

Although aside from encouraging every empty nester to make retirement planning a joint project, little can be done to change habits ingrained over many years of raising a family. We've already attempted to demonstrate the many benefits of budgets when involved in retirement planning as well as in trying to enjoy your empty nester status. Now consider one mistake made by so many empty nesters: no cash reserves.

The Credit Crunch

Americans have become consumers, not savers. Net national savings have declined from 7.1 percent of gross domestic product in the 1970s to 3.4 percent in the 1980s. In fact, in three of those years, the savings rate dropped below 2 percent of GDP.

The country, as a whole, has a budget deficit because we spend more then we make. That leaves us increasingly more in debt to other countries while dollars needed to pay interest on that debt reduce the amount of money available for our own economy's use.

Obviously, an empty nester must begin to curtail debt and begin to save and invest once again. Even if you have tried to reduce your own debt and failed, now it is time to begin again. After all, success is merely getting up one more time when you fall down.

Just as with dieting to lose weight, many of us try over and over again before we become successful money managers. The first step here is to learn to save.

How Much Should You Save?

Your current rate of savings is a combination of many factors. For example, you may feel that you aren't saving anything and yet be socking away money religiously into your employer's retirement plan. Perhaps you feel that you aren't getting ahead because you have no savings and yet you are reducing your credit card debt at a rapid clip.

As we have been stressing throughout this book, you need a total of all of your current savings that are earmarked for retirement. To determine this figure, begin with your personal retirement savings, including any bank, mutual fund or brokerage accounts. These are your basic savings.

To the above, you will ordinarily add any assets in tax-deferred retirement savings programs, including individual retirement accounts (IRAs), company 401(k) plans, or nonprofit 403(b) plans. Don't forget to count monies held in other employer-sponsored retirement plans, such as profit-sharing and other defined contribution plans.

> NOTE: When you have calculated your total savings, check to see that you have not double-counted any benefits in your employer-related retirement plans. For example, your employer's plan may allow you to convert your savings into a fixed pension at retirement. In this case, avoid overstating your retirement benefits, use either your current plan balance or the pension benefits estimate—but not both.

In order to compute your true savings rate, you must take all of these things and more into account.

How much you need to save depends on your particular situation. If you are heir to a great fortune, you may have no need for savings. If, however, your savings aren't enough to meet all your future financial needs, you will probably need to increase your savings rate a little each year to meet your financial goals.

Ideally, you will end up saving at least 15 percent of your income for future needs.

WHAT IS YOUR SAVINGS RATE?

Increase (decrease) in savings
and investments   _____

Amounts in savings and checking accounts   _____

New investments in mutual funds, stocks
and bonds   _____

Principal paid off on mortgage and car loans   _____

Credit card balance reductions (increases)   _____

Increase in cash value of life insurance
policies   _____

Contributions to retirement plans   _____

    Total savings and investments   _____

Less withdrawals from investments and
retirement accounts   _____

Less new debt incurred during year   _____

    Net savings and investments   _____

Your net income

    Your total income from all sources _____

    Less income taxes and Social Security _____

      Your net income   _____

Your savings rate (net savings and
investments, divided by net income)   _____%

No amount of savings is too small. If you save just $5 each day, in one year you will have nearly $2,000 to invest to grow for your future. As you supplement your investments with new savings year after year, the effect of compounding will be staggering.

The Power of Compounding, Again

When it comes to savings, the sooner that you get going, the better. Why? One word says it: Compounding. When you invest money and reinvest the earnings so that they feed on themselves, the money grows faster than you might imagine.

How fast? The most dramatic illustration (even if it is not very realistic) is the story of doubling a penny.

Begin with just one penny and double your investment each year. How long will it take that penny to become $10 million? A hundred years? A thousand? To give you a hint, after 14 years, you will already be up to $164.

The answer, surprisingly, is 30 years. That's right, by the 30th year you will have reached $10.7 million.

Naturally, no investment can provide a 100 percent return on your money every year. But the same basic wizardry applies even on much more modest returns of 6 percent, 8 percent or 10 percent annually. The compounding effect makes money work hard for you—even if you save a level amount or start with a simple sum and never add another penny. But it works hardest if you give it time.

If, for example, you save $100 each month for 30 years, earning 5 percent annually, your total will be $83,570 (ignoring taxes). That includes $36,000 of principal you saved plus $47,570 in earnings on that money.

How Can You Increase Your Own Savings?

According to the experts, there are five basic methods to increase your savings:

- Control taxes. The less that you pay the government, the more that you will have left over to save for your personal goals.

- Control debt. Imagine the money that you would save if you never paid a dime of interest again. By reducing debt and cutting interest rates, you can capture more of your money for yourself.

- Increase your income. Extra income from earnings or investment, means extra money to sock away into savings.

- Cut your expenses. Plug spending leaks and reduce nonessential expenditures.

What to do with the money saved using these strategies? First, you have to put sums aside for emergencies or until you have enough to invest rather than save. The basis of this ready cash is usually in the form of cash or cash equivalents.

Cash Equivalents—Just as Good as Cash

Cash equivalents are short-term interest-earning securities that can be readily converted into cash with little or no change in principal value. In other words, you get your original investment back—no more and no less—when you sell, plus you receive interest along the way.

Cash equivalent investments include money market accounts (sold by banks), money market funds (sold by mutual fund companies), savings accounts, certificates of deposit (CDs) and Treasury bills. They provide stability of principal and offer interest rates that change periodically.

> NOTE: In contrast, bonds or fixed income investments offer stable interest, but the principal can fluctuate.

The interest paid on cash equivalent investments fluctuates when overall interest rates change. However, if interest rates decline—as they did in the early 1990s—investors who had a lot of money invested in cash equivalents end up suffering from declining interest income on those investments.

Because the interest rates on cash equivalents are generally close to the inflation rate for the same period, they are best viewed as a temporary parking place for your money while you are awaiting a more attractive investment opportunity.

CDs: A Cash Consideration

Banks and other savings institutions may offer certificates of deposit at whatever amount, maturity and interest rate they choose. This means that you can shop among banks to find the CD package that is best for your current needs.

Since you can buy and redeem CDs by mail, it is just as easy to do business with a bank in another state as with one across the street. You can also purchase CDs from brokerage firms. You'll pay a brokerage fee, of course, but brokerage houses often pay a higher rate of interest because they buy in large quantities so they can frequently negotiate a higher rate.

> NOTE: When investing in CDs, some caveats are in order. If, for instance, the interest rate that a bank offers is substantially higher than the going rate for CDs of similar amount and maturity, be skeptical. The bank may be in a shaky financial condition and so must offer the higher rate to attract new money. Of course, if the bank is a Federal Deposit Insurance Corporation (FDIC) institution, FDIC insurance would cover your loss if the bank went belly up, but not necessarily the interest that is due you. Also, your money could be tied up for weeks or even months.

When buying a CD, it is important to make sure to find out about getting your money out before the CD matures. In some cases, a bank or savings and loan can slap you with an early withdrawal penalty that totals the entire amount of interest that is due you.

You may not be hit with a penalty if you withdraw your CD before its due date from a brokerage firm. That's because these firms make what is known as a secondary market in CDs so your broker can simply sell your certificate to some other investor.

The low interest rates sparked by the recession of the early 1990s made bank-issued certificates of deposit (CDs) anathema among savers. Interest rates that were well into double-digits in the early 1980s sank to the low single digits, spawning a mass exodus from CDs into higher paying investments.

When interest rates on one- to five-year CDs are in the 3 to 6 percent range and inflation is running at 3.5 percent, CDs offer little incentive to the long-term retirement investor other than their Federal deposit insurance up to $100,000.

But remember, rates change, so you should never say never to CDs. If rates push near or above the 10.4 percent historical average return for stocks, they could once again have a place in your retirement portfolio. The protection of government insurance is certainly one benefit. The other is that when CD rates jump, stocks sometimes run in the other direction.

Based on historical interest rate swings, one good approach might be: If five-year CD rates reach 10 percent, stock up for your portfolio. By staggering the maturities of the CDs you buy, you can protect yourself against rapid rate changes. If rates rise, the short-term CDs in your portfolio will mature in time for you to roll the money into new CDs at higher rates. If rates fall, your long-term CDs will continue earning your top CD dollars for up to five years.

Taxes, Savings Accounts and CDs

Boring old savings accounts and certificates of deposit. The tax treatment is fairly simple and straightforward: The interest that you earn is fully taxable. Naturally, as with all taxes, there are twists.

Interest earned by a savings account is taxable in the year that it is credited to your account, whether or not you withdraw the money. Even if a savings and loan or credit union labels the income on your account as dividends, the IRS says that it is interest and that is how it should be reported.

With certificates of deposit that mature in a year or less, the interest income is taxable in the year the deposit matures. This rule permits you to shift taxable income from one year to the next and hold off Uncle Sam from one April 15th to the next.

If you invest in a six-month CD in July 1997, for example, the interest will not be taxable until 1998, when the certificate matures. You would report this interest on your 1998 income tax return filed in the spring of 1999.

Interest paid on time deposits with maturities of more than one year is taxable as it is credited each year. The institution where you save should send you a notice of how much to report on your tax return (Form 1099).

If you withdraw funds early from a CD, the bank or savings and loan is likely to exact an early withdrawal penalty. You can deduct that charge even if you don't itemize your deductions. It is an "adjustment to income" claimed on the front of Form 1040.

Savings Bonds

Although it is probably too late for many empty nesters to take advantage of this incentive, if you redeem U.S. Savings Bonds to pay educational expenses, the interest on the bond is excluded from your gross income—if certain conditions are met.

- The bond must have been issued after 1989;

- You, the purchaser, must be at least 21 years old before the date of issuance; and

- You must use the bond proceeds for qualified educational expenses incurred by you, your spouse, or dependents for higher education.

Even if you cannot meet the requirements for this exclusion, you may still want to consider Series EE Savings Bonds. Series EE bonds issued after April 1995 mature in 17 years, but you can continue to hold on to them and receive interest until 30 years after the date of issue. (Bonds issued between March 1993 and April 1995 mature in 18 years; different maturity dates apply for bonds issued prior to March 1993, but the 30-year holding option applies to all issues.)

You can purchase Series EE bonds with a face value as little as $50 or as much as $10,000 through banks and savings and loans, payroll deduction plans, the Federal Reserve or the Bureau of Public Debt. The purchase price is one-half of the face amount ($50 for a bond with a $100 face amount).

There are no sales charges when you buy a Series EE bond. Also if you keep the bond until it matures, you'll receive at the very least its full face value and you may receive more.

The government guarantees that at maturity you will get at least twice the amount that you paid for the bond, even if interest rates have dropped precipitously (this equates to an interest rate of approximately 4 percent). With the extended maturity dates, the interest on the bonds may continue to accumulate—tax deferred.

Unless you choose to report it annually, the interest on these bonds is not taxed until the bonds mature and you cash them in. (If you cash them in before they mature, any interest that you accumulated to date is taxed at the time that you redeem them.) What's more, interest from Series EE bonds is not subject to state or local income taxes.

Warning: Series EE bonds issued after April 1995 no longer provide a guaranteed minimum rate of return if redeemed prior to their scheduled maturity. In recent years, Series EE bonds were guaranteed to provide at least a 5 percent return, no matter when they were redeemed.

The new Series EE bonds will earn market-based interest rates, with no guaranteed income return if redeemed before their scheduled maturity. Also, the new bonds will earn short-term–based rates only during the first five years, credited at six-month intervals.

The result? The new bonds are not quite as attractive as earlier Series EE bonds for long-term savings and if market rates fall below 4 percent. However, the option of being able to defer or possibly exclude some or all of the earnings remains, making Series EE bonds a savings vehicle that is still worth considering.

Money Market Accounts and Funds

Don't confuse money market accounts, offered by banks and savings and loans, with money market funds, offered by brokerage houses and mutual fund companies. Think of money market accounts as limited checking accounts (you can write only a few checks a month) that pay daily interest in relation to market rates.

Because they are offered by banks and savings and loans, these accounts carry Federal Deposit Insurance Corporation (FDIC) insurance up to $100,000 and are thus generally risk-free.

As you'll see in Chapter 12, unlike money market accounts, money market funds are not insured by a government agency. But that shouldn't cause you much concern because those accounts are invested in high quality U.S. Government securities, commercial paper, bankers' acceptances and other securities. And the funds themselves pay a higher rate of interest than bank money market accounts.

Guaranteed Investment Contracts

If you participate in a 401(k) plan at work, a guaranteed investment contract (GIC) will probably be one of your investment choices—nearly three-fourths of all 401(k) plans offer GICs as an investment option and 60 percent of employer contributions are put into GICs when the option is available.

GICs are similar to a giant certificate of deposit issued by an insurance company rather than a bank. It is not covered by FDIC insurance. The contracts generally run one to seven years.

Managers of 401(k) plans often buy many GICs and put them together into a GIC fund. The money you designate for a GIC in your 401(k) then goes into that fund.

The fund approach is good because it spreads the risk over as many as 20 issues. The different rates of return are blended to arrive at the yield you receive on your investment. When the term of any individual GIC contract is up, your pension fund recoups the principal and either reinvests it in another GIC or returns it to employees who are retiring or cashing out of the plan.

GICs have delivered what their name implies—a guaranteed return. The major risk is that a GIC is only as good as the insurance company that issues it. And some insurance companies, burdened with junk-bond investments, sour real estate loans and the like, have seen their creditworthiness dwindle.

Are you at risk? While there is a risk in every type of investment, the chances that big insurance companies will tumble and cost you money is remote. Because GICs in an individual's company plan are most likely drawn from a number of insurance companies, the failure of one insurer would not necessarily cause a significant drop in your 401(k) assets. And GIC contract holders are covered by insurance plans in most states under the same terms as holders of life insurance policies.

Strategies for Saving

Here are some savings strategies used to promote healthy savings habits:

1) Tithe to yourself. Each time you are paid, take 10 percent and sock it away into your savings account. With each bonus, do the same thing. Ditto for tax refunds, auto allowances, and any other extra income that comes your way.

2) Stash extra money into your employer salary reduction plan (which may be called a 401(k) plan, TDA plan, thrift plan, etc.) or into a tax deductible Individual Retirement Account (IRA). As you will see in Chapter 13, the money earned by an IRA or this type of plan won't be taxable until it is withdrawn. Plus, you'll garner a tax deduction for the money that you contribute.

> NOTE: These types of plans are not a good repository for money that you will need before retirement, because withdrawals before age 59 1/2, are subject to penalties.

IF YOU INVEST MONEY AT 9 PERCENT

Number of Years		5	10	20	30
Monthly Income	Monthly Savings				
1,000	100	7,500	19,400	66,800	183,100
2,000	200	15,100	38,700	133,600	366,100
3,000	300	22,600	58,100	200,400	549,200
4,000	400	30,200	77,400	267,200	732,300
5,000	500	37,300	96,800	333,900	915,400
6,000	600	45,300	116,100	400,700	1,098,400
7,000	700	52,800	135,500	467,500	1,281,500
8,000	800	60,300	154,800	534,300	1,464,600

3) Payroll deductions that go directly to your savings account or into U.S. Savings Bonds are another way of saving because it is money that you never see. This plan will only work if you let the money grow, so don't defeat your plan by raiding your savings account or cashing your bonds.

4) If you receive a substantial annual bonus, live on your regular income and save your bonus, or at least a significant portion of it. Saving part of your bonus for future needs is like saving part of your dessert from dinner to eat later. You won't really miss it now and it will give you great satisfaction later.

5) The next time you get a raise, don't tell your checkbook. Deposit the old amount of your paycheck into your checking account and put the extra net pay into your savings account.

You will be depositing the same amount into your checking account as before, so like the magician's rabbit, your raise is gone. Hidden in your savings account, it will multiply like rabbits and you won't miss it at all because you will have the same amount to live on as you did before.

6) When your automobile is paid for, continue making the car payments—to your savings account rather than to the finance company. In a few years you will have amassed enough in your fund to pay cash for your next car. Keep it up and this simple strategy will get you off the financing roller coaster forever.

7) Increase your income by working overtime, seeking a second job or starting a home-based business (see Chapter 8). Deposit your entire overtime or second job pay or the profits into your savings and watch it grow.

Savings Versus Investing

It has been said before, but many empty nesters consider savings and investing to be the same thing. You may not see any difference between saving for retirement and investing for retirement. Both words cover the process of putting money away for the future.

It can be helpful to distinguish between savings and investing. Try thinking about it this way: Saving money means not spending it. Investing money, on the other hand, means taking money that you have saved and doing something with it to earn a return.

Separating the two notions can do a world of good. Saving money becomes easier when the choice not to spend is separated from the choice about where to invest. That's because saving is a simple, onetime decision. After the decision has been made, saving can be put on automatic pilot through a payroll deduction plan and accomplished in small amounts that fit easily into your budget. If you are not ready to decide on an investment, you can leave the money temporarily in the bank.

Investing, on the other hand, is not a simple, onetime decision. It takes time, and possibly even help from a professional adviser, to research and select individual investments. Whereas it is perfectly okay to rush out and start a savings program as soon as possible, investing should be done deliberately.

By separating savings from investing, you can help make sure (1) you are setting money aside in a disciplined, regular way, and (2) your investments are chosen carefully and with due consideration for your overall financial goals.

Next, we'll begin reviewing the investment options available to you, the empty nester, with an eye toward how each type of investment can fit into your nest egg.

Chapter 12

INVESTMENT OPTIONS

Employing or using the money that you have saved involves investing. Before exploring the many strategies that can make investing so enjoyable—and profitable—it is probably best to take a look at some of the tools that you will use in investing. At the top of the list, of course, are stocks.

Stock Basics

The term "stock" usually refers to common stock, which represents an ownership share in the company that issued it. If you own stock in AT&T, for instance, you own a proportionate share (tiny though it may be) of Ma Bell's long-distance empire. That share entitles you to share in her profits or possibly help shoulder her losses.

Common stock may or may not pay dividends, which are profits the company distributes to its owners/shareholders. Divide the current annual dividend rate by the share price and you get the stock's yield—similar to the yield you earn on your savings in a bank.

> NOTE: Many companies also issue a special class of shares called preferred stock. These shares generally pay a higher dividend than common stock but don't have the same price appreciation potential of common stock. They appeal mainly to corporations which get a tax break on their dividend income. Individuals don't get that break, so there's no good reason to include this more esoteric stock investment in your retirement portfolio.

There are six basic, sometimes overlapping, common-stock categories to consider for your own retirement portfolio: growth stocks, blue-chip stocks, income stocks, cyclical stocks, small-company stocks and foreign or international stocks.

GROWTH STOCKS. These are so-named because they have good prospects for growing faster than the economy or the stock market in general. Investors like them for their consistent earnings growth and the likelihood that share prices will go up significantly over the long term.

BLUE-CHIP STOCKS. This is another loosely defined group; you won't find an official "blue-chip" stock list. Kellogg, Merck and some other large growth stocks are, for instance, also considered blue chips.

Blue-chip stocks are generally industry-leading companies with top-shelf financial credentials. They include such household names as AT&T, Coca-Cola, General Electric, Procter & Gamble and Xerox. They tend to pay decent, steadily rising dividends (many blue-chip companies have paid an unbroken string of dividends for 50 years or more), generate some growth and offer safety and reliability.

INCOME STOCKS. These securities pay out a much larger portion of their profits (often 50 percent to 80 percent) to investors in the form of quarterly dividends than do other stocks. These tend to be more mature, slower growth companies and the dividends paid to investors make these stocks generally less risky to own than shares of growth or small-company stocks.

Though share prices of income stocks aren't expected to grow rapidly, the dividend acts as a kind of cushion beneath the share price. Even if the market in general falls, income stocks are usually less affected because investors will still receive the dividend.

Utilities are good examples of dividend-paying stocks to consider for a retirement portfolio—especially if you are within 10 years of retirement. As earnings rise, the best of the utility companies raise their dividends regularly usually every year and they have brought investors steady, low-risk returns with bright prospects for more double-digit annual returns.

One measure of any income stock is its yield, which is the annual dividend calculated as a percentage of its share price at the moment. And the yields on utility shares over the past two decades have been double, sometimes triple, the yield of the average blue-chip stock.

Dividends are only one way that income stocks make money for your retirement nest egg. The key is their total return—the combination of dividends plus growth in the price of shares. In other words, if a utility stock priced at $20 and yielding 6 percent rises to $21 in a year (a 5 percent gain), and the dividend remains steady, your total return in the stock is 11 percent.

CYCLICAL STOCKS. A stock that tends to rise quickly when the economy turns up and to fall quickly when the economy turns down. Examples are housing, automobiles and paper. Stocks of noncyclical industries such as food, insurance and drugs are not as directly affected by economic change.

SMALL-COMPANY STOCKS. Shares in these companies are riskier than blue-chip or income stocks but, as a group, their long-term average returns are also higher. These are typically newer, fast-growing companies. Since 1926, small-company stocks have gained an average of 12.1 percent per year versus 10.4 percent for a 500-stock basket of the market's largest issues. Measured since 1960, the margin is even larger: 13.8 percent for small-company stocks versus a 10.4 percent average annual gain from large stocks.

The price of that long-term advantage has been greater short-term volatility. The best year for large stocks was 1933, with a gain of 54 percent; the worst year was 1931, with a loss of 43 percent. But the biggest ever one-year gain for small-company stocks was 143 percent in 1933, and they suffered a 58 percent drop in 1937.

FOREIGN STOCKS. These investments have a place in the retirement nest egg of many empty nesters and they are readily available through a wide array of foreign stock mutual funds. The two key benefits of adding an international flavor to your own nest egg are diversification and performance.

Looking beyond the U.S. market broadens your investment universe. And that is essential in this era of global interdependency when your personal property is ever more closely linked to the property of the world's economies.

Foreign shares help diversify your nest egg because international markets generally perform differently than the U.S. market does. When stocks in the U.S. are down, those in other countries may be rising. The reverse is also true, of course, but by investing in a mutual fund that owns stocks in many different countries, you can reduce the effects of a downturn in any one foreign market.

> NOTE: Because of the currency risk in owning foreign stocks, most empty nesters are better off in an international mutual fund that spreads the risk among many different countries and currencies.

Why Stocks?

Why is investing in stocks so important? If you are not investing in today's stock market you risk falling short of realizing your financial goals. Why? Stocks have consistently proven to be the best inflation-beating vehicle for long-term investors. And, if your investments aren't beating inflation, you are losing ground to the ever-increasing cost of living.

What Are the Risks?

There are risks to stock investing. For example, along with the opportunity of increasing stock prices, empty nesters must also accept the risk that stock prices will decline. The risks (which can occur for a variety of reasons) include the following:

- INDIVIDUAL STOCK PRICE FLUCTUATIONS. Many new investors become too preoccupied with short-term fluctuations in the prices of stock that they own. Individual stock prices are always changing; however, there are ways to control price risk. You can reduce risk by diversifying your holding among several different stocks and different industries.

- STOCK MARKET FLUCTUATIONS. Everyone knows about the volatility of the stock market. Surprisingly, in only five of the years from 1970 to 1992 did overall income stock prices actually decline. Sometimes, the yearly declines were substantial (almost 21 percent in 1974, for instance). Another way to look at it is that stock prices rose in 18 of the years from 1970 to 1992, including annual increases of 37 percent in 1975, 32 percent in 1989 and 30 percent in 1991.

While you shouldn't ignore price fluctuations, you shouldn't become preoccupied with them either because they may simply be responding to overall market fluctuations. To the extent that price fluctuations are covered by market forces, your willingness to accept the risks associated with stock investing are likely to be rewarded with good, inflation-beating returns in the long run.

Bonds as an Alternative

While the attention of the news media is usually focused on the stock market, bonds and bond mutual funds have been undergoing evolutionary changes that have made them both more complex and, at the same time, more attractive investments.

What is a bond? A bond is nothing more than an IOU issued by a government or by a corporation. It promises that the issuer or borrower will repay the principal to the lender (the bond purchaser) at a specified future date, plus pay any interest over the life of the bond to its owner.

Bonds are usually referred to as fixed-income investments because, in most cases, the interest rates that they pay remains constant for the life of the bond. An empty nester who purchases a bond locks in a specific interest rate for as long as he or she owns the bond. It also means that an investor is exposed to an element of risk if interest rates should rise during the holding period.

The value of fixed-income investments such as bonds moves in the opposite direction from changes in interest rates. Therefore, if interest rates rise, the value of your bond will decline, and vice versa.

Other fixed income investments include Treasury notes and bonds, U.S. savings bonds, mortgage-backed securities, municipal bonds, corporate bonds and convertible bonds.

Treasury Securities

These securities are the means by which the United States government borrows money. Treasury bills, notes and bonds are issued regularly by the Federal Reserve and are a popular investment for those who want very little risk. Since these are direct obligations of the U.S. Government, the interest paid on Treasury bills, notes and bonds is exempt from state and local income taxes.

Treasury bills are issued in minimum denominations of $10,000, while subsequent purchases may be made at $5,000 increments. Treasury bills are sold at a discount from their face (maturity) value. The amount of the discount is equal to the interest that will be paid at maturity.

Therefore, upon maturity, the investor receives the face value of the Treasury bill. Treasury notes and bonds are fixed-income obligations that have longer terms and pay interest semiannually at a fixed interest rate. They are sold at face value.

An interesting variation of U.S. Treasury securities is the so-called "zero-coupon" bond. These bonds pay no interest along the way. Instead, they are sold at a deep discount or at a price that is much lower than the maturity value of the bond.

Since you don't get any interest during the holding period, your profit comes at maturity in the form of a large increase in the amount that you receive.

The main advantage to zero-coupon bonds is that you are guaranteed a set return at the original interest rate. Therefore, if interest rates decline, you don't have to worry about reinvesting interest income at a lower rate.

This automatic compounding also avoids your having to decide on reinvesting the interest that you would receive on a regular bond although that, presumably, is why you have established vehicles for savings to park just such funds until they are sufficient for investing.

One major drawback of zero-coupon bonds is that even though you are not receiving interest along the way, the IRS assumes that you are for income tax purposes, so you have to pay income taxes on the imputed interest income.

The upshot? These are good investments for retirement accounts such as IRAs and Keogh plans because taxes are deferred until you withdraw the income at a later date.

Mortgage-Backed Securities

These securities have peculiar-sounding names like Ginnie Mae, Fannie Mae and Freddie Mac. These investments represent pools of mortgages backed by the specific government agency. In other words when agencies purchase mortgages, they are pooled. Shares in that pool are sold to individual investors.

The relatively high yields of mortgage-backed securities have been attracting a lot of investor interest. They can be purchased either individually or through a mutual fund, which offers a wider degree of diversification and safety.

Municipal Bonds

Municipal bonds are used to finance long-term projects for cities, towns, villages and even states. They are very popular investments because the interest that they generate is free from federal taxation. Sometimes, if you purchase bonds of issuing authorities in your own state (or the bonds of Puerto Rico or other United States territories), the interest is also exempt from state income taxes and, perhaps, local income taxes. These investments can also be purchased individually or through a family of mutual funds.

Corporate Bonds

Corporations issue bonds to raise money just like the U.S. Government and state governments. Due to changing economic conditions, some corporate bonds are no longer the safe haven for investors' money that they used to be. Too much borrowing and the sometimes rapidly deteriorating financial conditions of so many corporations requires careful selection and monitoring. Therefore investors of corporate bonds are well advised to stick with highly rated bonds.

Convertible Bonds

These are corporate bonds that can be converted into stock at a predetermined price. They are more attractive to some investors than, say, regular bonds because they enable investors to gain from the appreciation of the underlying common stock.

However, this conversion privilege usually means that their yields are one or more percentage points below those of a straight bond.

And Then There are Mutual Funds

A mutual fund pools your money with that of thousands of other investors to purchase stocks and bonds in a variety of publicly held companies. When you purchase a share in a mutual fund, you become part owner of a multibillion-dollar portfolio of investments that is managed by an individual fund manager or by a committee.

The fund manager decides what stocks or bonds to buy, when to sell and even when to sit on the sidelines, waiting to invest the fund's money.

The fund manager is guided by the investment parameters of the mutual fund, which defines the types of assets in which the fund can invest, how much uninvested cash is permissible, whether the manager can borrow money to invest and so forth.

Although there are many different mutual funds to choose from, you can narrow your choice by deciding what types of funds are best for you. Remember in the last chapter when we covered those banks' funds that invested in CDs and the like to provide a haven for your savings? A similar fund, this one a mutual fund, exists here.

Money Market Funds

Money market funds were the fastest growing fund when they were first introduced in the 1970s. The primary investment in these funds is commercial paper, that is, short-term unsecured corporate bonds and U.S. Treasury bills.

These money market funds usually price each share at $1.00 and since there is little or no credit risk to these investments and they are very short term, the share price should never deviate from $1.00. Most brokerage firms as well as mutual fund managers offer money market funds with no load and very low annual expenses.

Money market funds were designed by brokerage firms to be a competitive alternative to banks' savings accounts. Because money market funds encroach on bank accounts and because banks started offering mutual funds to their customers about the same time, money market funds were becoming popular, recent legislation has blurred the boundaries between the brokerage and the banking industries.

The Glass-Steagall Act, which defined the boundaries between banks and brokers, has been significantly weakened by legislation in the early 1990s.

Many bank holding companies now own investment company subsidiaries and may participate in most areas of the brokerage business except for investment banking. Banks are still excluded from participating in the primary (new issue) market.

Both brokerage firms and banks now compete as full-service financial organizations, with brokerages offering traditional bank account services and banks selling stocks and bonds, as well as issuing CDs and providing checking accounts for their customers.

In addition to money market funds, the typical empty nester can also choose from a variety of funds specializing in various segments of our economy.

What Type of Mutual Fund?

Mutual funds come in many shapes, sizes and investment objectives. They are roughly broken down into these categories:

- INCOME FUNDS. These mutual funds invest in assets that pay regular income. Most income-oriented mutual funds invest in bonds, though some invest in preferred stocks that are required to pay regular, generous dividends or in higher yielding common stocks, such as shares of utility companies. The fund's income (called its yield) is computed by dividing the fund's annual income by the unit price of the mutual fund share.

  You can compare the yields of income funds to each other and to the income yield of bank certificates of deposit (CDs), and the value of the mutual fund share will move up and down as the market price of the underlying stocks and bonds fluctuate.

- EQUITY INCOME FUNDS. These funds invest in high-dividend preferred and common stocks, convertible bonds and corporate bonds. Although these funds are more volatile than the others and generally produce smaller yields, equity income funds have a greater potential for growth.

- CORPORATE BOND FUNDS. These funds invest in corporate bonds and are generally less volatile than equity income funds. High-grade bond funds invest in the bonds of "A" rated or better companies, while high-yield bond funds invest primarily in junk bonds, which produce a high yield but a far greater risk of loss.

- GOVERNMENT BOND FUNDS. These funds invest in bonds that are issued by the U.S. Government and its agencies. Because of the government guarantees, these funds are less volatile than other funds and may yield somewhat less as well. These funds are not entirely free of risk, however, because small fluctuations in interest rates will cause the value of the bonds to move inversely. If you intend to hold bonds until maturity, you may wish to buy individual bonds or to invest in a target fund that buys bonds that all mature in the same year. If you hold a bond until maturity, the interim fluctuations in price will be meaningless.

- MUNICIPAL BOND FUNDS. These funds produce income that is free of Federal tax and free of state taxes as well—if you live in the state where the bonds purchased by the fund were issued. Municipal bond fund income is considerably lower than the income from other bond and equity income funds, so investing in municipal bonds makes sense only for those investors in top tax brackets.

  NOTE: Although the interest yield from municipal bond funds is usually free of tax, if you sell your shares at a gain, that gain will be taxable.

■ GROWTH FUNDS. Growth mutual funds are suitable for the empty nester who is seeking appreciation rather than current income. There are two types of growth funds:

—LONG-TERM GROWTH FUNDS. These funds are the least volatile of the growth funds. They invest in larger, well-known companies with a history of steady growth in earnings and share value.

—MAXIMUM CAPITAL GAIN FUNDS. Also known as aggressive growth funds or small cap funds, these funds invest in smaller, less well-known companies, often in new technology or potential takeover targets. These funds are very volatile and are not for the faint of heart. They can post spectacular gains but may suffer equally spectacular losses in a bear market.

■ TOTAL RETURN FUNDS. Total return funds blend the relative safety of income funds with the appreciation potential of growth funds, by investing in both stocks and bonds. They attract investors who don't need income but can't tolerate extreme volatility. There are two basic types of total return funds:

—GROWTH AND INCOME FUNDS. These funds emphasize growth more than income and therefore invest primarily in high-dividend stock and convertible bonds.

—BALANCED FUNDS. These funds balance their investments between stocks and bonds and usually guarantee that a significant portion of their portfolio will always be invested in bonds. Balanced funds are generally less volatile and less risky than growth and income funds—but not always. Some balanced funds allow investments in high-yield junk bonds and thus stray far from the conservative path.

■ SPECIALIZED FUNDS. Specialized mutual funds invest in a single segment of the economy.

—SECTOR FUNDS. These funds invest in a particular industry, such as health care, utilities, technology or banking. Investing in these fields is riskier than investing in other fields because you are predicting that a certain economic sector will outperform the economy as a whole. Past performance of the fund is often irrelevant, because particular sectors that did well in the past may be out of favor in the future.

■ INTERNATIONAL AND GLOBAL STOCKS. These funds provide the opportunity to invest outside the United States. International funds invest exclusively in foreign stocks and bonds, while global funds invest in both foreign and domestic securities. Your can also choose a fund that invests exclusively in one country or region, such as a Mexico fund or a Pacific basin fund.

■ PRECIOUS METALS FUNDS. These funds invest in mining company stocks and precious metals themselves. Many of the gold funds diversify their holdings among mining companies in several countries while some funds invest exclusively in silver.

■ INDEX FUNDS. These funds are weighted portfolios of all of the stocks of a particular index, such as the Standard & Poor's 500 stock index, which represents about three-fourths of the total value of shares traded by the New York Stock Exchange.

> NOTE: Although the goal of most mutual fund managers is to outperform the stock indexes, about half fail to do so. For that reason, index funds offer empty nesters the guarantee that their investments will perform as well (or as poorly) as the market index.

—SOCIALLY RESPONSIBLE FUNDS. These funds use negative screens to weed out traits of companies that they won't invest in. Negative screens include Environmental Protection Agency violators and polluters, nuclear power, weapons production, alcohol, gambling and tobacco.

Some socially responsible funds use positive screens as well, seeking companies that care about environmental protection, women and minority advancement, occupational health and safety, strong employee and customer relations and product quality and safety.

MUTUAL FUND OPTIONS AND RISKS

Type of Fund	Basic Objective	Type of Investment	Risk Level	Growth Potential
Money Market	Current Income	Cash Equivalents	Low	None
Municipal Bond	Tax-free Income	Municipal Bonds	Mid-Low	Mid-Low
Corporate Bond	Current Income	Corporate Bonds	Mid-Low	Mid-Low
Equity Income	Current Income	Stocks & Bonds	Moderate	Moderate

continues

MUTUAL FUND OPTIONS AND RISKS (cont.)

Type of Fund	Basic Objective	Type of Investment	Risk Level	Growth Potential
Balanced	Current Income	Stocks & Bonds	Moderate	Moderate
Growth & Income	Income & Appreciation	Stocks	Mid-High	Mid-High
Long-Term	Appreciation	Stocks	High	High
Aggressive Growth	Appreciation	Stocks	High	High
Sector	Appreciation	Stocks	High	High
Int'l & Global	Income & Appreciation	Stocks & Bonds	Moderate	Low
Precious Metals	Inflation Hedge	Stocks	High	Low
Index	Appreciation	Stocks	Mid-High	Mid-High
Socially Responsible	Income & Appreciation	Stocks	Mid-High	Mid-High

> NOTE: Mutual fund investors should also be aware that not all fund portfolios will be what they appear to be. In order for a mutual fund to be called a particular type of fund, it need only invest only 65 percent of its portfolio in that type of investment.

Gambling for Greater Rewards

Every investment provides safety, yield, or appreciation—but no investment provides all three. As a matter of fact, as you move toward investments that provide more than one of these three factors, you tend to move away from the other two factors.

Put another way, moving toward growth usually increases your risk of loss of capital. Moving back toward safety increases the risk that inflation will erode your money's purchasing power. Among the investments providing the biggest potential for both reward and losses are those we've categorized as real gambles.

Gambling with Hard Assets

Another category of investments is known as "hard assets." This is to distinguish them from paper assets such as stocks or bonds. Their common characteristic and the basis of their attractiveness is as an inflation hedge.

Hard assets include commodities, real estate, precious metals, timber rights, oil and gas leases—any of a variety of natural resources whose values tend to rise along with the overall level of consumer prices. Some hard assets such as commercial real estate or oil and gas properties can offer current income as well as the opportunity for pure appreciation. Others, such as gold bullion and raw land, provide no current income and may even carry expenses, such as real estate taxes, that give them a negative cash flow.

While most hard assets require some level of expertise, there are other investments that are, in the eyes of many, nothing but a gamble.

Real Gambles

A stock option is a contract that gives its purchasers the right to buy or the right to sell a fixed amount of stock (usually 100 shares) at a predetermined price and within a predetermined period of time. The contract that gives the purchaser of an option the right to buy the stock is called a "call" option. The contract that gives the purchaser the right to sell is called a "put" option.

Options originated as a way to give stock investors a means of insuring their portfolio and limiting market volatility. Shareholders could sell a contract guaranteeing delivery of their stock at a predetermined price above what they paid for it. By so doing, they would receive additional income from the sale of that contract that would reduce their loss if the stock dropped and had to be sold at a lower than purchase price. The option contract in this case would, of course, not be exercised. However, if the stock went above the price at which the investor had guaranteed to sell it, he or she would be limiting the upside potential from that stock but he or she would also be reducing the downside risk.

Options generally evolved into a highly leveraged short-term speculator's dream. You can still purchase either strategy—conservative hedging or outlandish speculation—using options.

Stock Rights and Warrants

Stock rights and warrants are similar to stock options in that they are relatively low-priced securities that can be converted into shares of stock, but there are significant differences between these securities and options.

Stock rights are usually issued if a company is planning to issue more new shares in the primary market. Prior to the issuance of those new shares the company will give its current shareholders the right to purchase additional shares of the stock.

These "stock rights" allow the owners to purchase enough new shares at a lower than market price to maintain the same percentage ownership of the company after the new shares are issued. By increasing the number of shares the company has outstanding, it is in effect "diluting" (or decreasing) the percentage of ownership of the current shareholders.

"Warrants," on the other hand, are more like long-term options. Warrants are contracts that allow the holder to convert them into shares of stock of the underlying company. At the time that they are issued, the conversion price of the warrants will be higher than the market price of the stock.

Warrants, like listed stock options, are highly leveraged contracts. For a relatively small investment like the option premium, a warrant will rise in value dollar-for-dollar as the price of the underlying stock rises above the exercise price.

Listed warrants will trade like stock, usually on the same stock exchange as the stock into which they can be converted. The leverage from investments in stock options or warrants pales, however, in comparison to the leverage from commodities futures contracts.

Commodities Futures Contracts

Futures contracts are similar to listed stock options in that they give the speculator the right to buy or to sell a specified quantity of a commodity within a certain period of time. There are, however, a great many differences between commodity futures and stock options.

First, futures are contracts to purchase or to sell a specific amount of an underlying commodity, not an equity security. This underlying commodity can be precious metals such as gold, silver or platinum. It can be consumable products such as wheat, corn, soybeans, cocoa, sugar, coffee, orange juice, live cattle or pork bellies (bacon). There are also such energy-related commodity contracts as crude oil, heating oil or natural gas. There are also foreign currency contracts and interest-rate and index contracts on Treasury bonds, Treasury bills, GNMAs or the S&P 500 Index.

Each contract on these commodities represents a specified quantity that varies from commodity to commodity. The quantities are not standardized as they are with listed stock options. A coffee contract, for instance, is 37,500 pounds. A wheat contract is 5,000 bushels. The quantities of the different futures contracts vary.

The main difference between commodities and stock options is that with an option you cannot lose any more than the option premium. With commodities futures contracts, the speculator has undefined risk.

The speculator deposits a small amount of equity when buying (or shorting) a futures contract. If the price of the commodity moves against that position, that is if the speculator is long and the price drops, or short and the price rallies, they will have to deposit additional equity in order to meet margin requirements.

The speculator will have to continue adding money to meet the equity requirements only if the commodity keeps going the wrong way.

Some commodities exchanges have introduced trading in options contracts. Options are similar to futures, but they do limit the trader's risk to the amount of the investment. In this sense, they are similar to options.

Using These "Tools" to Meet Your Financial Goals

In order to enjoy investing—and to profit from it—you must understand the basics. In this chapter we've attempted to explain the various types of investments that you will be using in your financial planning. Ranging from basic stocks to outright gambles such as commodities, these "tools" are essential.

The fun part of using these so-called "tools" comes later using the various strategies explained in Chapters 15 and 16 to really profit from these investments. But first, let's look at Uncle Sam's contribution to your financial planning arsenal: Tax Deferral.

SAVINGS ON SAVINGS
WITH TAX DEFERMENT

Inflation's Long-Term Threat

No discussion of time, money and compounding would be complete without a mention of inflation. Just as investment returns compound over the years and cause your savings to grow, inflation also compounds and causes the level of prices to grow.

As prices rise, the purchasing power of your investments decline. So, in a sense, inflation is also like a tax. The 2.7 percent increase in the consumer price level during 1994, for instance, was equivalent to a 2.7 percent tax on savings and investments. Since 1964, the price level has increased fivefold.

During your working years, you can cope with inflation by angling for a pay raise, seeking a higher-salaried job, working extra hours, etc.

Retirees, however, have stopped getting paychecks and salary increases. That makes them vulnerable to the relentless effects of rising prices on their standards of living. Their pensions tend to be fixed. And their investments must be largely directed toward safely generating income, not aggressively seeking growth to do better over the long run, in keeping up with inflation.

Recently an inflation rate of around 3 percent seems mild in comparison to the double-digit increases during the late 1970s and early 1980s. Yet, over time, even a 3 percent rate of inflation can still do considerable damage to the purchasing power of your savings and investments.

Tax Advantage of Tax Deferral

Like inflation, taxes work as a drag on the power of compounding by substantially reducing your effective rate of return. If, for example, you are in the 28 percent tax bracket, you keep 72 percent of all dividend or interest earnings that are exposed to tax. In the 36 percent bracket, you retain only 64 percent of pretax earnings, and in the top 39.6 bracket, just 60.4 percent.

As a result of taxes, you require significantly greater investment returns in order to reach a particular goal. If you are in the 31 percent tax bracket, for example, you will need a pretax return of 10.1 percent to attain an after-tax return of just 7 percent. In the 36 percent tax bracket, you need a 10.9 percent return to be able to keep 7 percent after taxes.

Obviously, the best outcome when taxes are concerned is not to have to pay them. That is a major reason why so many empty nesters favor municipal bonds. Interest on municipal bonds is not generally subject to Federal income taxes, although state and local income taxes may be due if you own municipal bonds issued outside your home state.

> NOTE: Capital gains on municipal bond investments
> are subject to Federal capital gains tax.

Unfortunately, municipal bonds may not be suitable for your investment strategy. You may, for example, need the long-term growth offered by common stocks. Don't forget, however, that all earnings from common stocks are taxable.

Which brings us to the next best strategy where taxes are concerned, and that is to delay or defer them as long as possible. The longer you can keep your money from being taxed and leave all your earnings free to compound, the easier it will be to reach your goals.

Once your assets are sheltered from taxes in a tax-deferred account, you will want to keep them sheltered as long as possible. As soon as you make a withdrawal, you immediately give up a portion of the proceeds to taxes and lose the advantage of further tax-deferred compounding as well.

If you change jobs, for example, you might receive a lump-sum distribution from a company retirement plan. Unless the distribution is rolled over within 60 days into another employer-sponsored plan or into an individual retirement account (IRA), you will owe taxes on the full amount of that distribution as well as a 10 percent penalty if you are under age 59$1/2$.

> NOTE: The cost of taking money prematurely from a
> tax-advantaged plan is substantial. Nonetheless,
> many employees still fail to take advantage of the
> rollover option.

Back in 1992, a survey conducted by the Gallup Organization for the Employee Benefit Research Institute asked Americans what they would do if they left their jobs and received a cash distribution from a retirement plan. Sixty-one percent said that they would continue to save the money for retirement in an IRA.

The remaining 39 percent, however, said that they would give up their tax deferral, pay taxes on the money and then use the proceeds to meet current spending needs

(12 percent), pay off credit card or other debt (12 percent) or bolster their regular savings (13 percent).

Spending retirement money to meet nonretirement financial needs may at first appear to make sense, especially when you are relatively young and retirement is years away. In the long run, however, doing so will make it harder to achieve your retirement goals, especially with the extra burden of taxes and penalties that are incurred whenever you spend a retirement plan distribution.

Recognizing the importance of retirement savings, Congress has authorized generous tax benefits for tax-deferred retirement plans. In order to reap the maximum benefit from these tax breaks, you will have to participate whenever possible in tax-deferred programs. You will also have to insulate your savings from taxes and curb your impulse to spend during your working years.

Defer Taxes Whenever Possible

If time is your greatest ally when investing or saving, taxes are your greatest enemy. The longer you can legally shelter your assets from taxation and keep your investment earnings compounding on a tax-free basis, the sooner you will meet your retirement investing goals.

How severe of a bite do taxes take out of your savings or investment return? Probably more than you expect.

Assume, for instance, that you are taxed at a marginal rate of 31 percent and you earn an 8 percent annual return over 10 years on an initial investment of $10,000. At the end of 10 years, your investment will have grown to $17,114, after taking into account taxes on your earnings.

Now consider the same set of circumstances, except this time we'll assume that your initial investment is placed in an individual retirement account (IRA). Since taxes on an IRA are deferred until you begin withdrawing money during your retirement, your earnings compound at a higher effective rate. At the end of the 10-year period, your final account value in the IRA would be $21,589—more than 25 percent higher than for the taxable account.

Of course, money that is growing on a tax-deferred basis will eventually be taxed upon withdrawal. However, even during retirement, you can make periodic withdrawals and continue to benefit from the tax deferral on your remaining balance.

> NOTE: You should also note that all withdrawals from a qualified retirement plan are taxed as ordinary income, regardless of whether the gain in the account accumulated from income or from capital

appreciation. What this means is that earnings that
may have been taxed at the capital gains rate (28
percent in 1996—but remember, capital gains will
change downward in 1998 and thereafter) will
instead be taxed at the income rate prevailing at
the time that the assets are withdrawn.

In addition to their tax deferral features, many qualified retirement plans also provide tax deductions for the empty nester's contributions—if they are in certain income brackets—up to certain yearly limits. These tax deferral type accounts include IRAs, 401(k) corporate savings plans, 403(b) savings plans for employees of public and non-profit organizations and Keogh and simplified employee pension (SEP) plans used by self-employed individuals and small businesses.

The arithmetic of this feature is fairly straightforward. To illustrate, assume that you are taxed at the 31 percent marginal tax rate and that you are eligible to make fully deductible contributions to an IRA.

If you contribute $2,000 (the present maximum allowed in any one year) to your IRA, the value of the tax deduction means that you effectively contribute only $1,380 (69 percent of $2,000), even though your IRA receives the full $2,000.

SAVINGS ON SAVINGS WITH TAX DEFERMENT

Individual Contributions

Limits For Tax-Deferred Investments

Tax-deferred investment	Individual Deductible Contribution Limit	Individual Nondeductible Contribution Limit
Company savings plan or 401(k)	Up to $9,240	May be possible
Employer pension plan	Not applicable	" " "
Nonprofit employer 403(b) plan	Up to $9,240	" " "
Individual retirement account (IRA)	Up to $2,000	Up to $2,000
Self-employed (Keogh)	Various limits	May be possible
Indirect tax-deferred annuity	Not applicable	No legal limit

continues

SAVINGS ON SAVINGS WITH TAX DEFERMENT (cont.)

Neither you nor your spouse can be eligible to participate in an employer-sponsored retirement plan. For others, deduction is phased out for higher income individuals and married couples.

Retirement Plans

Putting money into what is commonly known as a qualified retirement plan, either your employer's or your own, is one of the best ways to prepare for your financial future and to take advantage of tax deferral. It is also a great way to reduce your tax bill.

The variety of retirement plans that qualify for special treatment under our tax laws can be bewildering unless you understand that the underlying principal for most of them is the same: The money that you put in now will not be taxed until you take it out at retirement.

With that said, you should also be aware that there are important differences between retirement plans.

Types of Retirement Plans

There are really only three types of retirement plans: those that you create and contribute to yourself, those plans that your company runs and contributes to and those to which both you and the company may contribute. Many empty nesters often may participate in more than one type of plan.

Individual Retirement Plans (IRAs)

IRAs are retirement plans that you create and to which you contribute. Unfortunately, IRAs are no longer as beneficial as they once were to those individuals who are covered by employer-sponsored retirement plans. Still, they are not totally without value.

At the present time, the law allows you to contribute to an IRA the lesser of $2,000 or 100 percent of your compensation of each year; $2,250 if you and your nonworking spouse file jointly. However, you may deduct this contribution only if neither you nor your spouse is covered by a tax-deferred retirement plan or your adjusted gross income (AGI) falls below a certain level.

Whether your annual contribution to an IRA is deductible or not, the account earnings still accumulate tax-free until you withdraw your money.

Keogh Plans

If you work for yourself, you should have a Keogh plan for saving and sheltering part of your self-employment income—Keogh plans are bona fide nest egg building tools.

Since Keogh plans are for the self-employed, it should go without saying that in order to have a Keogh plan, an empty nester should be in business for him- or herself. In other words, you must have income from your own unincorporated business, such as a sole proprietorship or partnership. If you have employees, you generally must include them in your Keogh plan.

Having a Keogh plan does not preclude you from also having an IRA, but you should know that a Keogh is what is called a "qualified plan" under our tax laws. So, if you set up an IRA, your income must fall within certain levels or else your IRA contributions will not be tax deductible.

Once again, you may deduct your Keogh contributions and you will pay no tax on any earnings that accumulate until you begin to collect benefits, usually at retirement.

Keoghs come in two varieties: a defined-contribution plan or a defined-benefit plan. A defined-contribution plan allows you to contribute a specified amount—10 percent of your income, for instance—to the plan each year. To further complicate matters, the defined-contribution plans are further divided into profit-sharing plans and money purchase plans.

An empty nester may contribute up to 15 percent of his or her self-employment income with a profit-sharing plan, or up to 25 percent with a money purchase plan. In either case, however, your contribution cannot exceed $30,000.

You must subtract your contribution and your deduction for one-half of your actual self-employment taxes for the year to figure your net self-employment income. In reality, this means that you are contributing only 12.2 percent of your self-employment income to your profit-sharing plan or 18.59 percent to a money purchase plan.

For 1997, these percentages are for self-employment income that does not exceed $65,400. If your earned income tops this amount, the percentage varies slightly.

With a defined-benefit plan you contribute annually whatever amount is required to fund a specified retirement benefit or payment. The payment to be made during retirement is fixed, and the contribution is based on actuarial tables for your life expectancy.

The only limit: The annual benefit after retirement may not top the lesser of $150,000 or 100 percent of your average earnings for your three consecutive years of highest earnings.

> **NOTE:** Although the amount of your contribution to
> a profit-sharing plan may be more limited than it
> is for the other two types of plans, this type of
> arrangement does have one important advantage: You
> may vary the amount that you set aside each year
> and are free to base your contributions on how
> well your business performs. In other words, if
> your business does poorly one year, you aren't
> required to make a contribution. You are even free
> to skip a contribution any year you like. By con-
> trast, if you have a money-purchase or defined-
> benefit plan, you must make an annual contribution
> to the plan each year; otherwise, you may be sub-
> ject to an excise tax.

Employer-Sponsored Retirement Plans

Employer-sponsored retirement plans are created, and for the most part, funded by the company that employs you. As with Keogh plans, employer-sponsored plans come in two types: defined-contribution plans and defined-benefit plans.

As with all retirement plans, any earnings accumulating in employer-sponsored plans remain untaxed until you begin withdrawing funds at retirement.

401(k) Plans

When you participate in a 401(k) plan, your employer diverts a fixed portion of your pretax salary into a company-sponsored investment plan. There are two immediate advantages to this: Your overall taxable income is reduced and you've started investing in your future.

While 401(k) plans have long been available to employees of large corporations, it is only in recent years that they have also started to become popular with smaller companies. Many employees also match part of each employee's contributions to 401(k) plans.

401(k) plans save Federal income taxes in two ways. First, earnings placed into a 401(k) plan are deducted from your gross pay—before taxes are taken out. Thus, the more you put into your plan, the more income taxes you save each year that you contribute.

Because money in these plans is considered to be deferred compensation, it doesn't appear on your W-2 form and therefore avoids tax until such time as the money is eventually distributed. Also, depending upon where you reside, your 401(k) contribution may escape state and local taxes.

The second tax benefit of participating in or contributing to a 401(k) plan where you work is that earnings from the plan aren't currently taxed until you begin making withdrawals. Dividends, interest, and capital gains aren't taxed until withdrawal.

You have to choose how to invest your 401(k) investments. Depending upon your employer, you may be able to choose from among a limited number of mutual funds, or you may be able to invest your money in a wide variety of investment vehicles, such as an array of mutual funds and a guaranteed investment (or guaranteed income) contract (GIC). However, over the long run, a mix of stock and bond mutual funds will usually provide a superior return.

> NOTE: 401(K) LIMITS
>
> Unfortunately, for some high income earners, the IRS has put a cap on the amount of money that can be put into a 401(k) plan. For years after 1996, the maximum salary reduction allowed is $9,500. Even so, this is a very powerful retirement planning tool.

403(b) Plans

In many ways a 403(b) plan is the nonprofit sector's answer to the 401(k) plan. 403(b)s—also known as tax sheltered annuities—are a unique type of salary reduction retirement savings plan. They are available only to employees of educational institutions and other specified nonprofit organizations.

If you want to participate in a 403(b), you must agree to have your employer automatically reduce part of your current salary and transfer money into a 403(b) account. As with a 401(k) plan, you generally have several options as to how you can invest your 403(b) funds.

Since your paycheck will be reduced by the amount of money taken out of your salary, your income tax liability will decrease. Meanwhile, the funds invested in your 403(b) will generate dividends, interest and capital gains totally free of taxes until you begin making withdrawals during retirement.

Hybrid Plans

There are several retirement plans that combine some features of employer-sponsored plans with the IRA concept. For instance, 401(k) plans are a hybrid. Your employer will create and administer a 401(k) plan and may contribute to it.

Employees use 401(k) plans much as they do IRAs—as a place to deposit a tax-deferred portion of their salary or wage income until they need to withdraw it, usually at retirement.

Another hybrid, the simplified employee pension (SEP) plan, is very similar to an IRA. An employer, rather than maintaining its own pension fund, makes contributions to the IRAs of the employees and the employer may deduct its contribution. Moreover, you do not have to count the employer's contribution to that SEP as part of your income.

New . . . Simple Retirement Accounts

Beginning in 1997, certain small employers may maintain SIMPLE retirement plans. A SIMPLE plan may be maintained in any year by an employer who has 100 or fewer employees who received at least $5,000 of compensation from the employer the preceding year. The employer cannot maintain any other employer-sponsored retirement plan.

A SIMPLE plan may take the form of an IRA established for each participant in which case it is tax exempt like any other IRA—but it is not subject to nondiscrimination and other qualification rules that normally apply to "qualified" plans. Alternatively, it may take the form of a cash or defined 401(k) arrangement within a qualified plan.

Tax-Exempt Versus Tax-Deferred Investments

Yet another way to manage the tax exposure of your retirement nest egg is to invest a portion in municipal bonds. Interest from these securities, issued by state and local governments, is not generally subject to Federal income taxes and may, in fact, be free of state and local taxes as well. The same is true of dividends from mutual funds and unit trusts that invest in municipal bonds.

What's the catch? Municipal bonds offer lower yields than taxable bonds of comparable maturities and credit quality. For example, if a U.S. Treasury bond yields 7.5 percent, a high-quality municipal bond of the same maturity might yield 6 percent.

How Do You Compare Tax-Exempt and Taxable Yields?

In order to convert a tax-exempt yield to the equivalent taxable yield, divide the tax-exempt yield by 1 minus your Federal income tax rate, expressed as a decimal fraction. If your Federal tax rate is 28 percent, you would use 0.28. Here is an illustration using a 6 percent tax-exempt yield:

$$\frac{6 \text{ Percent}}{1 - .28} \quad \text{or} \quad \frac{6 \text{ Percent}}{.72} \quad = \quad \begin{matrix} \text{Equivalent} \\ 8.3 \text{ Percent} \\ \text{Taxable Yield} \end{matrix}$$

In other words, you would need to obtain an 8.3 percent yield on a taxable investment to match a 6 percent tax-exempt yield.

HOW TO COMPARE TAX-EXEMPT
AND TAXABLE YIELDS

Tax-exempt yield	Tax Bracket			
	28%	31%	36%	39.6%
4.0%	5.6%	5.8%	6.3%	6.6%
4.5%	6.3	6.5	7.0	7.5
5.0%	6.9	7.2	7.8	8.3
5.5%	7.6	8.0	8.6	9.1
6.0%	8.3	8.7	9.4	9.9
6.5%	9.0	9.4	10.2	10.8
7.0%	9.7	10.1	10.9	11.6

Last-Ditch Tax Deferral = Annuities

Other savings vehicles such as annuities, where you can obtain tax deferral on earnings but no upfront tax deduction on your contributions, may also make sense for some empty nesters depending on their circumstances.

Keep in mind, however, that higher costs and certain restrictions typically associated with annuities may offset some of the benefits of tax deferral.

Chapter 14

ANNUITIES

In the last chapter we explored the advantages of tax deferred investments centering on those tax deferred investments where contributions are also tax deductible. But what if this double benefit is not available?

Yes, you can make contributions to some employer-sponsored retirement plans and limited contributions to IRAs above the limits without penalties. Those contributions, while not tax deductible, will still enjoy tax-deferred earnings.

Tax Deferral with After-Tax Contributions

What if you aren't eligible for a tax-deductible retirement contribution. Let's say you have a pension plan at work but no 401(k) plan. If your income is above $50,000, for a married couple, you can't deduct an IRA contribution and probably don't have access to any other type of tax deductible retirement investment. Or perhaps you have a 401(k) plan at work but have contributed the maximum amount to the 401(k) and still want to invest more for retirement this year. What are your options?

Tax deferral is still available, but only for amounts that are invested on a nondeductible or after-tax basis. One possible option is to make after-tax contributions to your employer's retirement plan. Some employer plans permit after-tax contributions by employees up to certain limits. In these instances, employees can use the employer plan as a kind of tax-deferred retirement savings account.

Another option is to contribute up to $2,000 on a nondeductible basis to an IRA. A third option is to invest in an individual deferred annuity.

Deferred annuities, as you'll learn later, are a type of insurance contract that offers tax deferral of investment earnings and a minimum death benefit. There is no legal limit on the amount that you can invest.

But, without a tax deduction, does tax deferral still make sense? Or would you be better off simply investing on a fully taxable basis? The answer will depend on your own circumstances, particularly your tax bracket, your investment time horizon and the type of investment income that you intend to seek. Here's why.

Tax-Deferred Benefits and Pitfalls

Your tax-deferred income may end up being taxed at a higher rate. All income withdrawn from a tax-deferred account is taxed as ordinary income (maximum 39.6 percent) even if it resulted from long-term capital gains (otherwise taxed at a maximum rate of 28 percent).

Let's say, for example, that your tax rate for ordinary income is 31 percent, or 3 percentage points higher than the 28 percent maximum rate for long-term capital gains income. If you sold an investment that had increased in value by $1,000 over several years, the income would qualify as long-term capital gain and your tax bill would be $280.

If, however, that investment had been owned in a tax-deferred account such as an IRA, the $1,000 gain would be considered ordinary income even though it was derived from the gain on the sale of your investment. The result? Your tax at withdrawal would be $310.

In other words, as this illustration demonstrates, there may be circumstances where you are better off investing on a fully taxable basis outside a tax-deferred account.

A Further Example

Still on the subject of the differential between the tax rate imposed on long-term capital gain and the rates levied on ordinary income, let's use another example. Say that you invest $1,000 in a tax-deferred account and another $1,000 on a fully taxable basis. In each case, you use the money to buy stocks that appreciate in price by 6 percent a year and generate 2 percent a year in dividend income.

For the taxable account, each year you will pay taxes on the 2 percent dividend income at your ordinary income tax rate and reinvest the remainder. For the tax-deferred account, the dividends are reinvested without tax. After 10 years, you sell the stocks in both accounts, withdraw the money and pay all the taxes due.

Which approach provides the better return? Again, it depends on your tax rate. The higher your tax bracket—and thus the larger the spread between the rate you pay on ordinary income and the rate that you pay on long-term capital gain income—the more attractive it will be for you to invest for capital appreciation on a fully taxable basis outside a tax-deferred account. Here is what your gain would be net of taxes after 10 years, depending on your tax bracket.

TAXABLE VS. TAX-DEFERRED GAINS FROM $1,000 STOCK INVESTMENT OVER 10 YEARS

Tax bracket	Tax-Deferred Taxable gain	Tax-Deferred-Return to Taxable gain	Ratio of Full Taxable Return
28%	$751	$834	1.11
31%	741	800	1.08
36%	724	742	1.02
39.6%	713	700	0.98

Assumes 8% total return, 6% from unrealized long-term capital gain and 2% from dividends. Investments sold, funds withdrawn and deferred taxes paid at the end of the 10-year period.

Capital gains rate is 28% in this example.

As we have seen, the taxable versus tax-deferred equation depends on the type of asset in which you are investing. If the income generated by your investments is ordinary, fully-taxable income—not subject to the more favorable long-term capital gains tax rate—then tax deferral may be more attractive.

Let's take the example of an investment in a bond fund with a 7 percent return consisting of dividends taxed at ordinary income rates. In this situation, the higher your tax bracket, the more attractive tax deferral becomes.

A third factor is the extra cost, if any, that accompanies tax deferral. In many cases, that cost will be negligible. For example, you may have to pay a slightly higher annual fee to maintain an IRA account than you would pay for a comparable taxable account. Fees from accounts such as Keogh plans will be more substantial because of additional recordkeeping and reporting requirements. But in either case, the amounts involved will be relatively small.

In other instances, however, fees associated with tax deferral can become significant. Consider the popular tax-deferred investment, variable annuities, as an illustration of the impact that fees can have on return.

Variable Annuities

As we'll see later in this chapter, variable annuities can be thought of as tax-deferred mutual funds. They typically offer a choice of several mutual fund–like "subaccounts" with different investment objectives such as growth, growth and income, etc.

Like mutual funds, variable annuities levy annual fees for investment management and administrative costs. And, because they offer a death benefit, variable annuities charge an additional fee to cover the death benefit and related insurance costs. Those additional fees average about 1.3 percent a year. The higher the fee, the less attractive such annuities will be when compared to fully taxable investments.

A further factor in deciding whether to invest on a taxable or on a tax-deferred basis is your investment time horizon. If there is much likelihood that you will need the money before retirement, then the 10 percent penalty for withdrawal before age $59^{1/2}$ will make tax deferral much less attractive.

Likewise, if the tax-deferred investment that you are considering also carries a surrender charge in the initial years after you purchase it, as is the case with most deferred annuities, it becomes even less advantageous for anything but a lengthy investment time horizon.

On the other hand, the longer you keep your money in a tax-deferred investment, the more time there will be for the benefits of tax deferral to outweigh any extra costs that may be involved.

In the case of a deferred annuity, for example, you can estimate the length of the holding period that will be required before the tax benefits of deferral will outweigh the added insurance-related costs posed by the annuity. That breakeven holding period will vary depending, once again, on your tax bracket, the assumed investment return and the expenses charged by the insurance company offering the annuity.

Annuities: Another Tax-Deferral Option

Annuities certainly offer a number of advantages if you want tax-deferred growth. But they can sometimes be a very expensive way to buy your investments. Over and above any sales commissions that you pay to get in, these contracts (like mutual funds) charge investment management fees and have administrative costs. And, because they also offer a death benefit, these contracts charge for the life insurance protection they provide. There may also be surrender charges imposed if you take funds out of the contract too soon.

All of these fees are in addition to those charged by the funds themselves so you need to stay in the annuity for a long time before the benefits of tax deferral outweigh the commissions and additional costs. While your actual break-even period depends on the investment return and your tax bracket, 20 years is a good rule of thumb.

An annuity is, in general, a tax-deferred investment contract that is underwritten by an insurance company. In other words, these are life insurance products sporting tax advantages. In reality, however, there is usually almost no life insurance involved.

The hint of insurance—just enough to earn the tax break—guarantees that if you die before beginning withdrawals and the annuity is worth less at that time than the total of your investments, the insurance company will pay your beneficiary an amount equal to your investments.

Although annuities come in a variety of types, the two primary types are immediate annuities and deferred annuities. With an immediate annuity, you usually purchase the contract with a lump sum; you decide how frequently you want to receive payments (for example, monthly, quarterly or annually). Furthermore, those payments can be over a fixed period, such as 20 years, or for the rest of your life.

The most popular annuity for empty nesters is a variable deferred annuity. Variable annuities allow you to invest in a portfolio of investment options (such as guaranteed interest contracts or bond and stock mutual funds) that you select.

With a variable annuity, the interest dividends and capital gains you earn accumulate tax-deferred until they are entirely paid to you under the terms of your annuity contract. Unlike bank CDs and mutual funds, however, the annuity contract serves as an impenetrable wrapper that keeps the tax collector's hands off of your earnings.

With variable annuities, no tax is due until you pull funds out of the contract, presumably in retirement, either in a lump sum or by annuitizing the contract and having the company make payments to you for life.

Such tax-deferred growth gives funds invested in an annuity the same advantage as cash stashed in an individual retirement account (See Chapter 13). Unlike an IRA, however, you can't deduct amounts put into an annuity.

The price for tax deferral is the same 10 percent penalty that we saw earlier with the premature withdrawals from an IRA and other tax-deferred investments. You will pay ordinary income taxes plus a 10 percent penalty if you take the money out of an annuity before age $59^{1}/_{2}$.

CALCULATION OF BREAK-EVEN PERIOD
FOR VARIABLE ANNUITY

INVESTMENT RETURN

	7%	8%	9%	10%
TAX RATE				
28%	29 years	20 years	15 years	12 years
31%	31	23	18	14
36%	36	28	23	18
39.6%	39	31	26	20

Table assumes annuity expense of 1 percent.

Paying the Piper

If you cash in the annuity contract before retirement, you'll pay dearly as already mentioned. For one thing, most annuity contracts impose surrender charges during the first several years. Any earnings pulled out of the annuity are taxable and if you are under the age of 59½, you'll also be hit with a 10 percent penalty tax.

What portion of a withdrawal is earnings? That's easy—if you cash in the annuity and pull out all of the funds, you are taxed—and possibly penalized—on the difference between your original investment and what you get.

It is quite a bit trickier if you pull out only part of the money in an annuity. In many instances, the penalties for partial withdrawals are based on when you made the annuity investment. If it was purchased on or before August 13, 1982, the IRS considers the first money pulled out of the annuity to be a tax-free return of your investment. Only after you have recovered your full investment is any further withdrawal taxed.

For investments after that date, however, the rule is turned about. The first money out is considered earnings—taxable and potentially subject to the 10 percent penalty.

Suppose, by way of example, that you invest $10,000 in an annuity today and its value grows to $25,000 in 10 years. If you were to cash in the contract, $15,000 would be taxed, and if you were under age 59½, the 10 percent early withdrawal penalty would apply to that $15,000.

The other $10,000 would be a return of your original investment—untaxed and penalty-free.

If you simply withdraw $10,000 from the annuity contract, it would all be taxed and penalized.

The 10 percent penalty does not apply to payments to taxpayers under the age of $59^{1}/2$ who may be disabled. Nor does it apply to any payment that is part of a series of periodical payments based on your life expectancy. If you decide to annuitize a contract at age 50 and receive equal payments over the rest of your life, for example, you would dodge the early withdrawal penalty.

A key to shopping for an annuity is to watch that the fees charged by the insurance company don't devalue a good portion of the tax breaks. And, generally, investing in an annuity makes sense only after you've taken full advantage of other tax-deferred retirement plans that give you more bang for your buck.

```
NOTE: IRA ANNUITY

Retired empty nesters may use their IRAs to pur-
chase an annuity. Buying an annuity that begins
regular payments by age 70^1/2 satisfies the IRS's
IRA withdrawal rules. Like an annuity, it can be
purchased for your life expectancy or jointly for
the combined life expectancies of you and your
spouse or other beneficiary.

One advantage of this option is that it guarantees
payments for your lifetime, or in the case of a
joint annuity, for the lifetime of both you and
your beneficiary. There also may be a provision in
the annuity that provides for payments to heirs.
```

Fixed annuities are reliable in that they guarantee you a specified interest rate for a specified period of time, often one year. In the case of deferred fixed annuities, this rate is usually guaranteed for one, two or three years, or other specified period.

After the specified period (you need to be sure that you understand what happens after the guaranteed rate period expires), your interest rate will change in accordance with prevailing interest rates in the marketplace. However, there is often a minimum guaranteed rate per contract, often 4 percent.

A fixed-rate annuity may provide you with a reliable and predictable accumulation or monthly benefit, but when you factor in inflation, the purchasing power of the fixed return diminishes. Over many years, the purchasing power can diminish considerably.

Self-Directed Variable Annuities

Self-directed variable annuities are designed to protect your money from the diminishing purchasing power effects of inflation. The performance of a self-directed variable annuity investment is based not on a fixed interest rate but on the performance of a portfolio of mutual funds (called separate accounts) that you select.

What's the purpose? To provide you the opportunity for a return that far exceeds the return that you could get out of a fixed annuity contract. Moreover, unlike an IRA, 401(k) or other tax-deferred investments, there is no limit as to how much you can invest in a self-directed fixed or variable annuity.

Remember, however, while earnings may be on a tax-deferred basis, all amounts contributed or invested in annuities employ after-tax dollars, money on which taxes have already been paid.

The Role of Self-Directed Variable Annuities

Think of your self-directed variable annuity as an all-weather investment. How so? The fact that your investment is diversified in a portfolio of mutual funds provides you with the opportunity to outperform not only fixed annuities, but also other types of investments such as bonds and money market funds.

Effectively matching your investment needs to the right mutual fund portfolio is crucial to your ultimate financial well-being. First, you need to understand what portfolio options are available. Then you need to select the one that is right for you.

Many employer-sponsored retirement plans are either structured like an annuity or use annuities to pay benefits to retirees. Thus, payment is guaranteed to every worker after retirement.

Retirement Annuity Options

While some pension plans require you to take a monthly annuity payment at retirement, your plan may allow you the option of taking a lump-sum payment. There may be some advantage of taking a lump sum, but this option must be considered carefully.

Most annuities offer payments which are not adjusted for inflation. However, if you are confident that you or your investment advisor can invest the lump-sum amount more profitably, then this option may be a much better choice. You'll probably be able to generate more income than with the annuity and, at the same time, beat inflation.

But you must consider the drawbacks of taking a lump sum. For example, if you or your spouse should incur substantial uninsured medical expenses (i.e., a long-term nursing home stay), subject to the claims of creditors or the mismanagement of money, your lump-sum retirement fund may be jeopardized. In the worst instances, this could seriously erode or altogether wipe out your pension resources.

This eventuality must be weighed carefully in deciding on the lump-sum option as opposed to an annuity. Once more, money that is an annuity is usually protected from these adverse occurrences.

What's the solution? The decision may not have to be made for many years, but perhaps a partial lump-sum settlement and partial annuity may be a desirable compromise (if allowed by your employer). Be sure to examine all of the annuity options available to you. Payment rates on income annuities may vary widely. Shop around for the company that offers the most attractive terms.

If you take a lump sum, you have some homework to do as well. You may be able to take advantage of forward averaging to reduce the tax impact of the distribution, or you can postpone paying taxes on the distribution by rolling it over into an IRA. Only when you begin withdrawing money from the IRA will taxes be due.

Reconciliation

First, use all tax-deductible opportunities for retirement investing. If you employer matches part of your contribution, contribute enough to get the maximum available match. Once you have used up your tax-deductible retirement investing opportunities, carefully weigh the costs and potential advantages of making further tax-deferred investments on a nondeductible or after-tax basis.

With the role of annuities, even annuities as part of your employer's retirement plan, you have all of the tools necessary to invest for a comfortable retirement. In the next chapter, we will explore the various ways of allocating annuities and the other investment tools we've explored in order to reach your investment goals.

Later, we'll take a look at a number of strategies that can help make the management of your nest egg both profitable and enjoyable. What more could any empty nester ask for?

Chapter 15

ALLOCATING THE ASSETS

There is nothing mystical about asset allocation. Asset allocation, after all, is simply the process of dividing your investment assets among the various investments available to you in the most appropriate manner given your investment goals, your need for current income and the time horizon until you will eventually need the money.

The question you must ask, of course, is how much should you allocate to each category of investment? Obviously, the assets of every empty nester will be allocated differently depending on their age, need for current income and their goals.

Allocating Investments

Investing effectively is crucial to your financial success. Therefore, you need to develop a plan that will help guide you both in deciding on the type of investments to make and in reviewing your investments periodically. Periodically doesn't mean every day; otherwise, you'll be so concerned that you will end up making investment changes too frequently.

Remember, the idea is to enjoy your status as an empty nester while, at the same time, planning for your retirement. If you establish sensible criteria now, you will be able to invest wisely without needing to spend an inordinate amount of time worrying about your investments.

The four steps to allocating your investments are

1) First, decide how much of your retirement assets should be invested in stocks and how much should go into interest-earning securities (bonds and short-term securities).

2) Once you know how much of your nest egg you feel should be in each of the investment categories that you feel are right for your unique situation, you need to determine how to purchase the securities you want.

    You can buy individual stocks and interest-earning securities yourself or you can take advantage of professional management by investing in mutual funds. You may well want to use some combination of both approaches.

3) For each investment category, determine what types of investments would be appropriate for your portfolio objectives and confidence level.

4) Finally, you need to select and purchase the actual securities—such as a particular stock, bond or mutual fund—that will help you achieve your investment goals.

What is Asset Allocation?

There is often a great deal of confusion about what, exactly, is meant by asset allocation. Noted investment theorist William F. Sharpe has identified four different types of asset allocation:

- STRATEGIC ASSET ALLOCATION. The focus is on long-term asset mix with no attempt to outguess or time the market.

- DYNAMIC ASSET ALLOCATION. There is no market timing but active shifting among security markets limits downside risk (creates portfolio insurance). This strategy tends to have particularly high transaction costs.

- TACTICAL ASSET ALLOCATION. The express intent is to beat the market using market timing or other techniques.

Much of what you read in the investment media focuses on tactical asset allocation. Many professional money managers use asset allocation, but shift the asset allocation periodically in response to market conditions. However, since the majority of professional investment managers have been unable to consistently beat the markets, it follows those strategies that assume that you can outguess the market (tactical strategies) or have high transaction costs (dynamic strategies) should be avoided.

Strategic allocation, on the other hand, emphasizes that investment returns (net of transaction costs) equal to overall market returns are acceptable, especially if they can be obtained with less than overall market risk.

What is Diversification?

If asset allocation is simply the process of dividing your investment nest egg among the various asset categories in the most appropriate manner given your investment goals, need for current income and time horizon until you will need the money, it could also be labeled diversification. The basic idea behind asset allocation is to have a mix of assets over at least four investment categories that give you the best chance of achieving good returns with moderate risk.

Consider one study made a few years ago (1993) of the benefit of asset allocation and diversification. Conducted by Bailard, Biehl & Kaiser (B, B & K), a San Francisco investment management firm, that study showed that even a naive approach to asset allocation—that is, investing equally in asset categories—was effective in dramatically reducing the overall portfolio risk in any single year. B, B & K used five asset categories (treating international investments as a separate category) and a 20-year time horizon. The five asset categories were cash and cash equivalents, fixed income (government and corporate bonds), equities (Standard & Poor's 500 Composite Index), international securities (foreign stocks and bonds) and hard assets (real estate).

The study hypothetically invested 20 percent in each of these categories. At the end of every year, it reduced the amount in the winning asset category and purchased more in the losing categories in order to keep a constant 20 percent mix in each category.

THE NAIVE PORTFOLIO 1974-93

	Compound Annual Return	Standard Deviation (+ or -)
S & P 500 Index	12.8%	31.8%
Long-Term Bonds	9.9%	15.1%
Foreign Securities	14.5%	46.2%
T-Bills	7.4%	5.3%
Real Estate	8.0%	13.4%
Naive portfolio	11.1%	15.3%
Inflation	5.9%	6.8%

* 95% of the returns varied around the average by plus or minus the percentage shown.

Source: Bailard, Biehl & Kaiser

As you can see, the naive portfolio had excellent returns and only moderate risk, as measured by its standard deviation (For more on standard deviation, see Chapter 16). To further emphasize this point compare the return of the S&P 500 and the naive portfolio. In the 20-year period, 95 percent of the S&P returns was between -17.8 percent (or 14 percent minus 31.8 percent standard deviation) and 45.8 percent (or 14 percent plus 31.8 percent standard deviation).

On the other hand, 95 percent of the naive portfolio return was between -4 percent (or 11.3 percent minus 15.3 percent) and 26.6 percent (or 11.3 percent plus 15.3 percent). The naive portfolio was therefore half as volatile as the S&P 500, yet its compound rate of return was almost as great—11.1 percent versus 12.8 percent.

It is this ability to achieve close to market returns with less overall risk that makes strategic asset allocation the strategy of choice for most empty nesters.

Strategic Asset Allocation

The goal of strategic asset allocation is to determine the way that you will divide your assets among the four major asset categories so that you can obtain the long-term portfolio performance that you need in order to achieve your retirement goals with the least risk.

Asset allocation is by nature a long-term investment strategy and has its theoretical foundation in what has been known as modern capital market theory. This theory holds that:

■ Domestic and international capital markets are dominated by institutions with almost limitless access to information. It is increasingly difficult for individuals to get the information necessary to predict price movement given this institutional domination.

■ Economic analysis doesn't lead to consistently profitable investment results. Trying to outguess peaks and valleys in the markets based on economic data has proven fruitless since markets don't seem to respond consistently to similar economic trends.

■ Inflation is usually the best predictor of long-term investment behavior.

■ Different classes of investments respond uniquely to the various kinds of risk.

■ Holding periods greatly influence the suitability of particular types of investments.

■ Diversification is an effective way to control risk.

The Value of Diversification

Obviously, asset allocation is first and foremost a type of diversification, in this case, across asset categories. One of the most important methods of reducing risk is by having a diversified portfolio.

There are three levels of investment diversification. The first level is among asset categories (i.e., cash and cash equivalents, fixed income, equities and hard assets). This is the basis for asset allocation and is significant because the greatest differences in investment behavior exists between assets in different categories rather than between different investments within a class.

For example, bonds and real estate generally have opposite reactions to inflation. Having investments in each category will hedge the exposure to inflation present in both categories.

The second level of diversification is among subcategories. For instance, equities have subcategories of aggressive growth, growth, growth and income and international stocks. Diversifying among these subcategories recognized that each subcategory behaves differently during different parts of the economic cycle. Investing in more than one subcategory will cushion the blow when a particular subcategory is adversely affected.

The third level of diversification calls for the representation of an adequate number of individual securities within an asset subcategory so that the performance of the subcategory is reflected in your portfolio.

> NOTE: As a general rule, once you have about 12 to 15 individual securities in your portfolio, you should be sufficiently diversified against market risk. Good or poor performance of each stock should average out to approximate the market so long as an adequate number of securities is held.

Doing It

In general, you have several different ways in which you can diversify your investments:

- Buy mutual funds.
- Use a professional money manager.
- Buy individual securities through a full-service or discount broker.

Obviously each option has its advantages as well as disadvantages. In general, the experts believe that most younger investors should use mutual funds to implement their retirement investment strategies since they offer the lowest cost and highest flexibility of all investment options.

By contrast, if you're an older investor with large lump sums, you can use mutual funds or individual money management services, both of which can be obtained through investment advisers or on your own.

Getting Started, Gradually

One stone remains unturned in the all-important asset allocation process and it is a crucial one. Many investors, once they get serious about allocating their investments appropriately, find that they have made a major reallocation of their investments.

If, for example, you have been investing in conservative money market accounts and are now convinced that you need to invest in stocks and bonds, the crucial question is how fast should you do it? Additionally, if you have recently received a cash windfall, say an inheritance, how fast should you invest it?

If you invest all of it tomorrow, the risk, of course, is that you make a major investment in stocks just before the market declines or a major investment in bonds just before interest rates shoot up.

All too often, empty nesters become so wary of a possible loss amidst uncertain market conditions that they end up investing very conservatively—too conservatively. However, one way to reduce the risk of ill-timed investing is to devise a plan of gradual investment of your money rather than taking the chance of investing a significant portion of your money at a stock market high and/or an interest rate low.

Gradual investment of your money is, in essence, a form of dollar-cost averaging, which is widely and successfully used for investing in individual stocks or mutual funds. The following table shows how you might devise an investment timetable over the next two years. This allows for a gradual investment of the available money rather than an immediate commitment.

For the sake of our illustration, we'll assume that you eventually want an allocation of 50 percent stocks and 50 percent interest-earning securities. Also assume that you would like your distribution to be fully invested within two years.

GRADUAL INVESTMENT TIMETABLE

	Percent of Total Investment		
Investment Category	Now	Within Next 12 months	From 12-24 months
Stocks	15%	30%	50%
Fixed Income	25%	35%	40%
Cash equivalent	60%	35%	10%
Total	100%	100%	100%

As the timetable indicates, a large portion of the money initially sits on the sidelines in low-yielding cash-equivalent investments, e.g., money market funds, short term CDs, Treasury bills. Alternatively, if you are willing to accept some interest rate risk during the course of your investment program, you could use short-term bonds or short-term bond funds in lieu of much of the cash equivalent alternative which will probably enable you to get a somewhat better yield.

Within the first 12 months of the investment program, your stock exposure is increased from 15 to 30 percent and fixed-income exposure from 25 to 35 percent. The total column shows a fully invested allocation which would be achieved within a two-year period.

Gradual deployment of investments makes a lot of sense, particularly when you think stock prices are high and/or interest rates are low. Certainly opportunities may be missed by following such a timetable but costly mistakes may also be avoided.

Buying a portfolio of individual stocks or bonds can be an option if you have the time and patience to manage your own investments or want to pay the fees to have a broker or financial planner do it for you. In general, however, mutual funds or money managers provide the most cost-effective means to implement your investment strategy.

Risk Tolerance

Your asset allocation decisions will, to a great extent, be influenced by your attitude toward investment risk. Since perception of risk varies from one investor to the next, two empty nesters with essentially identical personal profiles—the same income level, the same financial goals, the same anticipated Social Security benefits and the same level of savings—may adopt quite different asset allocations.

Unfortunately, getting a feel for your level of risk tolerance is not a cut and dried issue. After all, there is no risk scale to indicate whether you are a conservative, moderate or aggressive investor. Nor are there set rules that link a specific asset allocation to your psychological attitude toward risk.

That is, for some empty nesters, a conservative investment posture may involve investing one-half of their savings in stocks; for others, a conservative posture may entail avoiding stocks altogether. Only you can provide a definitive answer to the question: What level of risk am I willing to assume?

Hopefully, with the help of this book and a better understanding of the financial markets, you'll be better able to responsibly address this question.

What Do You Have to Allocate?

In earlier chapters (7 through 13) we outlined a number of investment possibilities. To review your options:

- Stock returns are a powerful long-term creator of wealth. Historically, stocks are the only asset category whose returns have far outpaced inflation.

- Subcategories of stock offer markedly different patterns of return. Allocating a portion of your portfolio to each subcategory can enhance returns and reduce risk through diversification.

- Bonds provide predictable income from compounding and a cushion against the effects of stock price volatility or portfolio value. A so-called "laddered" portfolio (with various maturities) can mitigate against sudden changes in interest rates and inflation.

- As with stocks, subcategories of bonds exhibit different patterns of return. Allocating a portion of your portfolio to each subcategory may enhance return and reduce risk through diversification.

- Cash equivalents preserve capital but offer little or no real return.

- Hard assets are an appropriate investment even though they may be illiquid (real estate) or volatile (gold). They provide portfolio diversification because of their lack of correlation with the price movements of stocks and bonds.

Age 20—49

In your early and middle working years, when your investment horizon extends 40 years or more, your primary investment objective should be to accumulate capital for your retirement. At this point in your life, common stock should be your dominant investment option for two reasons: (1) stocks have provided the highest long-term total returns of any major asset class and (2) while stocks have also had the highest volatility level of any asset class, the passage of time has a dampening effect on their short-term fluctuations.

Although a 100 percent stock portfolio may be appropriate for accumulating investments in the earliest stages of the investment life cycle, few investors possess the necessary fortitude to commit all of their savings to stocks. For most investors, it's probably wise to maintain a modest investment in bonds as well. One possible allocation during the accumulation years might be 80 percent stocks/20 percent bonds.

Age 50—59

The majority of empty nesters find themselves in the so-called transition years between 50 and 59 years of age. Although most empty nesters will want to continue accumulating assets for retirement, they'll also want to preserve the capital that they have accumulated so far.

While stocks should continue to be your primary investment vehicle, it may be time to realize some of your stock market gains and gradually move to a more conservative investment stance. The recommended allocation might approximate 60 percent stocks/ 40 percent bonds.

The Early Retirement Years

During retirement you will begin to spend the capital that you have accumulated. At the same time, your investment horizon may still extend—given current life expectancies—20 or 30 years. So, some growth in savings is needed in order to protect your assets against the ravages of inflation. In this situation, it seems appropriate to reduce your common stock commitment while moving some of your assets into short-term reserves.

Your recommended asset allocation here might be 40 percent stocks/40 percent bonds/ 20 percent short-term reserves.

The "Right" Allocation Mix

Despite the above guidelines, there is no one "right" allocation. Ideally, most nest eggs or investment portfolios should contain a balanced combination of the various types of investment vehicles discussed in Chapter 12, such as interest earning investments (both cash equivalents and bonds), stocks and perhaps real estate.

Most portfolios should be sufficiently diversified so that all major asset categories are represented. Beyond that, allocation decisions depend largely on your investment time horizon.

Portfolios invested for longtime horizons can afford to accept the greater short-term price volatility that comes with a more significant allocation to stocks. Short time horizons call for less volatile mixes.

> NOTE: Long-term bonds are rarely recommended for individual investors because they have twice the volatility of intermediate-term bonds with little or no increase in the rate of return.

Once you have determined how to divide your portfolio, you can decide whether to directly—or indirectly—own your investments. Owing individual stocks or bonds is a form of direct investing, whereas buying stock or bond mutual funds is an increasingly popular form of indirect investing.

Indirect investing means buying shares in a fund where professional managers buy individual stock or bond issues for their fund investors.

Deciding how much of your hard-earned money to place in indirect as opposed to direct investments depends on several factors including how much you have to invest and how much time you and/or your investment adviser (see Chapter 18) want to devote to monitoring individual stock and bond investments.

Although we'll explore a number of strategies that can be employed to maximize your investment return and increase your profits, strategies that apply to both direct investments and indirect investments, let's take a closer look at the most favored means of indirect investing: mutual funds.

What Are Mutual Funds?

Mutual funds are open-end investment companies that pool money from individuals and invest in securities such as stocks and bonds. They must distribute earnings from the securities in their portfolio, both dividends and realized capital gains, to their shareholders each year.

A typical mutual fund invests in dozens of different securities; large funds own hundreds. As a result, even a small investment in mutual fund shares brings you immediate, broad diversification. Mutual funds enable every empty nester to go a step further by diversifying within a particular asset category.

Let's say, by way of example, you purchase $5,000 worth of shares in a growth mutual fund and its portfolio is invested equally in stocks of 75 different large companies. If one company went bankrupt and its stock became worthless, your share of the loss as a mutual fund shareholder would be less than a penny and a half on the dollar.

To purchase stocks on your own and achieve comparable diversification, you would need to invest in a substantial number of individual stock issues.

Selecting Mutual Funds

Selecting mutual fund investments might at first appear to be a daunting task. After all, with more than 5,000 funds available, where do you start?

Keeping in mind that 90 percent of the performance of your portfolio will be due to the mix of the investments that you select—your asset allocation—and less than 10 percent to the particular funds that you choose. In other words, once you have determined the appropriate asset allocation, 90 percent of your investment decision is behind you.

Here are the characteristics that you should look for when selecting mutual funds and completing the final 10 percent of the process:

1) A fit with your asset allocation. This is the starting point. You should be looking for funds that match your subcategory allocation.

2)   Above-average performance. Compare the fund's return to the average return of similar funds over different time periods. Select a fund that beats the average over long periods.

3)   Below-average risk. Likewise, look at risk ratings. Funds that beat the average in terms of return are also likely to experience greater-than-average volatility, or risk. You want to find one with above-average return and below-average volatility.

4)   A consistent track record. A mutual fund whose returns have consistently placed it in the first or second quartile among its peers and rarely in the bottom quartile, will be a better choice than an erratic up-and-down fund with the same overall average return.

5)   A complementary style. Make sure that your portfolio has a mix of styles. If you own two stock funds, for instance, make sure that one is a value style fund and the other is managed with a growth style. As you add stock funds, alternate between styles.

> NOTE: Value managers and growth managers differ markedly in their approaches to investing. Value managers look for stocks priced below some yardstick of their true worth. In essence, they are bargain hunters.
>
> Value managers tend to hold stocks for long periods, which reduces transaction costs and helps boost returns. And because value stocks, by definition, have low valuations in terms of price-to-earnings or price-to-cash flow return, they offer less volatility and risk in the short-term than growth stocks.

6)   Below-average expenses. Compare the expense ratio to the average for the fund's investment objective. Stick to funds with below-average expenses. Other things being equal, go with the fund that charges the lowest expenses.

7)   Consistency with investment objectives. Read the prospectus and check the composition of a fund's investment holdings to make sure that the fund will focus on the asset category that you want. For example, a growth fund may hold relatively large amounts of cash if the manager does not like the outlook for stocks.

Or a domestic fund may invest heavily in foreign securities. If you already have an appropriate amount of cash or foreign securities in other funds, you may not want funds that stray from their investment objectives. For instance, most funds employ an "active" investment approach, using a professional investment manager; other funds employ an "index" strategy seeking to match the performance and risk characteristics of a particular segment of the financial markets—without the use of an investment adviser.

Some funds emphasize technical factors hoping to identify trends from the past that will reoccur in the future; other funds emphasize fundamental valuation measures, such as price-earnings ratios, dividend yields and the like.

Fortunately, you need not allow the challenge of selecting particular mutual funds to distract you from your retirement program. Indeed, over the long run, the success of your retirement investment program will depend much more on how you allocate your assets among stocks, bonds and short-term reserves than which particular fund investment you choose.

Asset Allocation Funds

These funds are similar to the traditional balanced funds in that they invest in a mix of stocks, bonds and short-term reserves. But the similarity ends there. Unlike the traditional balanced funds, asset allocation funds retain the flexibility to substantially alter their allocation among the three asset classes depending on the fund manager's outlook for the relative performance of the different financial markets.

Even among asset allocation funds, investment policies may vary widely, with some funds permitted to hold up to 100 percent of their assets in stocks, while others have a much lower limit. In essence, all asset allocation funds engage in market timing to some degree, an endeavor that has rarely proved successful in the fallible world of investing. As a result, holding a particular asset allocation fund may entail much more risk than holding a particular traditional balanced mutual fund. In any event, you should carefully evaluate the investment portfolio of these funds before you invest.

Once you have allocated your nest egg among directly and indirectly owned investments, you need to divide those investment categories into specific industry, market and/or fund categories.

Directly-owned, interest-earning investments might consist of short-term investments (money market accounts, CDs), municipal bonds, corporate bonds and Treasury bonds. If you also decide to invest in interest-earning mutual funds, you might consider a Treasury bond fund and a municipal bond fund.

Finally, you will need to select specific investments within each of the industry or mutual fund categories that you have identified. One of the most important prerequisites for investment success is knowing the right questions to ask.

Familiarizing yourself with the array of commonly available investments in Chapter 12 will help you ask the right questions so that you can become a more informed investor—and have more fun.

You need not allow the challenge of selecting particular investments or mutual funds to distract you from your retirement program. Indeed, over the long-run, the success of your retirement investment program will depend much more on how you allocate your assets among stocks, bonds and short-term reserves than which particular mutual fund you choose.

Real choices, and perhaps for some, more enjoyment is to be found by personalizing your investment program by selecting and managing individual investments. Naturally, diversification and asset allocation will still play an extremely important role in the success of your retirement program.

Next, we'll take a look at some of the more popular and successful strategies that can help you manage either an individual portfolio or one invested in mutual funds—or both.

Chapter 16

INVESTMENT STRATEGIES

It should be remembered that empty nesters are rarely professional investors, nor do they really have to be in today's marketplace. In Chapter 18, we're going to be taking a look at all of the different types of professionals that are ready to advise any empty nester.

In addition to those who choose any independent path to investing, there are also empty nesters who prefer to know how their money is growing under someone else's guidance. For everyone, then, there are a number of investment strategies that are basic.

The Fundamentals of Investing

Many empty nesters don't fully understand the fundamentals of investing and therefore may have unrealistic expectations about an investment's future performance. For instance, money market funds represent a low-risk haven for emergency reserves and should not be expected to match the performance of more volatile bond funds.

In the same context, bond funds should not be expected to generate sustainable capital growth over the long run. While the steady decline in interest rates that began in the mid-1980s has resulted in substantial capital returns for bonds, inexperienced investors may view these yield driven earlier gains as a sustainable component of the investment return on bond funds. But they are not. When interest rates reverse this potential decline, those empty nesters/investors may be severely disappointed.

Buy Low, Sell High

It is easy to decide when to buy any investment: when you have the cash. You'll study your options, then pick the stock, bond, mutual fund or other investment that fits your empty-nester philosophy and that appears to have potential for appreciation.

Once you have decided which investment to buy, you might think that the hard decisions are over. Not so. Deciding when to buy an investment is much easier than deciding when to sell.

If your stock or other investment goes up in value, should you sell right away, or should you hold on for even more profit? If your stock goes down, should you sell now and accept your losses or wait for it to regain value?

A good rule of thumb in making that decision is to ask yourself, "If I didn't own this stock, would I buy it now at its present price?" If the answer is yes, hold it. If not, it's time to sell.

Investment Realities

In order to properly develop any investment strategy, you must first understand several investment realities:

- Investment categories and subcategories have different ranges of investment return and volatility.

- Your holding period (the amount of time you actually own the investment) affects both investment return and volatility.

- As you progress through the investment life cycle, your investment mix should change in both the accumulation and withdrawal phases.

Time Horizons

Now that you have seen examples of the volatility of the different types of investments as outlined in earlier chapters, the question becomes: how can you minimize volatility in your retirement portfolio? One possible answer is by designing a portfolio that makes sense given your unique investment time horizon.

When it comes to retirement investing, the time horizon is generally defined as your proximity to retirement age. If, for example, you are one year from retirement, it wouldn't make much sense to have your entire portfolio in small company stocks. They are simply too volatile—a short-term market downturn would have a devastating effect.

On the other hand, if you are 30 years from retirement, you shouldn't invest 100 percent of your money in Treasury bills that barely keep pace with inflation. Your time horizon will actually govern the amount of risk that you can afford. Since history shows that the passage of time will always smooth out short-term market fluctuations, the time horizon of your investments will have a significant impact on your planning.

Volatility/Standard Deviation

Make no mistake about it, investment markets are volatile. Look at what happened in 1994. Due to increases in interest rates, many bond portfolios lost value, and stocks, for the most part, broke even.

Now look at the first six months of 1995. Both long-term bonds and blue-chip stocks rose about 20 percent. For an individual investor, these short-term peaks and valleys take their toll.

Unfortunately, this investment risk is frequently misunderstood because it is so difficult to measure. Some people would just say that risk means the likelihood that you will lose the entire value of your investment. Others look at the probability that the actual return will turn out to be different than what was expected. A more accepted definition equates risk with volatility (fluctuations on investment returns over a given time period).

In assessing volatility of return, one of the most common measurements used by investors is a statistical concept called the standard deviation which means the degree to which annual returns from a given investment varied above or below an average. Generally speaking, the more volatile the investment, the larger the standard deviation.

HISTORICAL ASSET CLASS RETURNS AND RISK 1926-93

Asset Class	Compound Average Annual Return	Standard Deviation*
Small-company stocks	17.6%	34.6%
International stocks	15.8%	23.8%
Large-company stocks	12.3%	19.6%
Government bonds	5.4%	8.6%
Treasury bills	3.7%	3.3%
Inflation	3.2%	4.6%

* 95% of the returns varied around the compound average by plus or minus the percentage shown.

Source: Ibbotson Associates

As the table above illustrates, using historical performance as a guide, we can get a sense of how different investments perform as a class and how returns vary among those investments.

Over time investors have been rewarded for taking on the risk posed by more volatile returns. In the table above, for instance, large company stocks posed more than twice the risk of U.S. government bonds, at least as measured by the standard deviation of their return. But the returns of large-company stocks were also more than twice as large as those of government bonds. Even more volatile, but more rewarding, were small-company stocks.

Stock Tips

Obviously, there are no guarantees of success with any type of investments. When it comes to stocks, however, there are a number of strategies that have proven profitable for investors in the past:

1) Never buy stocks indiscriminately. Many empty nesters buy stocks haphazardly simply because they have money to invest. This is a very bad practice; investments should be made only when you have a good reason to buy them.

2) Select a promising industry. At any given time, most industries in the economy are either on the upswing or the downswing. When choosing a stock, an empty nester should start by selecting a promising industry with a good future outlook. Then it is time to look for a specific company within that industry whose prospects look the most promising.

3) Diversify. As we've mentioned repeatedly, try to own stocks in several different industries. The danger of too many eggs in one basket can't be overemphasized. However, overdiversification is also unwise. It is easier to keep track of 5 or 10 stocks than it is to track 25 stocks. As a general rule, you can achieve excellent diversification with about 10 well-chosen stocks.

4) Buy low and sell high. You don't really have to be a contrarian (see later in this chapter) in order to condition yourself to buy stock when a company's share price is down and sell it when the price is up. Stocks can gain when prices are low and major selling opportunities can come when the stock is hot (everybody wants to own it) and prices are high. This is the famous buy low, sell high rule mentioned earlier in this chapter; it is recommended that you use caution when following even his basic stock market axiom or strategy.

5) Stay abreast of market trends. Look at the general trend in the market. A stock that has already risen in value might be a good candidate for continued gains if the market is still rising. Conversely, a stock that does not respond to a general market rise might turn out to be a candidate for selling.

6) Use stop-loss orders to protect against loss. Potential losses can be effectively limited by using stop-loss orders (they are not available on over-the-counter

stocks), which fence in gains by restricting the effects of a market downturn on your stock.

> NOTE: Stop-loss orders or simply stop orders are orders to a securities broker to buy or sell at the market price once the security has traded at a specified priced call the "stop price." They are intended to either protect a profit or limit a loss.

Stop-loss orders can also be used to force you to sell. If, for example, you buy a stock at $12 per share and it rises to $18 per share, you might put a stop-loss order in at $15 per share to lock in your gain. The risk of this strategy is that you might get left behind at $15 per share if that stock continues rising, but this may be less risky than a loss due to a sharp decline.

7) Buy value. Companies with strong finances (not too much debt) and solid earnings growth are consistently better long-run performers.

8) Buy stocks with low price/earnings ratios and high dividends. Many successful long-term investors use the investment strategy of purchasing common stocks of companies with relatively low price to earnings multiples and relatively high dividend yields. The logic behind this strategy is that the stock price is depressed (a low price/earnings multiple) and hence, the stock is being purchased when no one else wants it.

   This in itself is a good strategy as long as the company with the low price/earnings and high dividends has no major long-term problems. Moreover, when the stock price rises, the company probably will attempt to maintain its high dividend yield by raising its dividend. Investors, therefore, get the best of both worlds: rising stock prices and higher dividend income.

9) Buy stock in companies with strong dividend payment records. Consider stocks in companies that have a consistent history of paying generous dividends. In a bear market (in which the stock price has declined), those companies tend to decline less in price than companies that pay no dividend at all or pay dividends erratically, since investors are confident that the dividends will keep coming through thick and thin. Some companies have paid annual dividends for more than 100 years.

10) Rely on your own experiences and judgment. Often, looking for successful companies to invest in doesn't require that you go to Wall Street. Investment ideas can come from your own observations of how things are selling on Main Street.

This common-sense strategy (on Wall Street it is labeled "real economics") has been used by some of the most successful investors and money managers for years. The next time that you go to the mall, keep your eyes open for new investment opportunities.

Technical Analysis

Technical analysis involves studying indicators that are intended to predict whether the supply of shares of stock which will be offered for sale will be satisfied by the expected demand for those shares. A pure "technician" is one who doesn't care what a company's future earnings will be.

A technical analyst or "technician" is usually only concerned with interpreting chart patterns and other supply and demand related indicators. Most analysts, however, are not really "pure technicians," even if they claim to be technical analysts.

The majority of analysts, even those claiming to be technicians, are usually somewhat eclectic. Most technical analysts would admit that they take into account the earnings forecasts for a company as well as their own technical analysis.

Most investors use what is called fundamental analysis in order to select what to invest in and use technical analysis to help them decide when to invest in it. Technical analysis is most valuable for offering guidelines on investment theory.

"Market efficiency" is the term used to describe the concept that the market, and the price of any stock at any time, is always fully valued. In other words, the market is always selling at exactly the right price at any given time.

The market continually and quickly adjusts to reflect all of the facts that would go into evaluating the price of any security. Market efficiency is one of the major criticisms of technical analysis. It implies that there is no such thing as an undervalued or overvalued investment, since the price of all securities would be fully valued all the time.

Technical analysts, however, would point out that although a security may be fully valued at any point in time, that value will change as circumstances change in the future.

Some critics of technical analysis take the extreme approach of market efficiency and have pursued what is often called the "random walk hypothesis." That random walk hypothesis states that the direction of any particular stock is no more predictable than the steps of a drunken man. Just as there is no logical way to predict where a drunk's next step will fall, there is no basis for predicting where the price of any given security is going.

Whether the market truly follows a random walk or a predictable path is a debate that will never be resolved to the complete satisfaction of all concerned. The empty nester should keep both theories in mind when developing their investment plans, strategies and courses of action.

Short Interest

The so-called "short interest ratio" used by many professional investors operates on the same premise. Short interest is the percentage of the outstanding shares of stock that have been sold short. The short interest on most major companies is reported weekly in financial publications such as the *Wall Street Journal* or in *Barron's,* a weekly investment newspaper.

> NOTE: A short sale is a sale of a security without
> ownership in the hopes of a price decline that
> will allow repurchase at a lower price. The broker
> typically borrows the stock from another customer
> to deliver for the short sale.

If a large percentage of a company's shares have been sold short, you would assume that a large number of speculators believe that the stock is going lower. Logically, this sounds like a bearish indicator. After all, a short seller would make money when the stock dropped in price.

To a technician, however, this is a contrary indicator and a high short interest would be a bullish indicator. The rationale is that the more speculators who have sold a stock short, the more investors there are who will have to be buyers of that stock in the near future. The short sellers are all going to have to cover the short sales. So, like high mutual fund liquidity, high short interest also represents built-in demand for that stock.

Market Timing

There are two basic market timing techniques used by some investors: dollar-cost averaging and fixed amount investing. If you are investing in individual stocks, these timing techniques may not be practical. These strategies can, however, be useful for timing mutual fund investments.

"Dollar-cost averaging," is a strategy for investing the same dollar amount in the same investment at fixed time intervals. Investors usually have the option of investing in mutual funds in relatively small dollar amounts. So, sometimes, they will make an agreement with a fund to send in a fixed dollar amount every month to that fund. This adds discipline to the savings strategy, but it could also help the investor establish a better cost basis for the fund.

If an individual had originally put in the whole $2,000, rather than invest one-half of that amount and time average the other half, they would have had a total of 200 shares

REGULAR INVESTING THROUGH
DOLLAR-COST AVERAGING

Quarterly Investment	Average Price per Share	Number of Shares Purchased
Year 1		
$2,000	$13.00	153.85
2,000	11.85	168.78
2,000	10.46	191.20
Year 2		
$2,000	$17.87	111.92
2,000	18.10	110.50
2,000	20.33	98.38
2,000	16.06	124.53
Year 3		
$2,000	$23.61	84.71
2,000	33.79	59.19
2,000	40.17	49.79

Total Investment	Average Price per Share over 3 Years*	Average Cost for All Shares Purchased+
$24,000	$21.24	$17.68

* Add the 12 quarterly prices and divide by 12

+ Divide your total investment by the total number of shares purchased.

at $10 per share. At the lowest point of the price decline, April 30, the $2,000 investment would have had a market value of only $1,450.

However, by cost averaging, the investor ended up purchasing a total of 215.84 shares, at an average price of $9,375. Because of the price decline after the initial purchase, the investor in this case benefited by cost averaging. That strategy reduced the price per share and increased the number of shares.

When you send in a fixed dollar amount every month, you will buy fewer shares when the price of the shares goes up and more shares when the price goes down. So you end up dollar-cost averaging your price per share. If the investment goes through a down cycle, you will be buying more shares while it is down, reducing your average cost per share over that time. If it goes up, you will be buying fewer shares at the higher price.

The Empty Nester as a Contrarian

Your emotions are always going to be working against you when it comes to making good decisions concerning market timing. The best time to buy is when everyone is selling and the best time to sell is when everyone is buying. That is being a contrarian.

If you had been a buyer of securities after the "Crash of '87," you could have doubled your investment over the following 12 months. There weren't, however, all that many investors scrambling to buy on that day. It goes against the grain to buy when everyone else is selling, or to sell when everyone else is buying. This is true regardless of whether you are an individual investor or a so-called "institutional" investor—we are all individuals.

If you want to avoid falling victim to the cycle, you will need to make investment decisions based on logic and research, not on emotions.

Remember, a contrarian is likely to be an investor who is buying when the majority is selling and who is selling when the majority is buying. That is a good position in which to be.

Consider a few contrarian strategies:

The "mutual fund liquidity theory" measures the percentage of mutual fund assets that are not invested in equities but, instead, are kept in money market funds. At first glance, it might appear that if mutual fund managers are not investing a large percentage of their funds' assets, then they must have a very bearish outlook on the market.

In other words, the logical conclusion to high mutual fund liquidity is that this represents a bearish outlook. This, however, is a contrarian indicator. To a technical analyst, the higher the percentage of mutual fund liquidity, the more bullish the indicator. The reason this is a bullish indicator lies in the basis for all technical indicators—supply and demand.

To a technician, the more investments that mutual fund managers have in cash, such as money market funds or Treasury bills, the more money they have that is going to be invested some time in the future. So, to them, it means that high mutual fund liquidity represents pent-up demand.

Paired Investments

Only you can decide whether a particular investment is right for your unique situation. Paired investments, on the other hand, appeal to many investors.

As their name implies, they are limited partnerships with two distinct businesses. One business generates income and, hopefully, cash. The other business generates losses—at least for tax purposes—to offset that income.

Paired investments are just another variation on the tax shelter theme. Therefore, empty nesters should invest in one of these vehicles only if it makes economic sense.

Fundamentals of Investment Strategies

Investment theories are much like bellybuttons, almost everyone has one. Armed with the fundamentals of what you would be best advised to invest your own retirement portfolio in, how it should be allocated and over what period of time, every empty nester will need an ever-changing strategy to maximize the return from those investments. Or they will find it necessary to understand basic strategies in order to understand what their advisers are doing in their name.

In the next chapter we'll explore the subject of advisers. Not only will we take a look at investment advisers, who they are, how you find them, and how much you can expect to pay them, but we'll go one step further. Since man (or woman) does not live by investments alone, we'll also take a look at other types of professionals and advisers who can help every empty nester enjoy and benefit from their newly discovered lifestyle.

BEWARE OF EMPLOYERS

We've already outlined some of the benefits that employers can and do furnish their employees. These benefits not only help fund your retirement nest egg, many of those benefits help you enjoy your empty nester lifestyle and continue it even after retirement. Unfortunately, today's economy doesn't bode well for employer-provided benefits.

First, just who is an employee? Using the general definition of an employee, anyone performing services is considered to be an employee if the services are under an employer's control as to both what must be done and how it must be done. However, if the employer has the right to specify the work to be performed, but not the manner and materials of achieving the result, the person performing services may be an independent contractor. Although everyone wants to be labeled as an independent contractor, if only for the additional tax deductions, there is a great deal of controversy over the Internal Revenue Service's definition of who is an independent contractor and who is an employee. Employer's, too, often prefer to deal with independent contractors because of the reduced paperwork and employment tax burden.

The risk of having independent contractors labeled as employees as well as the threat to pension and fringe benefit plans frequently prevents many employers from being too aggressive in labeling workers as independent contractors. And the IRS, in their efforts to ensure payment of employment taxes and enforce withholding tax rules, are also quite aggressive in examining the status of workers labeled as independent contractors. Fortunately, Congress has slowed the IRS's efforts in this area until new legislation can be created.

The Importance of Fringe Benefits

As many employers have discovered, it would be difficult to imagine better recruiting and retention tools than fringe benefits. Tops on the list of why anyone would prefer status as an employee over the more flexible independent contractor status are stock options and stock appreciation rights.

Both stock options and stock appreciation rights let employees share in the success of their employer and, at least from the company's perspective, both boost employees' incentives to work for their company's success.

Some companies restrict options to top executive. Others spread this benefit down the line. Often options are a negotiable part of a total compensation package. Most empty nesters can use stock options and stock appreciation rights to their best advantage only if they understand the tax rules that govern them.

How Options Work

When your employer grants you a stock option, you've gained the right to purchase a specific number of shares of your company's stock at a specific price within a specified period of time. You don't have to buy, but you may—at your option.

Options come in two varieties: incentive stock options (ISOs) and nonqualified stock options (NQSOs). The difference lies mainly in the tax benefits provided by ISOs.

There is no regular tax due on an incentive stock option until you eventually sell or exchange the stock you've purchased and then only if you sell or exchange it for more than you paid for it. Naturally, you must hold ISOs for a specified amount of time if your profits are to be taxed as capital gain.

Generally, with NQSOs, there is an immediate tax bite when you exercise the option, as well as the tax you pay when you sell the stock at a profit. To illustrate, if you were granted NQSOs instead of ISOs, you would have incurred a tax liability when you exercised them. The IRS taxes you on the difference between the option price and the market price at the time you exercise the NQSO options. In other words, you are taxed on the difference between the price you pay to exercise the option and its market value at that time. Even worse, this income is treated as ordinary, fully taxable income.

The advantage of an ISO is that you pay no regular tax until you actually realize a gain when you sell or exchange your stock and all of that gain is then treated as a capital gain. With the NQSO you generally pay tax on your paper profits as ordinary income when you exercise the option. That means that you not only must have cash to buy the stock when you exercise a NQSO, you also need additional funds to pay taxes due.

Which is the better deal? ISOs or NQSOs? The answer, surprisingly, is that it depends. You may, for instance, be better off from a tax perspective with ISOs. But ISOs do come with a set of rules that can make them less desirable for other reasons.

The Restrictions on ISOs

Specific rules and restrictions define an ISO. If a stock option doesn't conform, it is, by definition, a NQSO and is automatically treated as such. Even if an option qualifies as an ISO, however, you may be able to treat it as an NQSO—if its terms give you that option and if to do so is to your advantage. Naturally, if you violate the rules, your ISO will be automatically treated, at least for tax purposes, as an NQSO.

Generally, from the day you receive the ISO until three months before you exercise it, you must be employed by the company (or a related company) granting it. However, you may, if your employer's plan allows, exercise the option within three months after you leave the company and still retain the favorable tax treatment.

Although stock options are relatively rare among middle level employees, everyone today seems to have the opportunity to invest in their employer's 401(k) plans. Thus far, it has proved to be an excellent tool for funding the retirement plans of most empty nesters.

Those 401(k) Plans

We've explored the value of 401(k) plans (Chapter 13) but there is also an often-overlooked downside. Not surprisingly, there are limits on the amount of money that you and your employer may contribute to a 401(k) plan each year. But those limits seem rather generous when compared, for instance, to the $2,000 cap on IRA contributions.

The government sets two limits on 401(k)s. One cap is the amount that you may contribute to your own retirement plan. The other restricts the amount that you and your employer together may contribute. The Federal government adjusts both of these figures annually.

With proper planning, you can ensure that your plan receives the maximum, total contribution. As far as the first limit is concerned, for years after 1996, the maximum amount an employee may salt away annually, tax deferred, in a 401(k) plan is $9,500.

Accident and Health Benefits

In today's economy, one of the most important fringe benefits that any employer can offer is that of health insurance. A major reason is that amounts received by employees under employer-financed accident and health plans may qualify for exclusion from income. A self-employed person, on the other hand, is not an employee for purposes of this unique exclusion.

Amounts received by employees as reimbursement for medical care and payments (computed without regard to the period of absence from work) for permanent injury or loss of bodily function under an employer-financed accident and health plan are also excludable.

Money, other than reimbursements for medical expenses, received by an employee from accident and health insurance because of personal injuries or sickness generally must be included in income if the amounts (1) are attributable to contributions from the employer to an insurance plan and were not included in the employee's income or (2) are paid directly by the employer.

Payments from an accident and health plan are also excludable from an employee's gross income to the extent that the plan providing the benefits is funded by the employee.

But what if your employer doesn't offer a health plan or underwrite medical expenses? A unique option is a test program created by our lawmakers that will allow many empty nesters to set up special savings accounts, much like IRAs, which can be used, tax-free, to fund medical expenses.

Medical Savings Accounts (MSAs)

That's right, employees of small businesses and self-employed individuals will be able to take advantage of MSAs to pay health care expenses, provided that these accounts are used in conjunction with "high deductible" health insurance. The program is a test of the MSA concept and will be available only to the first 750,000 participants each year—unless expanded or extended—from 1997 through the year 2000.

MSAs are like IRAs created for the purpose of defraying unreimbursed health care expenses on a tax-deferred basis. Contributions are tax deductible, medical expenses withdrawn from these accounts to pay medical expenses are not taxed and the amounts in the MSA continue to grow, tax-free, until withdrawn after the empty nester reaches the age of 59 $1/2$—just like an IRA.

A Dark Cloud on Every Employee's Horizon

Every empty nester faces enough threats to their retirement security to make worrying about independent contractor status a moot point. Much has been written about a retirement crises that will affect members of the baby boom generation sometime after the turn of the century. Much more will be written by the time the first wave of baby boomers begins retiring around the year 2010.

You don't have to be an alarmist to agree that there is a significant cause for concern. Signs of weaknesses are apparent in each of the legs of the "three-legged stool" that has, up to now, supported retirees: employer pensions, Social Security and individual savings.

The number of employees covered by traditional pension plans is shrinking and some of the remaining plans have become underfunded. Meanwhile, Social Security is headed for trouble. Experts agree that Social Security payroll taxes will have to be raised and growth of benefits will have to be trimmed over the coming decades; the great debate is over how much and when.

To offset pension and Social Security shortcomings, all of us ought to be saving more. But we aren't. The personal savings rate in this country declined sharply beginning in the early 1980s from a previous range of about 9 percent of national income to about three percent today.

NOTE: A SUGGESTION

Realize that you, not your employer or the government, will be responsible for providing your retirement security. Don't count too much on a pension or Social Security for retirement income.

What if Your Company's Pension Plan Fails?

During the 1980s, the problem of pension underfunding became acute in the U.S. Underfunding is where employers have an obligation to pay money into pension plans but substitute IOUs instead. At the end of 1992, corporate pensions were underfunded by $53 billion in the aggregate, although 75 percent of that underfunding was centered in about 50 companies.

If a pension fund actually goes bankrupt, however, there is a payor of last resort: the Federal government. The Pension Benefit Guaranty Corporation (PBGC) insures pensions in a way roughly similar to how the FDIC insures bank accounts. PBGC charges each covered plan a premium (called a head tax) for each participant covered by PBGC insurance.

Remember, however, this insurance applies only to defined benefit plans. Other types of retirement plans are not insured. And you may not get the full value of your pension. The maximum benefit payable by the PBGC is currently around $27,000 per year.

Taking Early Retirement

What if you decide to retire before the company—or its pension fund—goes belly up? Many empty nesters dream about retiring while they are young enough to enjoy it. Of course, early retirement may not always be optional.

Although our economy is by all indications booming, companies continue to restructure their work forces through voluntary—and sometimes involuntary—early retirement offers. Often these programs offer tempting sweeteners to encourage employees to retire early.

The terms of an early retirement offer may vary depending on whether it is a true voluntary early retirement program or an involuntary severance program. Many voluntary early retirement offers provide employees with a host of benefits from cash severance payments and enhanced pensions to post-retirement medical coverage and offer of outplacement counseling or help in finding a new job.

Many companies routinely provide early retirees with financial planning assistance to help them evaluate the offer. Other benefits, such as educational assistance and ongoing life insurance coverage, may also be available.

Should you, an empty nester, receive such an offer, your first step should be to check the specifics of the early retirement offer. Keep in mind that this list explains the most common benefits based on experience. Your company has no legal obligation to offer these payments and its program may be very different.

First, if you are surprised by an early retirement offer, don't feel singled out or feel that it reflects on your job performance. Particularly over the past 10 years, companies have increasingly used early retirement programs to reduce workforce levels across the board.

The truth is that in many companies, offering enhanced early retirement programs is more cost-effective than continuing the work force at present levels. Harsh as it might seem, early retirement has become an economic fact of life in corporate America.

You might also keep in mind that you do have a choice. Under Federal law, you can't be forced to take the package that is offered. However, nothing prevents your company from later eliminating your job, demoting you or otherwise making you wish that you had taken the offer.

Many companies routinely follow up a voluntary early retirement program with a less generous involuntary severance program within a year or so. In fact, one company that shall remain nameless offered a generous voluntary early retirement program to 6,000 workers and, within two years, followed it with involuntary layoffs of more than 10,000 workers.

Some empty nesters want to—or have to—work after they leave their current employer. If you are one of those individuals and if you receive an early retirement offer, think about your odds of finding another job. That's when a professional outplacement counselor comes in handy. If your employer doesn't provide this service, you may want to foot the bill yourself.

If you have good prospects of finding another job or starting your own business, the decision to retire may become easier. For many empty nesters, however, the question is whether you can afford to retire now.

If you do receive an early retirement offer, look at the pension benefits that you will receive. Will you get fewer benefits because you're retiring early or do enhanced age and years of service make up the difference? Will you receive enough to adequately fund your retirement until you qualify for Social Security? How do your early retirement benefits compare with those that you will collect if you continued to work for your company? Are they more generous or less generous?

Suppose that you hadn't planned to retire for another 5 or 10 years from now. Your early retirement benefits might be considerably less than those you'd anticipated receiving. If they are, you may have to take on another job to make up the difference.

In analyzing your employer's early retirement offer, don't avoid the tough questions. Does the bank still hold a mortgage on your house? If it does, can you still make the mortgage payments without working full-time? What about health care expenses? You'll need to pay for medical coverage if it is not part of your early retirement offer.

Also, do you anticipate income from other sources—an inheritance, perhaps, to up your income in your retirement years?

Golden Parachutes

We've all read about company executives that walk away from takeovers and mergers with huge amounts of money. In most instances, they've written clauses into their employment contracts that guarantee them these huge payments in the event that their company is taken over or sold to another company that might not want to utilize their services. Unfortunately, our tax laws now impact on those so-called "golden parachute" clauses.

Any company that enters into a contract whereby it agrees to pay an employee amounts in excess of the employee's usual compensation in the event that control or ownership of the corporation changes hands is barred from taking a tax deduction for an "excess parachute payment" made to any "disqualified individual."

The disqualified individual, who just might be an empty nester, is subject to an excise tax of 20 percent of the excess parachute payment in addition to the income tax due.

Under these tax rules, a disqualified individual is considered to be an employee or independent contractor who performs personal services for any corporation and is an officer, shareholder, highly compensated person or personal service corporation.

> NOTE: A parachute payment is any payment in the nature of compensation to a disqualified individual if: (1) the payment is contingent on a change in ownership or effective control of the corporation or a substantial portion of the corporation's

> assets, and (2) the aggregate present value of
> such contingent payments equals or exceeds three
> times an individual's base amount.

Amounts that an empty nester establishes to be reasonable compensation for personal services to be rendered on or after the date of change or for personal services actually rendered before the date of change are not treated as parachute payments. Additionally, parachute payments do not include payments to or from certain qualified plans.

Lump-Sum Distributions

When you retire—or are forced to retire—you may be offered an opportunity to take the retirement benefits you've accumulated in a lump sum. Temper your excitement about the prospect of getting a big hunk of cash with the thought of the huge tax bill that it will trigger. Our tax law gives you several options on how to handle such a payment and the choice that you make can have a lot to do with how financially secure you are in retirement.

When you receive a lump-sum payment, the first thing that you should do is subtract from that distribution any after-tax contributions that you made to the plan. That is your money and it is tax-free. As for the taxable portion:

- You can simply take the cash and pay tax on it in your top bracket. Obviously, that's not always the best choice, tax-wise.

- You can roll over the funds into an IRA, a move that postpones the tax bill until you later withdraw the funds from that tax shelter. This choice is attractive if, as with most empty nesters, you won't need the bulk of the money for at least a few years.

You may be eligible to apply a special computation formula—there are two versions, 5- or 10-year forward averaging—to the payment and perhaps treat part of the distribution as tax favored capital gain. This could be your best bet if you plan to spend a substantial part of the payment fairly soon.

Rollovers

In the past, there was a slew of rules to wade through to make sure that a company plan payment qualified to be rolled over. Now, basically, any lump-sum payment can qualify.

> NOTE: Any part that represents your after-tax con-
> tributions to the plan can't be rolled over. You
> get that money tax-free. If you want to use the
> rollover option, your best bet will be to have

```
your employer ship the money directly to the
IRA—or IRAs—of your choice. The direct rollover
lets you avoid the 20 percent withholding neces-
sary with most distributions.
```

If you handle the rollover yourself, you have 60 days from the time that you get the money to have it safely ensconced in an IRA. Once the money is there, you can't move it around as often as you like. If you want to diversify your investments, you can roll the money into several IRAs.

The advantage of the rollover route is that you continue to hold the IRS at bay. Funds that otherwise would go to pay taxes remain in the account and continue to enjoy tax-sheltered growth.

Choosing an IRA rollover does prevent you from using the special averaging methods. Whether that is a significant loss would depend on how quickly you will need access to your funds. Holding off the tax bill by using an IRA for just a few years could more than compensate for skipping the chance to pay a reduced tax bill now.

```
NOTE: If you have a Keogh plan—set up with self-
employment income—you can hold off the IRS and
retain the right to averaging. the company-plan
distribution can be rolled over tax-free into the
Keogh. If you later take a lump-sum distribution
from the Keogh, it would qualify for averaging.
```

Averaging

Five- and 10-year averaging of pension plan distributions can significantly reduce the tax bill of any empty nester. These special computation methods tax the distribution all at once, but the bill is figured as though you received the money over a number of years. Although you must actually pay the tax right away, the amount of tax due will be significantly less than if the full amount was heaped on top of your other taxable income.

Unfortunately, generally speaking, this special treatment will no longer be available for lump-sum distributions made after 1999. Of course, in the case of benefits earned by any employee who attained age 50 before January 1, 1986, the averaging options will continue—except that five-year averaging may not be utilized.

```
NOTE: In recent years, several pension distribu-
tion rules have been simplified, five-year averag-
ing has been replaced, exclusion of employer-
provided death benefits is now permitted, etc.
Currently, up to $5,000 paid by the employer can
be tax-free—although Congress is, once again, con-
sidering ending this tax break.
```

Job-Hunting Expenses

We've already mentioned that many of the retirement packages offered by employers contain counseling and job placement services. But what about a situation where the empty nester attempts to find employment on his or her own?

As mentioned, the value of services paid for by an employer who is letting you go is a tax-free fringe benefit. This might include motivational seminars, resume writing and counseling aimed at helping you find a new job. Or you may foot the bill for these job-hunting expenses yourself.

When you look for a new job, the IRS might pick up some of your costs—via tax savings. The key to tax deductions is to seek a new position in the same line of work, rather than try to switch careers.

Perhaps our lawmakers worry that someone changing occupations might be willing to take a pay cut to make the change, while a job hunter looking for a different job in the same field is likely to do better financially and in the process produce more income for the government to tax.

Whatever the reasoning, job-hunting expenses are tax deductible when you confine your search to the same line of work you are in—whether or not you wind up changing jobs. The cost of seeking a job in a different occupation is not deductible, nor are expenses connected with landing your first job—or of reentering the job force after a lengthy absence.

If you qualify for job-hunting deductions, your write-off can include travel expenses if your search takes you away from home overnight. That includes the cost of food, lodging and transportation. Your meal expenses are covered by the rule that limits the deduction to 50 percent of the cost (this may be increased to as much as 80 percent under pending tax legislation). In addition, deductible job-hunting costs encompass what you spend for employment agency fees, want ads, telephone calls connected with the job hunt and the cost of printing and mailing resumes.

NOTE: THE 2-PERCENT RULE

There is a catch, though. Job-hunting expenses are miscellaneous itemized deductions, which means that they're subject to the 2-percent rule: You may claim a deduction only for the amount by which the total of all miscellaneous expenses exceeds 2 percent of your adjusted gross income.

Again, Beware of Employers

Today, no job can be considered as safe. The empty nester who enjoys his or her work and employer is lucky. They should also be aware that those good times could end at any time. Fortunately, the empty nester who is properly prepared can consider this lack of job security as merely a potential stumbling block on the way to retirement.

With a little caution, such as not relying too heavily on your employer's assistance in reaching your retirement savings goals, every empty nester can factor this uncertainty into their plans. If the worst does occur, and your job is lost, you've planned for it, hopefully, and possess the basic knowledge to cope with the situation.

Next, we'll take a look at the many professionals who can help you cope with or even profit from the uncertainties of job security. Those same individuals can also help you better enjoy your empty nester status today and increase your retirement savings for tomorrow.

Chapter 18

FINDING A PROFESSIONAL

The goals of many empty nesters are increased savings and/or an improved lifestyle. Increased savings create the need to determine good from bad investments. However, in addition to advisors who can help with investments, there are also a number of professionals who can provide badly needed help and guidance in other areas that will make your life a lot easier.

Certified public accountants (CPAs) and attorneys, for example, can assist you with other aspects of your personal financial planning as well as taxes. Unfortunately, many empty nesters fail to select appropriate financial advisers or neglect to take full advantage of the services they offer.

Taking a more active role in making sure that your advisers are providing the best possible advice and service will help make your professional relationships work better and more effectively. Remember, it is up to you to define the role that your family financial advisers will play.

Many people can and do benefit from the services of a financial planner. If you have a complex financial planning matter that needs evaluation, a consultation with a planner who is experienced in your particular area of concern may be well worthwhile.

In addition to evaluating specific concerns, financial planners can comprehensively review your total personal financial situation, either on a one-time or an ongoing basis.

Other professionals—such as bankers, insurance agents and stockbrokers, to name a few, who practice in specialty areas of financial planning also may be able to assist you in attaining your specific goals.

A Key Ingredient of Investment Portfolios: Stockbrokers

Many people think of stockbrokers as investment advisers. However, stockbrokers may have a conflict of interest when advising you on your investments—their income is dependent upon the type of investments that you buy and the frequency with which you buy or sell. Nevertheless, there are many excellent stockbrokers who can deal with these conflicts and still act in your best interests. The problem is finding them.

The brokerage industry today is sharply divided between full-service brokers and discount brokers. A full-service brokerage account can provide such benefits as professional securities analysts' recommendations, portfolio evaluation, banking services, such as checking accounts and credit cards, and, of course, the advice of the broker.

Discount brokers will primarily act as order takers only. They may provide some of the banking services, but the investment recommendations they would make, if any, would be on the basis of outside sources such as Standard & Poor's or ValueLine. They generally do not offer advice on what to invest in or when to buy or sell.

The commissions that a full-service broker charges to execute a transaction will generally fall in a range from 1 to 5 percent of the amount of money being invested. The average commission will generally be about 2.5 percent.

Discount brokers often advertise that they can save investors from 40 to 90 percent off full-service brokerage fees. As dramatic as that may sound, the investor's actual savings are usually only about 0.5 to 2 percent of the amount of the investment. For example, a 50-percent discount on a 2 percent commission would be 1 percent.

Competition within the brokerage industry has benefited consumers such as empty nesters. Since discount brokers became popular around the late 1970s, this competition has forced full-service brokerage firms to deliver extra services for the extra commissions that they charge.

As a direct result of competition from discount brokers, the professional analysis available from most full-service brokers today is about the best it has ever been. In addition, the price differential between discount brokers and full-service brokers is about as low as it has ever been.

Free Advice on Ownership

An important consideration when you establish a brokerage account is what legal designation you would like on the account. If you wish to have more than one name on the account, such as husband and wife, there are several choices that will clarify how you would like the investments distributed in the event of your death.

The most commonly used designation is "joint tenants with rights of survivorship," which is sometimes abbreviated "JTWROS" or "Jt. Ten." This designation simply means that the property is jointly owned by both individuals named on the account, and if one tenant dies, the account will become the sole property of the surviving tenant.

Other options for account designations are "community property" or "tenants in common." These designations both denote that if one tenant dies, half of the property goes to that tenant's estate and the other half goes to the survivor.

A community property designation means not only that half of the property goes to the estate, but also that it will take a court order to transfer it out of the estate. This type of designation is usually used by individuals who arrange prenuptial agreements for keeping their personal property separate or who do not want their property to go to their spouse after their death.

The laws governing the legal disposition of an individual's wealth after his or her death are set by the states. Not all states have community property laws.

There is no "and/or" designation for security account titles as there can be for bank accounts because securities are legally defined as property, whereas bank accounts are not. Because securities are defined as such, these types of investments must be owned either by one party or by both parties jointly.

Property cannot be legally owned both by two parties jointly and also by either one party or the other, as an "and/or" designation would indicate. However, all the standard joint-account designations allow for one party or the other to make investment decisions. So your broker will not require both parties to tell him to buy or sell a security. Either party can make a decision. Naturally, both signatures will be required on written transactions. If a stock certificate is requested in joint names, it must be properly endorsed by both parties before it can be negotiated.

Stock certificates, however, do not have to be held in the investor's name. If the broker holds the certificates for the client, he will usually hold it in street name. A stock certificate that is held in "street name" is held in the name of the brokerage firm, or the nominee name of the brokerage firm. This means that the security can be sold without the owners having to sign the certificate. The owner can simply tell his broker to sell the stock and the transfer to the new owner can be accomplished without the seller's signature.

Your legal proof of ownership of the stock is represented by your brokerage account statements—in the same way that the proof of your bank account balance is represented by your bank statements. However, you will probably have a much closer and more personal relationship with your stockbroker than you have with your banker.

The Umbrella Investment Adviser

Finding the right advisers is well worth the effort. Word-of-mouth recommendations can be an important first step. It's also important to know that the person you are dealing with has your best interests at heart.

The umbrella term, "investment adviser," covers all of those who provide investment advice for a fee—from mutual fund managers to publishers of investment newsletters and the more familiar personal money advisers.

Investment advisers must register with the Securities and Exchange Commission (SEC) although there is no specialized training or financial qualifications.

Some investment advisers operate individually, while others operate under the auspices of financial organizations such as insurance companies.

Charges for the services rendered by investment advisers can be either fee-based or commission-based. Commission-based investment advisers charge you a commission on the investments that you purchase. Fee-based investment advisers charge you either an hourly fee for the work that they perform on your investment accounts or a fee based on a percentage of the total value of the investments that they manage for you.

A good investment adviser can be an important part of your team of financial advisers. He or she can be keep you current on economic trends that may affect the market, as well as keep a watchful eye over your investments' performance.

Getting the Necessary Help

A professional financial planner can help you and your spouse or partner overcome the emotional roadblocks that may be keeping you from making decisions for your future. You may feel uneasy about setting your life's goals down on paper and then dealing with them in dollars and cents.

Or you may be reluctant to confront the reality that your financial resources are limited and you must make choices between current and future consumption. Often spouses or partners have different priorities that may be hard to discuss, let alone reconcile.

If you face any of these personal or emotional barriers, an experienced financial planner can help. Of course, a planner will also assist you with technical advice on such issues as asset allocation, selecting investments, reviewing your insurance needs and planning the transfer of your property in the event of your death.

Choosing a Financial Planner

Choosing a financial planner is no different from choosing any other professional who provides you with advice and services. The best means of locating candidates is through referrals from people such as your lawyer, accountant, banker or business associates.

You want a planner who is experienced, established in the profession and highly knowledgeable about the issues and technicalities of personal finance. You also want someone with whom you can feel comfortable, someone who has a good "bedside manner," in the parlance of the medical profession.

In other ways, however, choosing a financial planner poses more of a challenge than picking a doctor, lawyer or accountant. Unlike these other fields, financial planning is a still-emerging profession. Financial planning practitioners are not uniformly trained, licensed or regulated as are other types of professionals. In most states, for instance, you can set up shop as a financial planner without obtaining a license or meeting any particular professional requirements.

That's not to say that financial planners as a group are not well trained, or that they operate without any regulation. Many financial planners are licensed accountants, insurance agents, stockbrokers or lawyers and must follow the regulations that apply to those professions. The absence of uniform professional training and regulations, however, means that you must take particular care in evaluating the credentials of any planner that you hire.

There is also a lack of uniformity in the way that professional planners are compensated. Some charge fees for their services and others earn their money solely through commissions on the sales of financial products such as life insurance or investments. Still others charge a combination of fees and commissions. Following are the three principal categories of planners:

- FEE-ONLY PLANNERS. These are compensated solely by the client. Neither the planner nor any related party receives compensation that is contingent on the purchase or sale of any financial product.

- COMMISSION-ONLY PLANNERS. These are compensated from commissions on the sale of financial products such as insurance or investments to the client.

- FEE-BASED PLANNERS. These are compensated from fees paid by the client or commissions on the sale of products. Typically, commissions are offset against the fees charged for financial planning. If the commissions are not large enough to cover the planner's services, the client pays for the difference in the form of a fee.

The important thing is the quality of the service that the planner provides, not the form of the compensation. Fee-only planners, for instance, have no financial incentive to recommend a certain type of product/investment or to favor one financial provider's product over another's.

The trend recently has been away from commission-based compensation and toward compensation through fees. A major reason is that consumers increasingly are demanding objective advice and information. They want to be fully informed and to shop and compare before committing their money. They also understand the conflict of interest when a planner is being paid by a third party to sell them a product.

Before choosing any planner, try to define the scope of your needs. Among the options:

- A comprehensive financial plan addressing all of your financial goals;

- A single-purpose plan, such as a retirement plan or estate plan;

- Coaching/review of a financial plan that you develop on your own; or

- Investment advice on money management services.

Your Adviser's Credentials

As mentioned, financial advisers are not covered by any uniform state or Federal regulations; their qualifications and business practices vary considerably. Top-flight financial planners are highly trained, with knowledge of accounting, tax and estate laws, pension planning and investment management.

They will also have certification from one or more professional organizations in the financial planning field. You should be wary of individuals who hold themselves out as financial planners but do not have appropriate training or certification.

The wide variety of professional certification for financial planners can lead to confusion for those who are not familiar with the planning profession. Here's a summary of the relevant certifications:

CERTIFIED FINANCIAL PLANNER (CFP). This designation is awarded by the International Board of Standards and Practice for Certified Financial Planners in Denver, Colorado.

CHARTERED FINANCIAL CONSULTANT (CHFC). Planners with the ChFC designation are also insurance agents or have an insurance industry background. The ChFC is awarded by the American College in Bryn Mawr, Pennsylvania.

CHARTERED FINANCIAL ANALYST (CFA). The CFA designation is awarded by the Association of Investment Management and Research in Charlottesville, Virginia. Financial planners who are CFAs often have a background as stock market analysts and professional money managers.

PERSONAL FINANCIAL SPECIALIST (PFS). This designation is awarded by the American Institute of Certified Public Accountants in New York City to CPAs who meet certain qualifications. Financial planners with the PFS designation often have a background as tax specialists.

Inexpensive Financial Advice

When empty nesters invest in a mutual fund they are, in essence, hiring a financial adviser. Someone has to make the investment decisions. That is the role of the fund manager.

Each mutual fund has a stated purpose. Whether the fund's goal is long-term growth, immediate income tax-free income, or speculative foreign stocks, the fund's manager makes the decisions necessary to achieve that goal. Those professional managers are taking the burden off of the empty nesters' shoulders to find, investigate, invest in and ultimately sell stocks, bonds or other investments desired by the empty nesters who places their money with that fund.

The cost of this advice is hidden among the various costs of owning a mutual fund. Whether labeled management fees, investment manager fees, or whatever, those costs are often well worth the small percentage charged.

> NOTE: Since there is some evidence that successful mutual funds tend to exhibit continuity of fund management, every empty nester should be aware of the name, qualifications and tenure of a mutual fund's portfolio manager. A study by COA/ Wiesenberger Investment Companies Service found that changes in investment advisers can have a big impact on a fund's performance.

The study found that funds with above-average past performance that changed investment advisers were much more likely to experience below-average returns than funds with above-average performance in which the managers stayed put. On the other hand, funds with below-average performance tended to improve their results following a change in fund management.

In any event, you should know whether a fund's record was achieved by the present management.

Suppose, however, that the empty nesters want to go it alone. They can, of course, use the services of a stockbroker, but how do they know what to buy or sell? That is where investment managers come in.

The All-Purpose, All-Around CPA

Certified public accountants, or CPAs, are not the only type of accountant, of course. They are simply accountants who are regulated by state licensing boards. Regular accountants and public accountants offer many of the same types of services.

CPAs practice in about every town and city. A CPA provides a variety of services and most are well qualified to advise you on tax matters and/or prepare your income tax returns. If your tax situation has become complex—for example, you've started a business, just sold your home or received a lump-sum pension payment—then you may benefit from the help of a CPA at tax time.

Many CPAs have also become proficient (and even certified) in personal financial planning. The APFS designation denotes a CPA who is qualified to help you with your financial planning needs.

NOTE: ENROLLED PRACTITIONERS

These individuals are tax professionals. They have either worked for the Internal Revenue Service in the past or passed a two-day test and met the IRS's experience requirements in order to be recognized by the IRS as tax practitioners or "enrolled agents."

Attorneys

A family attorney is essential for preparing necessary estate planning documents such as wills and powers of attorney. It is often best to use an attorney who is approximately your age or younger, because you don't want to be burdened with having to find a new attorney when your current one retires.

However, you may outgrow your attorney's expertise if your estate grows to a level that will require more sophisticated estate planning techniques. Larger estates require the expertise of an attorney who devotes all or most of his or her time to estate planning matters, rather than general practice.

Insurance, Just in Case

A catastrophic loss can scuttle any financial plan. Every empty nester will need to insure himself or herself against medical costs, sudden loss of life and loss of property or earning power. Are you adequately insured?

1) Do you know how much life insurance you have on you and your spouse— and to whom it will be paid if one of you dies?

2) Have you calculated the lump-sum amount your family would need if one of the family's income earners died?

3) Have you purchased disability insurance on the family's income earner to provide continuing income if he or she becomes disabled?

4) Does your health insurance cover all major medical expenses with a high upper limit for lifetime benefits?

5) Is your home insured for its full replacement value?

6) Do you carry high upper limits on your auto liability insurance, or an extra umbrella liability policy to supplement casualty policies?

If you answered yes to each of these questions you are better informed about insurance matters than most people. Many empty nesters are mostly in the dark when it comes to insurance coverage. In fact, many empty nesters worry that they are underinsured but they don't think that they can afford additional insurance or don't know where to turn for answers to their insurance questions.

Insurance Help

If you use an insurance agent, you want one that you can trust with your life—or at least your life insurance. When considering what kind of agent you need—and whether you need an agent at all—keep in mind that each option has its pros and cons:

■ EXCLUSIVE AGENTS work for just one company.

   Pros. Policies are somewhat less expensive than those sold by independent agents due to the commission structure. To lure the agent, insurance companies pay higher commissions—and charge you a higher premium—for policies sold by independent agents.

   Cons. You'll have to do more footwork in order to compare policies between companies.

■ INDEPENDENT AGENTS work for a number of companies.

   Pros. The agent can show you a wider variety of policies.

   Cons. Policy prices may be higher since the companies pay more to lure independent agents to their products.

■ INSURANCE BROKERS sell insurance as well as other financial products.

   Pros. One-stop shopping for all of your financial and insurance needs.

   Cons. Because they are financial generalists, brokers may not know as much about life and disability insurance as an insurance agent.

■ SHOPPING FOR YOURSELF allows you to cut out the middleman and buy direct from the insurance company.

Pros. You can save the cost of a commission.

Cons. You need to know exactly what kind of policy and coverage you need. Some companies won't sell to individuals; others will provide only term life insurance, no cash-value policies.

Before buying from any insurance agent, ask about the commission structure. If the agent balks, walk. The agent is asking you to be forthcoming about your financial circumstances and you deserve the same respect.

Also check with the state department of insurance to find out if there have been any complaints filed against the agent you are considering. The agent should be on file, since all insurance agents and brokers must be licensed by the state.

NOTE: PICKING THE RIGHT INSURANCE COMPANY

When choosing an insurance company, financial strength is important. Look up your prospective insurance company at the library in a current copy of Best's Insurance Reports, which is published by A.M. Best Co., an organization that rates the financial health of insurance companies.

The rating for your insurance company is very important, since you want to insure with a company that will survive to pay the benefits due your beneficiaries.

Banks

The first thing to realize about a bank is that it is in business to make money. It sells a number of services for which you pay. How much you pay depends upon the amount of time you are willing to spend investigating different institutions and their fees.

The seductive convenience of using the bank on the nearest corner is no longer the only criterion for picking a bank. You also need to consider services (which have proliferated), costs (which have steadily been rising), financial stability and, of course, whether there are usually long lines at the time you'd be using that bank.

Many empty nesters may be thinking about opening accounts at several banks—perhaps one is nearby, another pays higher rates and a third has long hours. That's the approach taken by the late W.C. Fields. He had 700 accounts in banks all over the world, so that if he was ever stranded somewhere, he'd have cash.

Fields also reportedly worried constantly about being penniless and starving to death. The 700 bank accounts apparently helped ease his mind.

When he died on Christmas Day 1946, his executors found only 30 of the 700 accounts. Although many were in his own name, he also used fictitious names such as Figley E. Whiteside, Sneed Hearn and Dr. Otis Guelpe.

Few, if any empty nesters, should follow this example. Open no more than one or two accounts and have them in your legal name. With the proliferation of ATMs, every empty nester can get cash about anywhere in the world.

In fact, there are many real reasons for doing all of our banking at just one institution (this is called "relationship banking").

Banks impose stiff fees on most types of accounts and about the only way to avoid or reduce them is to keep a certain amount of money in the bank. It pays to not only shop around but to consolidate—you may find a bank that waives fees for customers who keep more than one account at the bank and whose combined balances exceed the minimums.

When it comes to finding the bank you will use, one of the first banks to investigate is the one your employer uses—you may find it easier (or at least faster) to open an account there and most likely you will be given special consideration.

Other reasons for consolidation: It makes you more important to the bank, so you are more likely to get preferential treatment such as immediate crediting of your deposits and overdraft protection. If you gain the reputation as a good customer, it will often ease the way to getting a loan. And don't forget that larger account balances often earn higher yields.

Appraisers

Often ignored among the professionals that every empty nester should know and use is the appraiser. Yes, those professionals who place values on everything from Mother's vase to the family homestead are extremely important in today's economic climate. Consider our tax rules as just one illustration of an appraiser's importance.

Our tax laws allow you to contribute either money or property to a charity. If you donate money, you write-off or deduct the amount of your gift. If you donate property, however, you deduct an amount equal to the fair market value of the property at the time that you make that donation.

The government defines fair market value as "the price at which the property would change hands between a willing buyer and a willing seller, neither being under any compulsion to buy or sell and both having reasonable knowledge of relevant facts," which means only the amount that the property would bring if you sold it in the open market.

Unfortunately, fair market value is not always easy to determine. If you donate a painting to your local museum just after a comparable painting by the same artist sold at auction for $100,000, you may be fairly confident that you'll be able to write-off or deduct $100,000. However, you must still obtain a qualified appraisal to protect that tax deduction. Plus, you may also be subject to charitable deduction limits.

The opinion of an appraiser is also valued. In fact, appraisals are required if you donate property with a total value of $5,000 or more. If, for example, you donate two automobiles, valued at $3,000 each, to an area vocational school, you would be required to get an appraisal because the value of the two cars tops the $5,000 limit.

The IRS requires you to attach to your income tax return a complete copy of a signed appraisal to support charitable donations of works of art with a total value of $20,000 or more. A color photograph must also be provided upon request.

The IRS wants to make sure an appraisal is not made by someone with a stake in overstating your gift's value. So appraisals may not be made by you, the organization receiving the gift, the party from whom you received it or any related entity—that is a member of your family or a corporation that is controlled by any of the above individuals or organizations.

For the same reason, the appraiser must not base his or her fees on the gift's appraised value.

> NOTE: Don't forget the importance of appraisals of closely held businesses and various types of property when it comes to estate tax purposes. Closely held businesses enjoy reduced values and help contribute to reduced estate taxes. Similarly, an appraiser who is familiar with your property may place a more realistic value on it than one who is not.

Competent Adviser

Finding competent advisers is well worth the effort. There is no ideal way to locate these professionals, but word-of-mouth recommendation referrals can be an important first step. You should expect your financial planner or attorney to be responsive to your needs and to conduct their work ethically. If you are unhappy with one of your advisers, it may be because you have not taken an active role in establishing the relationship.

First, try to resolve the problem with your adviser. But, if the problem persists, don't hesitate to make a change.

Chapter 19

GONE BUT NOT FORGOTTEN

The children are on their own, your financial affairs are beginning to shape up and an enjoyable retirement looms on the horizon. You have it made! But didn't you forget something?

Your own financial health may be looking pretty rosy, but what about the financial pictures of your children? Or how healthy or enjoyable is the lifestyle of your parents or others close to you?

Fortunately, with a little planning, some help from our tax laws and the cooperation of your children and/or parents, you can cope not only with these potential worries but you may also profitably factor any future crises into your present lifestyle and retirement planning. One key solution may be found in our tax laws.

Dependents and Taxes

Our income tax rules permit any empty nester to claim a dependency exemption on their income tax return—if their children, parents, relatives or even unrelated parties take up residence in the empty nest. More to the point, that dependency exemption is also available where the child or parent doesn't actually reside in your empty nest. Naturally, there are rules and regulations, but even the relatively small deduction that each "dependent" creates can help financially.

On a negative note, any person who can be claimed as a dependent on someone else's tax return can't claim a personal exemption on his or her own. This primarily affects children claimed on their parents' returns—but it also applies to anyone who can be claimed as a dependent such as elderly parents who are being supported by their children.

The dependency exemption must be earned by passing a series of tests. That is not so difficult when it comes to a minor child who lives with you. The IRS takes that for granted. However, many empty nesters have found that it is not so simple as children grow older or when you try to claim adult relatives—your parents say—or unrelated people as your dependents.

Who qualifies as a dependent? There are five so-called "hoops" that every empty nester must jump through in order to win the right to claim someone as a dependent on their income tax return:

- Member-of-household or relationship test;

- Citizenship test;

- Joint-return test;

- Gross-income test; and

- Support test.

Membership of Household or Relationship

Perhaps the most important thing to note about this test is that someone need not be related to you in order to qualify as your dependent. If you pass the other four tests, then a friend that you are supporting can be a tax dependent.

When an unrelated person in involved, the IRS demands that he or she be a member of your household, which means living with you for the entire year. When it comes to relatives, however, the IRS doesn't demand that they live under your roof in order for you to qualify for the tax break. In fact, the IRS is pretty broadminded when defining relatives. Included are:

- Children, grandchildren or other lineal descendants;

- Stepchildren;

- Brothers, sisters, half brothers, half sisters, stepbrothers or stepsisters;

- Parents, grandparents or other direct ancestors (but not foster parents);

- Stepfathers or stepmothers;

- Brothers or sisters of your mother or father (your dad's brother—your uncle—counts, for example, but not his wife—your aunt);

- Sons or daughters of your siblings; and

- Fathers-in-law, mothers-in-law, sons-in-law, daughters-in-law, brothers-in-law or sisters-in-law.

The list probably contains everyone who you think of as a relative—except perhaps cousins. To claim a cousin as your dependent, he or she must live with you for the entire year, something most empty nesters probably want to avoid if at all possible.

Citizenship

A person really doesn't have to be a citizen in order to pass this test. Someone can qualify if he or she is a U.S. citizen, resident or naturalized, or a resident of Canada or Mexico.

Joint Return

This test usually raises its ugly head only in the year that a son or daughter that you've been supporting gets married. The law prohibits claiming a dependency exemption for someone who files a joint return.

Thanks to an exception to this rule, however, if the couple owes no tax but files jointly simply to reclaim money withheld from paychecks during the year, the joint return doesn't scotch your right to claim the exemption.

Gross Income

Someone who earns more than the exemption amount—$2,650 for 1997—generally can't be claimed as someone else's dependent. Let's say, for instance, your elderly mother lives with you and the value of the food and lodging that you provide and the medical bills that you pay amount to more than 50 percent of her support. If she earns more than the exemption amount—say from interest on her life's savings—you can't claim her as your dependent.

Because too much income can obliterate an empty nester's right to a dependency exemption, it is important to understand just what is included in gross income—and what is not.

Essentially, gross income is all income that's not exempt from tax. Earnings from a job or taxable investments count; Social Security benefits generally don't unless they are taxed. Gifts and insurance proceeds are not included either, nor is tax-free interest.

If someone's interest income is tripping you up, consider whether it would make sense to suggest a switch to tax-free bonds. Although there may be little or no tax benefit to a low bracket investor, the exemption could be worth more to you than the amount of income lost to a lower yield.

Support Test

To claim someone as a dependent, you must provide more than half of his or her support. When the children lived at home, there was generally no question that the parents could pass this test. However, as the kids got older and got jobs to generate their own spending money, the 50 percent test often toppled your right to the exemption.

When it comes to figuring the support that you provide for someone living with you, include the fair rental value of the housing that you provide. That means what you would expect a stranger to pay for it. Count what you spend for food, clothing, transportation, education, medical bills, etc.

In other words, a person's total support is what it costs for him or her to live during the year; your share is the amount of the total that comes out of your pocket.

When you tote up what the person paid for his or her own support, don't assume it includes everything earned during the year. Money that goes into savings—even Social Security benefits set aside for a rainy day—does not count as support.

Multiple-Support Agreements

There is a notable exception to the hard-and-fast rule that you must provide more than half of someone's support in order to claim that person as a dependent. When two or more persons together provide more than half of someone's support, one of the providers can claim the exemption if the other agrees not to.

The multiple-support agreement generally comes into play when two or more adult children support a parent. Assume that a brother and sister each provide 40 percent of their mother's support and that either one could claim her as a dependent if it weren't for the 50 percent test. Form 2120, "Multiple Support Deduction," will permit one of them to claim the tax-saving exemption. The form is filed with the tax return of the person claiming the exemption and must be signed by the other provider, certifying that he or she provided more than 10 percent of the dependent's support and could have claimed her on his own return except for the 50 percent support stipulation.

Taking It Back

Our lawmakers have decided that once your income reaches a certain level, you don't need the tax-saving assistance delivered by exemptions. If your adjusted gross income (AGI) exceeds the levels shown in the table below, your exemptions may be jeopardy:

LOSS OF EXEMPTIONS (1996 THRESHOLD AMOUNTS)

Filing Status	
Married filing jointly	$176,950
Single	117,950
Head of Household	147,450
Married filing separately	88,475

For every $2,500 your AGI exceeds the threshold for your filing status, you lose 2 percent of your exemption. If you claim just one exemption, each additional $2,500 of AGI reduces the value of your exemption by $51 (2 percent of the 1996 exemption value of $2,550). If you claim 10 exemptions, each additional $2,500 of AGI cuts the value of your exemptions by $510 (2 percent of $25,500).

Keeping the Nest Empty

It is currently estimated that more than eight million Americans provide personal care to their parents. Given the aging population, this number seems destined to increase. Unfortunately, few of us plan ahead effectively or prepare for the probability that our parents will, at least to some extent, rely on us during their old age.

Fortunately, aging empty nesters can plan for their own senior years while helping their parents plan for theirs.

Unpaid bills, unfilled prescriptions, an overdrawn bank account or other indications of forgetfulness are all possible first signs that an elderly person's ability to take care of himself or herself may be waning.

While your parents are still healthy, it is important that you have a frank discussion with them about plans for and worries about the future. However, including the possibility of moving if the current location is inconvenient is a critical topic.

> NOTE: Remember, many retirement homes and other older-care facilities have long waiting lists. To avoid having an elderly parent placed in an unsatisfactory home because of a sudden illness, you and your parents should discuss the alternatives and possibly apply to a home before the need actually arises. Even if your parents are healthy, they should consider any housing decisions in anticipation of possible future health problems.

Meeting Major Medical Costs

One of the most important things for many empty nesters to consider is how their parents expect to meet any major health care costs. Do they have sufficient health insurance? Remember that Medicare has many gaps in its coverage.

Whatever the deficiencies, the fact remains that Medicare is the core of most retired persons' medical coverage. The Medicare program provides health care benefits to every American over age 65 who is eligible for Social Security, plus some disabled persons.

What Medicare Covers

Medicare consists of two parts: Part A pays for the costs of a hospital stay—it is provided at no cost for everyone who is automatically eligible for Social Security. Part B is an optional medical insurance plan designed to pay doctor bills.

Medicare Part B participants pay a monthly premium, which is automatically deducted from their monthly Social Security checks. Like any private insurance plan, Medicare does not cover all procedures, medicines or doctor bills. It is important to know the ins and outs of the system in order to avoid unpleasant surprises.

Incapacity

It is difficult to raise the unpleasant issue of what will happen if your parents become incapable of managing their own affairs. They (as well as you) should have durable powers of attorney or similar documents prepared.

Ask your parents how well they have been meeting expenses, keeping in mind that they may not wish to reveal any financial problems. Also, be sure that your parents have a file, kept in a location known to you, containing copies of their wills, insurance policies, real estate papers, past tax returns and other important documents.

Financial Crises

Evaluate an elderly parent's future financial situation as well as current situation. Even an elderly parent who is currently financially secure may eventually run into trouble. After all, a retiree's typically fixed income is always in danger of having its purchasing power eroded by inflation. Of course, medical care and nursing care can reduce anyone's income and savings drastically.

It is important to consider what measures you are willing or able to take to assist your parents financially. You should discuss with them how they are currently managing their own investments. Many elderly people either invest too conservatively or are susceptible to unscrupulous salespeople.

Options

The National Association of Area Agencies on Aging (NAAAA), 1112 16th Street, NW, Washington, DC 20036, can help. You can write NAAAA to request information on agencies and elder-related services in your parents' locale. Services that can be arranged include:

- Emergency medical response system;

- Daily visits by local residents;

- Home care (e.g., laundry, housecleaning, cooking, small repairs, errands and snow removal);

- Legal assistance;

- Hot meals (at neighborhood centers or delivered to the home);

- Transportation services; and

- Day care centers.

Further help can be sought through senior citizens centers, religious organizations, welfare services, nursing homes, local branches of the United Way and major hospital social services departments or elderly outreach programs.

If an elderly person requires substantial health-related assistance, a hospital-based social worker is often the best alternative. Naturally, in choosing among these options, parents should be included in all important discussions to the greatest possible extent.

Housing Options Outside the Empty Nest

As many older Americans have discovered, healthy habits and good medical care have broken the link between advanced age and poor health. With the aging of the nation, more and more alternatives are being developed for the relatively healthy elderly—that increasingly large group who need a modest amount of help with the chores of daily living but can still manage pretty well by themselves.

The following alternatives vary in the lifestyle they promote and in the amount of medical and custodial care they offer:

HOMESHARING. Homesharing is a means for an older person to share expenses and household tasks with a younger person who needs affordable housing. A younger person might agree to do cleaning or yard work in exchange for inexpensive or free room and board.

Local community groups or government agencies in most areas match homeowners with potential homesharers. Naturally, you'll need to check the references of any potential homesharer thoroughly—from credit checks to personal references.

HOME CARE. Home care may be appropriate for people who wish to remain in their own homes but for whom the unskilled companionship and guardianship of a homesharer will not be adequate. Of course, when you remain in familiar surroundings, you usually feel more at ease, more in control and more comfortable.

Home care is particularly appropriate for persons with Alzheimer's or other debilitating diseases and people who are recovering from recent hospitalization and still require nursing care or help with life's daily activities.

CONGREGATE HOUSING. This is a group living situation for older people who are basically in good health, but whose functional abilities are somewhat limited. Basic services usually include one to three meals per day in a central dining area, light housekeeping, laundry services and organized recreational activities.

Residents share common areas such as the living room, bathroom, kitchen and dining room. The services of a social worker and/or housekeeper, meal delivery, transportation and recreational programs may also be available.

CONTINUING CARE COMMUNITIES. Designed to meet the changing needs of their residents, these communities offer a variety of alternatives in one location: town houses for independent, active older adults, apartment buildings with meals, housekeeping and laundry services and, in many communities, a nursing home.

Continuing care communities usually require a sizable entry payment as well as a sizable monthly fee.

ADULT DAY CARE. Adult day care is often appropriate for elderly persons who are still mobile and have their facilities but who may not be entirely self-sufficient. Adult day care is available at a lower cost then residential care and many retirement communities offer this care daily or several times a week at much lower cost than nursing home or home nursing care.

Transportation, games and puzzles, exercise, physical therapy, field trips, performances, classes, snacks and hot midday meals are the staples offered by many adult day care centers, in addition to having registered and licensed practical nurses on hand to monitor the patient's health.

NURSING HOMES. The decision to enter a nursing home—or to place a spouse or parent in one—is a difficult one and can be very traumatic. However, once the decision is made, the trying task of selecting an appropriate nursing home begins.

It is important to realize that few homes will offer everything that you want. Since every home that you visit will present its best features, it is important to know exactly what to look for and what to ask when you make your visit. Only after you have established that the nursing home is clean, well-kept, and treats its patients decently do you compare the estimated monthly costs (including extra charges) with those of other homes.

Make sure that the financial terms are clear and in writing and that the contract specifies that the home will provide a refund for unused days paid for in advance. The rate when you sign up should be guaranteed for a reasonable period of time.

Is the home certified to participate in Medicare and Medicaid programs? Will the patient be able to remain if he or she is forced to fall back on Medicaid?

An Incapacitated Heir

Special steps are required to plan for the needs of a handicapped child, an aged parent or another family member who might be incompetent. If your heir is a minor child, you will obviously name a guardian and successor guardian in your will. If, however, a child is incapacitated after reaching the age of majority, a court may have to approve any guardianship.

The wills of empty nesters should anticipate this contingency. Often the best step is to establish a trust and give the trustee the power to distribute income to your heir, to the guardian and to caregivers as needed.

If you will be funding the heir's support needs through life insurance, you may want to consider the use of a life insurance trust for this purpose. You should also consider the requirements of any government assistance programs for which your incapacitated heir might be eligible. Special provisions may have to be added to the trust so your heir retains eligibility for such assistance programs.

You may also want to take precautions in leaving your money to an adult child who is financially irresponsible or who may be suffering from addictions to alcohol or drugs. Again, this may be best accomplished by using a trust and giving the trustee authority to withhold or vary distributions to the heir as the trustee sees fit.

The trust document should include a "spendthrift" clause to help shield the trust assets from potential creditors by preventing the beneficiary from using income or assets of the trust as collateral for a loan.

Life Insurance Trusts

Life insurance can be used as a financial tool to generate cash to pay estate taxes as we'll see in the next chapter. Extra cash is essential when a major portion of an estate's value consists of illiquid assets such as real estate or a family business. Otherwise, these assets might have to be sold in order to pay the estate tax bill.

Although life insurance proceeds are free of income tax, they are not free of estate tax. Insurance proceeds from a policy that you own are included in your estate and are subject to Federal estate tax.

For this reason, a life insurance policy purchased to help pay estate taxes may not provide the help that you expect. For example, proceeds from a $1 million life insurance policy payable to your children might add $500,000 or more to your estate tax bill, making this a costly way to raise extra cash.

One way to avoid this problem is to establish a trust that owns life insurance covering you and your spouse. The proceeds from an insurance policy owned by a life insurance trust can be kept out of your estate and out of the estate of your spouse as well. Your spouse, children and other heirs are beneficiaries of the trust.

When you die, the trust receives the life insurance proceeds without a tax bite. The trust can (but cannot be specifically directed to) use the proceeds to help pay estate taxes by purchasing assets from or lending cash to your estate.

The premiums that you pay on policies owned by the trust are considered gifts to your beneficiaries. But if structured properly, the gifts will qualify for the annual exclusion of $10,000 per beneficiary ($20,000 if your spouse joins in the gift).

If you have three beneficiaries, for instance, you and your spouse could pay annual insurance premiums of up to $60,000 for a policy in a life insurance trust without incurring gift taxes.

Gifts Affect Estates

Taxable gifts made during your life also come into play when figuring the tax on your estate. For gifts made after 1976, the taxable portion is included in the amount on which the estate tax is based.

At first that might appear to be double taxation, but is not that sinister. Instead, as with the requirement that previous gifts be taken into account when calculating the gift tax, the provision is to prevent you from using the lower estate tax brackets more than once.

Although you have to bring gifts back into the estate, you also get to use the full credit to offset the estate tax bill—even though part of it was used during your life to shield you from the gift tax.

To illustrate:

Assume that during your life you made $600,000 of taxable gifts, using up your entire credit. When you die, your taxable estate is also $600,000. Without the requirement to "gross up" the estate for taxable gifts, the tax on $600,000 would be $192,800.

To prevent you from using the 18 percent through 34 percent brackets a second time, the law requires you to find the tax on $1.2 million (the total of taxable gifts plus the taxable estate). Stacked on top of the gifts, the estate is taxed in the 37 percent through 41 percent brackets. The bill on $1.2 million is $427,800. Subtracting the $192,800 credit amount leaves your estate with a $235,000 liability.

Although putting taxable gifts back into the estate may seem to defeat the tax-saving aim of gifts, it does not. The assets are counted in your estate at their value at the time of the gift. Any appreciation between that time and your death avoids being taxed in your estate. That can be extremely important, particularly when rapidly appreciating assets are involved.

> NOTE: If you are supporting your parents, give them appreciated securities rather than giving them cash. They can sell the securities and pay tax on the gain at their low tax bracket rather than at your higher tax bracket—even with the new capital gains tax rates.
>
> OR
>
> There are obvious income tax advantages to making gifts as discussed earlier (Chapter 6). But you should be aware of a potential income tax draw-back, too. The IRS figures the tax on any profit that has built up on assets that you own at the time of your death. (This is sometimes called the "Angel of Death" tax break.)
>
> Assume that the stock that you purchased for $50,000 is worth $100,000 when you die. That $50,000 profit escapes the income tax. If you were to give away the stock before death, however, the recipient would be responsible for the income tax on the appreciation that accrued while you owned the stock.

Keeping the Nest Empty—Humanely

The pressures posed by children clamoring to return to the nest and by parents in need of attention or care can be almost overwhelming. They are the rare empty nesters who can completely turn their backs on family. Fortunately, there are numerous options that can be used to either buy the care needed by those family members or, if all else fails, help compensate the empty nester for the expense of caring for those family members.

In the next chapter, we'll explore a strategy to help care for family members when you are gone. Estate planning allows every empty nester to direct their money and assets where they feel they will do the most good. And, handled properly, estate planning will not only reduce the taxes on any money passed on but may well reduce today's tax bill as well.

Chapter 20

SIMPLE ESTATE PLANNING FOR PERMANENT SAVINGS

Having, hopefully, established a retirement plan; discovered the many ways that the empty nest lifestyle can be enjoyed, perhaps even used to create a "tax business" with its attendant tax benefits and profits; and after coping with a potential return migration, it is time to think of the future.

Taking care of those you will leave behind is something that many of us prefer to postpone or ignore. However, even the most basic estate planning can ensure that your heirs benefit with a minimum of interference from the tax collector. That same estate planning can also ensure that your assets are used in the way that you want them to. Plus, handled properly, estate planning may even reduce your current tax bill.

What is Estate Planning?

Estate planning is the process of organizing your financial and personal interests, in accordance with prevailing laws so that your wishes are met with a minimum of inconvenience and expense to your family. Estate planning can also ensure that your estate incurs the minimum possible estate tax.

> NOTE: First things first. The estate tax applies
> to the transfer of property at death. The tax is
> paid by the estate, not by the person who inherits
> the property.

Effective estate planning need not be complicated. It has several straightforward objectives, including:

- Minimizing the problems and expenses of probate and to pass on your estate in accordance with your wishes.

- Providing your spouse with as much responsibility and flexibility in estate management as desired, consistent with potential tax savings.

- Providing for the conservation of your estate and its effective management following the death of either or both spouses.

- Minimizing taxes at the time of death as well as estate taxes after death.

- Avoiding leaving children too much, too soon.

- Providing for adequate liquidity to cover taxes and other expenses at death without the necessity of a forced sale of assets.

- Providing for estate management in the event of the incapacity of either spouse.

- Organizing all important papers affecting your estate plan in a location known to all family members and reviewing them at least annually.

- Briefing family members about the overall estate plan.

Many empty nesters don't complete even the most basic estate planning documents, nor do they revise their estate plan to reflect changes in personal circumstances or new laws and regulations. One reason for this, as mentioned, may be a general reluctance to confront the fact that we are all mortal. While it is unpleasant to contemplate the possibility of our own demise, however, it is far more satisfying to know that our affairs have been put in order and that our children have been taken care of.

Beyond the basics there are several more sophisticated estate planning techniques of which every empty nester should be aware—and which you don't have to be wealthy in order to take advantage of.

Don't Underestimate Your Estate

Don't let the $600,000 (soon to be more than $1 million) amount where estate taxes are assessed lull you into thinking that you will never have to worry about estate taxes. One of the greatest threats is to underestimate the size of your estate and blissfully ignore planning opportunities.

In reality, your estate—as the law defines it for tax purposes—may already be much larger than you imagine. It includes the value of your home and other real estate holdings, obviously, as well as your savings and the value of your investments, cars, boats, jewelry and other personal property.

Also included are benefits from retirement plans, whether an IRA, Keogh or company-sponsored plan. Another amount that can go into your taxable estate, but which you may not think about because it doesn't exist until after your death, is life insurance. If you own the policy—which you do if you can change the beneficiary or borrow against cash value—its proceeds are considered part of your estate.

Minimum Estate Planning

A simple estate plan can help save legal fees as well as all unnecessary and costly probate delays and ensure that your estate is distributed in accordance with your wishes. It also may have some potential effects while you are still alive.

Since it is unlikely that an estate will be distributed in accordance with any individual's wishes should they die before creating an estate plan, empty nesters need to make adequate plans for the distribution of their estate.

A minimum estate plan usually consists of the following four documents:

A Valid and Up-to-Date Will

Everyone knows that preparing and maintaining a will is important. But surprisingly, many adults do not have wills. A will specifies exactly how your estate is to be divided. It should be drawn up by an experienced attorney.

Intestate estates (those of individuals who die without a will) may incur higher than necessary legal fees and unnecessary probate delays. Additionally, if you die intestate, a probate judge, rather than you, will decide how your estate should be distributed.

Most importantly (for empty nesters) you should periodically review and revise your will to reflect changes in your personal circumstances (including moving to another state) or changes in state and Federal laws.

A lawyer can help you draw up a will to specify exactly how you want your estate divided. Your will does not protect you from doing whatever you'd like with your property while you're still alive. If your circumstances change, you can always amend your will with a codicil or with a new one.

Durable Power of Attorney

There are basically two ways to protect personal assets and ensure that they will continue to be managed appropriately should you become incapacitated and unable to manage your financial affairs because of an accident, illness, or age. You can appoint a person to act for you by signing a durable power of attorney or you can establish a living trust.

Your right to manage your financial affairs may be revoked by a court order and, if you haven't provided for one in your durable power of attorney (or living trust), a court-appointed conservator (perhaps not the one you would have chosen) will oversee the management of your affairs.

Signing a durable power of attorney ensures that if you ever become unable to manage your own financial and personal affairs, someone that you trust will be able to act on your behalf. A power of attorney may be either special, applying to only certain situations, or general, giving the attorney-in-fact virtually limitless control over the financial affairs of the principal (the person who created the arrangement).

General powers of attorney should be appointed with caution as they can be subject to abuse; moreover, they're usually unnecessary. A power of attorney may be either indefinite or for a specific length of time. No matter how the time is designated, it may be canceled at any time as long as you're not incapacitated and it terminates immediately upon the death of the principal.

Living Will

Medical dilemmas surrounding terminally ill patients abound and compound the difficulty of trying to accommodate the patient's wishes. Drafting a living will informs family members and physicians that under certain conditions you do not wish to be kept alive by artificial means.

The fundamental shortcomings of living wills is that under most state laws, the circumstances are prescribed by law and you are not free to define the circumstances. Health care proxies and medical durable powers of attorney have appeared on the scene to provide this control.

Living wills are legally recognized in most states. But even where they are not, experts suggest that preparing one anyway can be very helpful if and when the need to make these difficult decisions arises.

Letter of Instructions

A letter of instructions is not as critical as other essential estate planning documents but your heirs will be thankful that you prepared one. A letter of instructions is an informal document (you don't need the services of an attorney to prepare it) that gives your executor information concerning important financial and personal matters.

Although it does not carry the legal weight of a will, the letter of instructions is very important because it clarifies any further requests to be carried out upon death and provides essential financial information, thus relieving the surviving family members of needless worry and speculation.

The four basic estate planning documents described above—a will, durable power of attorney, a living will and a letter of instructions are the essential components of an estate plan.

Only for the Wealthy?

There is a threshold at which you will pay no estate or gift taxes at all—$600,000 (soon to increase to over $1 million). Called the "unified credit equivalent," it is the maximum amount of property that any one person can pass on free of estate taxes. That threshold applies to lifetime gifts too, so you could give away up to $600,000 during your life (not including the $10,000 annual gift tax exclusion discussed in Chapter 6) without incurring gift taxes—but you wouldn't have the exclusion available to your estate.

> NOTE: Over the next 10 years the unified estate and gift tax credit will be gradually increased so as to be worth $1 million by 2006. After December 31, 1997, family-owned businesses and farms will be eligible for an additional exclusion. Coordinated with the unified credit, the exclusion and credit combined would be worth $1.3 million from 1998 on.

The term unified credit equivalent means that our tax laws give each person a tax credit of $192,800, which is exactly the tax on today's $600,000 exclusion. Subtracting the credit from the tax on $600,000 equals zero, which means that the IRS collects no taxes from your estate—one goal of estate planning.

If you are married, each person gets one $600,000 exclusion during life or at death so you and your spouse combined can pass up to $1.2 million free of Federal estate taxes.

While many empty nesters will never end up paying estate taxes thanks to this unified credit equivalent, don't think that you don't need any estate planning simply because the combined assets of you and your spouse are currently less than $600,000. Chances are that your assets will grow over time and you'll eventually be over the $600,000 or even the $1 million mark by 2006. Planning techniques can save the heirs of your estate from writing a big check to the Internal Revenue Service.

Federal Estate and Gift Tax

In Chapter 19, we briefly touched on the role that gifts (and the taxes incurred as a result of those gifts) play on the tax bill of an empty nester's estate. Minimizing or eliminating Federal estate and gift taxes is the main reason many people do estate planning. In a nutshell, estate planning can ensure that your heirs—not the IRS—get the property that you worked so hard to acquire.

Generally, the amount of your estate tax liability is directly linked to the size of your estate. In other words, the lower the value of your estate, the lower the potential liability. Rates go as high as 55 percent. Obviously, failing to plan to minimize estate taxes at your death can be a very expensive mistake.

Obviously, the simplest estate plan is to give your property away during your lifetime so that there is nothing to tax at death. Unfortunately, the IRS is way ahead of you—there is also a gift tax on lifetime transfers over certain levels to prevent you from avoiding estate taxes through lifetime transfers.

Thus, a more realistic approach is to plan for both types of transfer taxes so that you minimize the amount of gift taxes during life and ensure that the value of your estate is as low as possible at death.

One Successful Strategy

If you are married, you can leave everything that you own to your spouse, free of estate tax. Relying too much on the marital deduction to protect the estate of the first spouse to die, however, could set up the survivor for unnecessary taxes.

To illustrate this potential problem, and a solution to it, consider one scenario. Assume that you have a taxable estate of $1 million and your spouse owns property worth $200,000. If you leave everything outright to your spouse, the unlimited marital deduction will permit it to pass tax-free.

But if the $1 million plus the $200,000 remains intact when your spouse dies, the taxable estate will be $1.2 million. The unified credit (at the time) will protect just half of that amount, letting the IRS claim $235,000 in tax on that extra $600,000. That's money that, with a little planning, could have been passed on to the next generation.

One of the most common estate planning strategies for a couple with more than $600,000 in assets is to make sure that the first spouse to die takes advantage of the unified credit as well as the marital deduction.

Note that in our example by relying fully on the marital deduction, the first spouse effectively threw away the $192,800 credit.

In order to avoid forfeiting that tax break, you can use what's variously known as a bypass or exemption-equivalent trust. Basically, in our example, you would split your estate, putting $600,000 in a trust and leaving the other $400,000 outright to your surviving spouse. (Naturally, you can split your estate however you choose, but the goal is to make maximum use of the unified credit.)

Although the money put into these types of trusts would not qualify for the marital deduction, it would be protected from tax by the credit. The $400,000 left outright to your spouse would be shielded from tax by the marital deduction. As in the first example, then, no tax is due on the death of the first spouse.

A key factor of the bypass trust is that income from the trust can go to your survivor—just as if he or she inherited the assets outright—but at his or her death the principal would be distributed to other heirs, such as your children, without being included in your spouse's estate.

In our example, the estate would include the $400,000 left under the marital deduction plus the $200,000 of personal assets. The unified credit would shelter the full amount from the estate tax. Bottom line: The family comes out $235,000 ahead.

QTIP Trusts

Until recently, in order to qualify for the estate tax marital deduction, assets had to be left to the survivor in a way that permitted him or her to control their ultimate distribution. In other words, if you left $1 million to your spouse, that spouse would get to decide who would inherit what remained at the time of her death.

Today, however, every empty nester can use a qualified terminable interest property (QTIP) trust that qualifies for the marital deduction without giving away ultimate control of the property. A QTIP trust gives the surviving spouse income for life and possibly some principal, but after his or her death, the distribution of the assets is controlled by your wishes as expressed in the trust document rather than by your spouse's will.

Although the QTIP trust is similar to the bypass trust in that the survivor receives income for life and assets are then passed on according to the trust, there are two big differences. One is that the QTIP protects property from the estate tax with the marital deduction rather than the unified credit used by the bypass trust (and, therefore, the transfer of other property can be protected by the credit). And unlike a bypass trust, assets in a QTIP trust are included in your survivor's taxable estate.

QTIP trusts may be especially appropriate for those who have children from a former marriage. A husband, for example, can use such a trust to provide for his second wife while ensuring that when she dies, the assets will pass on to the children from his first marriage.

Childless couples can also use the QTIP trust so that either spouse can be sure that, after providing for the survivor, his or her blood relatives will ultimately inherit specified assets.

Property Ownerships

For most people, the will is the means by which property is usually passed to heirs. But the will operates to pass only property that is not effectively passed using some other means. Often property passes to heirs in other ways, such as through beneficiary designations or legal forms of property ownership. This is commonly referred to a "passing property outside the will."

These alternative ways of passing property, particularly property ownership, can also greatly influence the cost of administering your estate and the amount of Federal income taxes your estate ultimately pays.

The way that you own an asset, what lawyers call the "form of ownership," will determine how much of the asset will be included in your taxable estate and who will inherit your share of the asset. Lawyers refer to ownership of property as "titling." (For example, the owner holds title to the property.)

The different forms of property ownership include:

■ Individual ownership;

■ Joint tenancy;

■ Tenancy in common;

■ Community property;

■ Trusts; and

■ Beneficiary designations—for example, in a retirement plan or life insurance policy

How Asset is Held	Included in Estate	Who Gets Property	How is it Transferred
Individually owned	100%	Beneficiary	By will
Special joint tenancy with right of survivorship	50%	Spouse	By form of ownership
Other joint tenancy	Up to 100%	Other joint tenant	By form of ownership
Tenancy in common	% owned	Beneficiary	By will
Retirement plans	100%	Named beneficiary	By contract
Life insurance	100%, if deemed	Named beneficiary	By contract

These forms of ownership determine how much of the asset's fair market value is included in your estate for estate tax purposes and how your property legally passes to your heirs at death.

INDIVIDUAL OWNERSHIP. Individual ownership simply means that you alone own and control the entire interest in a piece of property. For example, if you purchased 100 shares of stock and own the shares individually, only your name is on the stock certificates. On the day that you die, whoever you name in your will will get those shares.

JOINT OWNERSHIP. Joint ownership means that you own property with one or more other people; for example, instead of owning that stock individually, you can buy those shares with your spouse as joint tenants. The stock certificate should indicate that you own it as joint tenants with some notation, such as "as joint tenants with right of survivorship" or "JTWROS." In this case, your spouse automatically inherits your shares, regardless of what your will says.

The titling on the stock will overrule your will because your joint tenant has a right of survivorship—that is, if she survives you, she will inherit your portion of the stock.

TENANCY IN COMMON. Another way to own an asset jointly with someone is as tenants in common. Tenancy in common is somewhat similar to joint tenancy in that two or more people have an ownership interest in property. But unlike joint tenancy, tenants in common do not have right of survivorship; therefore, the other "tenants" do not inherit your share of this property. Instead, it is your will that determines who receives your share of the asset.

COMMUNITY PROPERTY. The last form of joint ownership is community property. It does not depend on titling but rather is the result of living in one of the nine community property states (Arizona, California, Idaho, Louisiana, Nevada, New Mexico, Texas, Washington and Wisconsin.)

Community property is all assets that you acquired during your marriage; except for gifts and inheritances, which are considered individually owned property. Under community property rules, the asset does not actually pass to your spouse. Instead, it is your will that determines who receives the property.

Don't Overlook the Impact of State Taxes

Most states impose some form of estate taxes and/or inheritance taxes. However, this isn't as bad as it might at first appear because you get a credit for state death taxes paid against the Federal estate tax. In fact, most states only impose a tax in an amount that equals the credit allowed for Federal purposes; this is commonly called a pickup tax and the net effect to you is zero.

Keep in mind though, that some states impose their own estate taxes or inheritance taxes. Inheritance taxes differ from pickup taxes in that they are assessed against the recipients of your estate, not against the estate itself. Therefore, in those states that have an inheritance tax, state death tax planning becomes much more important.

Estate Administration and Probate

Next to reducing estate taxes, minimizing probate costs is an important goal since estate administration can be time consuming and expensive. How can you plan your estate to minimize the cost of administering it?

First, what exactly is probate? Probate is a court process in which the executor of an estate, accumulates probate assets, pays debts and taxes and distributes assets to beneficiaries. During the probate process, your executor is responsible for submitting your will to the court as well as preparing an inventory of your estate's assets and liabilities.

Tax elections and returns will be prepared and filed and taxes will be paid as part of the probate process. Debts and claims against the estate will also be settled. Once the will is approved by the court, the probate process generally takes from six months to two year to complete.

There are some advantages to the probate process. For one, beneficiaries are protected because a court oversees the process and makes sure that the right person inherits the proper assets. Also, statutory notices are given that cut off creditors from presenting claims after a certain period (usually four to six months). Also, the court is available to interpret any ambiguous portions of your will and settle claims or disputes, such as will contests. Finally, the transfer of title will be properly recorded in the probate process.

In spite of these many benefits, many people want to avoid probate because it is time-consuming, cumbersome and expensive. The cost of probate will usually be based on the amount of your property that actually passes under the will and thus goes through the probate proceeding.

Remember, the entire value of your estate will not necessarily go through probate. Assets that you own under joint tenancy, retirement accounts, life insurance proceeds, and assets held in trust, don't go through probate.

So, avoiding the probate process requires that you analyze the way that your assets will pass and structure your estate so that everything passes outside of your will. The most common way to achieve this objective is by employing a revocable trust (see Chapter 6).

After the Basics

Now that you've begun thinking about retirement planning, delved into the many types of investments that can help you achieve your retirement goals and even explored the possibility of a so-called "tax business" to help you enjoy the planning and your empty nester lifestyle more, all is not done. Even learning how to cope with a return migration to the empty nest and planning to pass on your assets to your heirs does not finish your chores.

Just as the empty nester lifestyle will hopefully be an ongoing one, planning for your future should also be an ongoing—although not onerous—process as you'll see next.

Chapter 21

SUMMING IT UP: DEVELOPING AN ONGOING STRATEGY

You're not free yet. Realizing that every empty nester needs to begin thinking about retirement was a good first step. Actually planning for that retirement was a good move, too. Incorporating the enjoyment than can be found as an empty nester and, perhaps, incorporating a spare-time "tax business" into your empty nester lifestyle for profits and tax benefits was smart.

Planning to cope with family members and their financial and health problems ensures that your retirement plans will proceed on track and that you can continue to enjoy your empty nester lifestyle. You may even have begun thinking about the future and incorporated estate planning into your lifestyle. But that doesn't mean that you can rest yet.

Setting your plans into motion was the difficult part. Now you have to insure that your retirement financial plan stays healthy and on target. To do that, you'll have to keep taking your plan's pulse—and monitor your own as well.

Monitoring Your Personal Behavior

In order to know if your retirement assets will be sufficient to reach your goals, you must first know how long that retirement will last. Clearly, no one can answer that question with any degree of certainty. However, a fundamental understanding of what influences longevity and fitness is critical to fully enjoy your empty nester lifestyle—and to make knowledgeable decisions regarding the adequacy of your retirement reserves as you age.

The Aging Process

Your overall health and wellness is a combination of many factors, both physical and mental. While aging is inevitable, it is important to recognize that everyone ages differently—at different rates—because of our unique genetic makeup and lifestyle. Although not much can be done about your genes, your empty nester lifestyle is something you do have some influence over.

Exercise

Twenty-five years ago, experts believed that physical conditioning after the age of 40 had little or no effect. And after age 60, the experts assumed that exercise produced no observable improvement in functioning. In fact, people in those age categories were considered by many experts to be "untrainable."

In 1967, Dr. Herbert A. deVries, professor emeritus of exercise sciences at the University of Southern California, challenged this notion. Studying men and women in the Leisure World community in Laguna Hills, California, Dr. deVries found that healthy older people who engaged in appropriate physical exercise benefit as much as younger people. Today, his results have been corroborated by scientists all over the world.

More recent studies show that men in their 80s can still build muscle mass, which means that they can get stronger. Frail older people have been found to benefit from training designed to increase their strength. With strength training programs, nursing home residents, averaging age 87, increased their walking speed and ability to climb stairs. Some no longer needed their walkers, relying on canes instead.

Slowing Down the Aging Process

Exercise decreases body fat as well as heart rate and blood pressure. It improves endurance with increased circulation. It increases strength, thus building up muscles. And it increases flexibility. Some studies show that exercise can even decrease certain kinds of depression, particularly if the individual exercises with someone.

Unfortunately, not everyone likes to exercise. You may be one of them. You may, in fact, agree with a quote attributed to James Thurber: "Oh exercise! When I feel like exercising, I lie down until the feeling goes away."

In general, however, people do not continue with a particular physical activity that they don't like. The key is finding an exercise that's enjoyable and fun. And, of course, continuing with it as a regular part of your empty nester lifestyle—especially after retirement.

Nutrition

Research has long confirmed the link between nutrition and health. As the late George Burns said, "If I had known I was going to live so long, I would have taken better care of myself."

Consider the Dietary Guidelines for Americans published by the U.S. Department of Agriculture:

- Eat a well-balanced diet.

- Maintain healthy weight.

- Choose a diet that's low in fat, saturated fat and cholesterol. It is recommended that 30 percent or less of your calories per day come from fat.

- Choose a diet with plenty of vegetables, fruits and grain products.

- Use sugar in moderation.

- Use salt and sodium in moderation.

- If you drink alcoholic beverages, do it in moderation.

In other words, elevate your health plan to an equal level of importance as your financial plan. You need both for an enjoyable, healthy lifestyle.

Your Ongoing Financial Health

Although we have minimized the effects of inflation, the financial health of every empty nester's retirement portfolio demands that they watch out for inflation. Like termites eating silently and steadily away at the framework of your house, inflation can inflict irreparable damage by steadily chewing up a chunk of your nest egg's value. Even seemingly low levels of inflation can cause big-time damage.

At a "modest" 4 percent annual inflation rate, a 40-year-old empty nester earning $50,000 today will need an income of $109,500 in order to enjoy the same buying power 20 years from now. If inflation averages 5 percent, the figure will jump to $132,500.

Owning stocks and stock mutual funds will be many empty nesters' best long-term defense against inflation. They've managed to gain a yearly average of 10.2 percent since 1926—a comfortable margin above the rate of inflation.

Admittedly, you may have to pay tax on some of your stock earnings each year if the investments aren't locked into a tax-sheltered account such as an IRA, Keogh or 401(k) plan. But stock and stock mutual funds will usually generate the bulk of their return as appreciation and there is no tax due on that gain until you sell.

> NOTE: When taxes are due, you should consider paying the bill from a separate fund rather than using the money in your retirement nest egg. That keeps your retirement money compounding at top speed and puts you well ahead of those inflation termites.

And don't forget that those built-in or built-up gains that remain untaxed in stocks and stock mutual funds until they are eventually sold are now taxed at special tax rates. That's right, thanks to recent legislation, the tax rate for capital gains, that is, gain on investments that have been held for the minimum required period of time, qualify for extremely preferential tax rates.

Reassess and Reassess

A change in jobs, a big promotion, an inheritance—all of these events, as well as any number of other changes, can change the shape of your retirement finances. In order to keep your plan on track and your empty nester lifestyle intact, you must occasionally recalculate your retirement income goals and the assets that you have available to meet that goal whenever a major change happens.

In fact, it may be a good idea to recalculate every couple of years even if there haven't been any big changes.

Track Your Investment Progress

It is crucial to keep taking the pulse of your investment portfolio—especially the stocks and stock mutual funds that you own. Don't be a fanatic about it, no need to eyeball the stock and fund tables in the newspaper every day. This is a long-term proposition after all.

However, long-term project or not, no empty nester can afford to ignore investment performance and the fact that everyone makes a bad choice now and again. Keeping tabs on all of your investments along with periodic comprehensive reviews will allow you to gradually weed out nonperforming investments as well as take advantage of investments that may contribute more to your ultimate goal.

Keep Tabs on Your Debt and Savings Schedule

Damaging debt—in the form of credit card balance creep—can sap funds that would otherwise go to retirement savings. Watch those plastic balances in order to avoid paying needless interest and channel the savings into your nest egg. Consider a plan to pay off any outstanding loans early and save thousands of dollars in interest.

Check Your Social Security Records

Call (800) 772-1213 to request Form 7004-SM, "Request for Earnings and Benefit Estimate Statement." About four weeks after you complete and return that form, you should receive an estimate of your retirement benefits, along with a year-by-year listing of your Social Security wages. Check for mistakes and request a change if you find any. This should be done every three to five years.

Review Your Insurance Coverage

Checking your insurance coverage means coverage that you buy yourself as well as what you have at work. Coverage at work is subject to change. A promotion, for example, could boost the amount of life insurance coverage you receive. And a job change could completely alter your insurance picture.

At a minimum, you should plan to review your insurance every two years; fill any gaps and cancel overlapping policies.

Monitor Your Company's Pulse, Too

Your own retirement plan's pulse may be closely linked to your company's health. That's especially true if you participate in a profit-sharing plan at work, hold any of your retirement assets in company stock or participate in an employee stock ownership plan (ESOP).

Obviously, you'll want to read the company's annual and quarterly reports as well as monitor outside media or analyst reports on the firm. If the company's growth prospects dim and other investment options are available for that money, consider switching your assets elsewhere.

And the Beat Goes On

By now, you probably have an appreciation of how uncertain your retirement can be, especially if you do not take responsibility now for your own financial security. The future of the Social Security system is tenuous and it is unlikely that the promises made to today's generation of wage earners can be kept if the system remains in its present state.

Even worse, the tradition of career employment capped by a guaranteed pension has become somewhat fractured as a result of the economic dislocation of recent years. Rather than spend their careers at one company, employees today tend to switch jobs frequently, often losing critical pension benefits along the way.

In this dynamic and challenging environment, we all must start early in our working lives to establish a retirement investment program. The change into empty nester status provides a much-needed incentive to enjoy the new lifestyle—and, hopefully save and invest at the same time.

In order to be successful, any retirement program requires considerable savings discipline and should take advantage of all tax exemptions. For instance, in addition to maintaining a regular monthly savings program, you will probably need to save in larger amounts than you are currently. Thus, the need for ongoing evaluation of your retirement portfolio.

The exceptional investment returns of the 1980s are unlikely to be repeated and empty nesters today seeking to accumulate retirement benefits for tomorrow will find that they must set aside considerably more of their yearly income in order to build the same size nest egg as their parents.

With lower returns in prospect for financial assets, it is even more critical that you establish and follow a thoughtful investment plan for your own retirement. The following "rules" for empty nester retirement investing rely on the methods and strategies covered earlier.

BE KNOWLEDGEABLE. Every empty nester should develop a basic familiarity with the workings of the economy and the fiscal markets—both at the outset of their investment program as well as on an ongoing basis. Think about investments from a historical perspective and consider the likely long-term tradeoffs between reward and risk. When considering a mutual fund investment, evaluate that fund on the basis of its investment objectives and policies, its continuity of management, the reputation of its sponsor—and its costs.

BE STEADFAST. Every empty nester must develop a basic financial plan for their investments and "stay the course," allowing nothing to distract them from their long-term goals. When financial markets turn against them, as they inevitably will, the long-term investment plan should be kept in mind and temptation to abruptly change course should be avoided.

The ability to remain steadfast in the face of market challenges will be a significant determinant of the long-term results of your retirement investment program.

BE CONSISTENT. It is generally better to build your retirement portfolio by contributing on a systematic basis (i.e., dollar-cost averaging) rather than making large, all-at-once investments. While a regular investment program will not entirely isolate anyone from portfolio losses, dollar-cost averaging provides a disciplined investment approach. An IRA, 401(k) or 403(b) retirement plan presents an easy to use investment vehicle for systematic—and tax advantaged retirement investing.

BE BALANCED. Having a balanced portfolio of stocks, bonds and short-term reserves is the most suitable way to hedge against the vagaries of the financial markets. Overseas securities and real estate holdings may also be appropriate for further diversification.

BE DIVERSIFIED. Diversification is simply common sense. Whatever investment balance is selected, it should spread the investments among a large number of stocks and bonds. Often, the best way—and typically least expensive way—for any empty nester to accomplish this objective is through mutual funds. In a single portfolio, every empty nester can achieve a level of diversification that likely could never be attained by investing in individual stocks.

BE AWARE OF RISK, BUT DON'T AVOID RISK. While every empty nester should analyze the potential risks of every possible investment—and measure that risk against their personal financial circumstances—be wary of stockpiling your retirement portfolio with "risk-free" investments.

Many investors view risk primarily as the chance that they will lose money and therefore hold money market instruments or certificates of deposit to eliminate the possibility of principal losses. But on a long-term basis, risk is more accurately thought of as the possibility that your accumulated assets (adjusted for inflation) will be insufficient to meet your financial goals. In this light, although stocks clearly have the highest risk—in terms of long-term protection of your assets against the erosion of inflation—they can't be beat.

PLAN FOR A TOMORROW THAT YOU HOPE WILL NEVER COME. The number of empty nesters and others who have planned their futures only to be surprised in one way or another when that future finally arrived are legion. The ongoing, all-encompassing strategies we have presented offer an excellent way of both planning and coping with unexpected changes.

Every empty nester who combines their newly discovered free time and financial resources with an ongoing financial plan should be able to cope with the unexpected changes that face us all in the years ahead. Whether you, as an empty nester, take up investments as a hobby or employ some other enjoyable hobby or activity as a part of your retirement financial plan, you must invest time in order to continue with the empty nester lifestyle in a manner to which you are just becoming accustomed.

GLOSSARY

Acquisition debt—Acquisition debt is a loan secured by your primary or second home and which is incurred when you buy, build or substantially improve your home. Acquisition debt is limited to $1 million ($500,000 if you are married and file separate income tax returns).

Adjusted gross income (AGI)—The intermediate step in calculating taxable income—the amount used for computing deductions based on or limited by a percentage of income, such as medical expenses, charitable contributions and miscellaneous itemized deductions.

Annuity—A contract sold by commercial insurance companies that pays a monthly (or quarterly, semiannual or annual) income benefit for the life of a person (the *annuitant*), for the lives of two or more persons or for a specified period of time.

Appraisal—Professional opinion or estimate of the value of a property.

Arm's length transaction—A transaction among parties, each of whom acts in his or her own best interest. Transactions between the following parties would, in most cases, not be considered arm's length: a husband and wife, a father and son and a corporation and one of its subsidiaries.

Assessment—Amount of tax or special payment due to a municipality or association.

Balance sheet—A financial statement that gives an accounting picture of property owned by a company and of claims against that property on a specific date; or the statement of an individual's personal assets and liabilities (personal balance sheet) in order to determine their net worth.

Basis—Amount representing an individual's cost in acquiring an asset. It is used for a variety of tax purposes including computations for gain or loss. (*book value*).

Bear—A person who thinks that a market will fall. Bears may sell a stock short or buy a put option in order to take advantage of the anticipated drop.

Bond—An obligation to pay. A bond is an IOU issued by a government or by a corporation. It promises that the issuer or borrower will repay the principal to the lender (the bond purchaser) at a specified future date, plus pay any interest over the life of the bond to its owner.

Budget—An estimate of revenue and expenditures for a specified period. A budget provides a moving picture of your financial situation.

Bull—A person who thinks that prices will rise. One can be bullish on the prospects for an individual stock, bond or commodity, an industry segment or the market as a whole.

Cafeteria Benefits Plan—An arrangement under which employees may choose their own employee benefit structure from a list of benefits provided by the employer.

Capital Expenditure—An expense that adds to the value or useful life of property is considered to be a capital expense and generally cannot be claimed as a current tax deduction. Capital expenditures include those for buildings, improvements or betterments of a long-term nature, machinery, and architect's fees, as well as the costs of defending or perfecting title to property.

Capital gain—Gain on the sale of a capital asset.

Cash equivalents—Investments considered to be of such high liquidity and safety that they are virtually as good as cash. In other words, short-term, interest-earning securities that can be readily converted into cash.

Cash flow—Net income plus depreciation and other noncash charges. In this sense, it is synonymous with cash earnings. Investors focus on cash flow from operations because of their concerns with a firm's ability to pay dividends.

Cash reserve—Cash kept by a person or business that is beyond immediate needs.

Casualty losses—Losses arising from fire, storm, shipwreck or other casualty or from theft. A loss from a casualty arises from an event due to some sudden, unexpected or unusual cause.

Certificates of deposit (CDs)—A debt instrument issued by a bank that usually pays interest.

Common stock—A security representing an ownership interest in a corporation. Ownership may also be shared with *preferred stock* which has prior claim on any dividends to be paid, and, in the event of a liquidation, to the distribution of the corporation's assets.

Community property—Property acquired during marriage and recognized to be the product of the joint efforts of the married couple.

Compensation. Direct and indirect monetary and nonmonetary rewards given to employees on the basis of the value of the job, their personal contributions and their performance.

Compound interest—Interest earned on principal plus interest that was earned earlier.

Convertible bonds—Corporate bonds that can exchanged for a set number of another form of security (usually common shares of stock) at a prestated price.

Convertible term life insurance—Insurance that can be converted into permanent insurance regardless of an insured's physical condition and without a medical examination.

Corporate bonds—A debt instrument issued by a private corporation.

Crummey Trust—Called a "Crummey Trust" after the court decision that recognized it, this trust basically allows the distribution of principal and income at the trustee's discretion but does not require the mandatory termination of the trust when the child reaches 21. Instead, the trust documents may allow for the distribution of the principal in stages.

Decedent—A person who has died.

Deferred payment annuity—Annuity whose contract provides that payments to the annuitant be postponed until a number of periods have elapsed—for example, when the annuitant reaches a certain age.

Defined benefit plan—A plan (such as a pension plan) that promises to pay a specified amount based on a predetermined formula to each person who retires after a set number of years of service. In other words, with a defined-benefit plan you contribute annually whatever amount is required to fund a specified retirement benefit or payment. The payment to be made during retirement is fixed, and the contribution is based on actuarial tables for your life expectancy.

Defined contribution plan—A deferred retirement plan that provides a separate account for each person covered by that plan. Future benefits are based only on amounts contributed to or allocated to each account. These plans usually allow you to contribute a specified amount—10 percent of your income, for instance—to the plan each year.

De minimis—Of insufficient significance to warrant judicial or tax attention, as in the case of nontaxable, de minimis fringe benefits.

Dependent—Any person who a taxpayer can claim a dependency exemption. Defined by the IRS, as any individual supported by the taxpayer who is related to the taxpayer in specified ways or who makes his principal abode in the taxpayer's household.

Depreciation—A systematic write-off of the cost of an asset over a period of time allowed by tax law.

Disability income insurance—A health insurance that provides income payments to the insured wage earner when income is interrupted or terminated because of illness, sickness or accident.

Diversification—The reduction of risk by putting assets in several categories of investments—stocks, bonds, money market instruments, precious metals and real estate, for example—or several industries, or a mutual fund with a broad range of stocks in the portfolio.

Dividends—Profits that a company distributes to its owners/shareholders.

Dollar cost averaging—A strategy for investing the same dollar amount in the same investment at fixed time intervals. More securities will be bought when prices are low, resulting in lowering the average cost per share.

Donee—The recipient of a gift or trust.

Double taxation—The effect of Federal tax law whereby earnings are taxed at the corporate level, then taxed again as dividends of stockholders.

Employee stock ownership plan (ESOP)—A program encouraging employees to purchase stock in their company. Companies with such plans may take tax deductions for ESOP dividends that are passed on to participating employees and for dividends that go to repay stock acquisition loans.

Energy conservation subsidies—Subsidies for energy conservation measures. The value of any subsidy provided (directly or indirectly) by a public utility to a customer for the purchase or installation of energy conservation measures for a dwelling unit is specifically excluded from the customer's gross income. There is no income tax on energy conservation subsidies.

Estate planning—Planning for the orderly handling, disposition and administration of an estate when the owner dies. In a broad sense, it is the art of designing a program for the effective enjoyment, management and disposition of property at the minimum possible tax cost.

Estate tax—The amount that results from deducting the following: (1) unified credit, (2) state death taxes, (3) gift taxes paid on gifts made before 1977, (4) foreign death taxes, and (5) estate taxes on prior transfers to decedent from the estate tax before unified credit.

Exclusion—In insurance, an item not covered by a policy. With taxes, an amount that otherwise would constitute a part of gross income, but is excluded under a specific provision of the tax law.

Fair market value—The price which property will bring when offered for sale by a willing seller to a willing buyer, neither being obliged to buy or sell.

Federal Deposit Insurance Corporation (FDIC)—Independent Federal agency that insures deposits up to $100,000 in member commercial banks. It has its own reserves and can borrow from the U.S. Treasury and sometimes acts to prevent bank failures.

Federal Insurance Contributions Act (FICA)—The Federal law that provides for the imposition of the Social Security tax.

Federal Unemployment Tax Act (FUTA)—Provides for Federal unemployment insurance and is paid by employers.

401(K) plan—Allows an employee to contribute pretax earnings to a company's pool, which is invested in stocks, bonds or money market instruments; also known as a *salary reduction plan*. The contributions as well as earnings are only taxed when withdrawn.

403(b) plan—Also known as *tax-sheltered annuities*—is a unique type of salary reduction retirement savings plan. They are available only to employees of educational institutions and other specified nonprofit organizations.

Futures contracts—Agreement to buy or sell a specific amount of a commodity or financial instrument at a particular price on a stipulated future date. A futures contract obligates the buyer to purchase the underlying commodity and the seller to sell it, unless the contract is sold to another before the settlement date.

Gifts—A voluntary transfer of property without consideration, that is for which no value is received in return.

Gross income—The total of a taxpayer's income from any source, except items specifically excluded by our tax laws and other items not subject to tax.

Hard assets—Hard assets include commodities, real estate, precious metals, timber rights, oil and gas leases—any of a variety of natural resources whose values tend to rise along with the overall level of consumer prices.

Home-equity loan—A loan secured by a second mortgage on one's principal residence, generally to be used for some nonhousing expenditure. Home equity loans up to $100,000 above the cost of purchase and improvements generate tax-deductible interest.

Imputed interest—Implied interest. In a mortgage that states an insufficient interest rate, tax law will impute a higher rate and a lower principal, which will increase taxes on the receipt of payments. The imputed interest is based on the difference between the rate the Federal government pays on new borrowings and the interest charged on the loan.

Income replacement—A benefit in disability income insurance whereby an injured or ill wage earner receives a monthly income payment to replace a percentage of his lost earnings.

Independent contractor—A worker or contractor who is self-employed. The contracting party need not pay Social Security taxes and the like; the independent contractor must instead pay a self-employment tax.

Individual Retirement Account (IRA)—A trust fund to which any individual employee can contribute up to $2,000 per year. However, income level and eligibility for an employee pension plan determines whether or not the employee's contribution is tax-deductible.

Inflation—A rise in the prices of goods and services, as happens when spending increases relative to the supply of goods on the market; in other words, too much money chasing too few goods.

Inheritance taxes—A state tax based on the value of property passing to each particular heir. It differs from the Federal estate tax in that the degree of kinship of the heir to the decedent generally determines the exempt amounts and tax rates. An estate tax is based on the value of all property left by the decedent, whereas an inheritance tax is paid by the benficiary.

Interest—The cost of using credit or another's money, expressed as a rate per period of time, usually one year, in which case it is called an *annual rate of interest.*

Intestate—A person who dies leaving no will or leaving one that is defective. Property goes to the legal heirs of the intestate. If there are no heirs, the property will escheat (pass to the state).

Invest—To transfer capital to an enterprise in order to secure income or profit for the investor.

Investment advisers—This umbrella term covers all of those who provide investment advice for a fee—from mutual fund managers to publishers of investment newsletters and the more familiar personal money advisers. Investment advisers must register with the Securities and Exchange Commission (SEC).

Investment portfolio—Diversification of investments in various securities and other investment instruments to maximize opportunities while minimizing risk exposure.

Joint tenancy—Ownership of an asset by two or more persons, each of whom has an undivided interest with the right of survivorship. Typically used by related persons.

Junk bonds—Junk bonds are on the opposite side of the safety coin. Bonds with a speculative credit rating of BB or lower by Standard & Poors and Moody's rating systems. They have lower ratings and are high-risk investments.

Keogh Plan—A tax-deferred pension account designated for employees of unincorporated businesses or for persons who are self-employed either full or part time.

Lifetime gifts—An effective means of transferring property for estate planning purposes. Gifts eliminate all probate and administrative expenses on the property transferred.

Liquid wealth—Liquid wealth includes bank accounts, certificates of deposit and money funds. Some people include as liquid wealth the cash value of their life insurance and the credit available on their credit cards and home equity loans, because these are all money sources that can be quickly tapped.

Liquidity—The ability of an individual or company to convert assets into cash or cash equivalents without significant loss. Investments in money market funds and listed stocks are much more liquid than investments in real estate, for instance.

Living benefit riders—Under these riders, the policy's owner can receive from 25 percent to 100 percent of the policy death benefit; the exact amount depends on life expectancy (usually 12 months or less) and state regulations. According to the Internal Revenue Service, the proceeds will not be considered income for Federal income taxes.

Living trust—A trust established and in operation during the settler's life. This trust can be canceled or revoked so you have the power to get back any assets that you transfer to it. For most purposes, you retain control over the property; you've simply changed title to it from yourself to the trust.

Long-term care insurance—Provides income for the day-to-day care that a patient (generally older than 65) receives in a nursing facility or in his/her residence following an illness or injury, or in old age, when the patient can no longer perform at least two of the five basic activities of daily living.

Lump-sum distributions—Payment of the entire amount of retirement benefits due at one time rather than in installations.

Marital deduction—A Federal estate tax deduction permitting a spouse to take, tax free, the decedent spouse's total estate. The marital deduction permits property to pass to the surviving spouse without being depleted by the Federal estate tax.

Market efficiency—The term used to describe the concept that the market and the price of any stock at any time is always fully valued.

Maturity—The date at which legal rights in something ripen. In case of an investment, the date at which the underlying investment matures or may be passed to the recipient.

Medicaid—Medicaid is a state-run program designed primarily to help those with low income and few or no resources. It provides a safety net of sorts for retirees—but only those in the most dire situations. Yet, about 61 percent of retirees rely on Medicaid to cover at least a portion of the cost of custodial care.

Medical Savings Accounts (MSAs)—MSAs are like IRAs created for the purpose of defraying unreimbursed health care expenses on a tax-deferred basis. Contributions are tax deductible, medical expenses withdrawn from these accounts to pay medical expenses are not taxed and the amounts in the MSA continue to grow, tax-free, until withdrawn after the empty nester reaches the age of 59 1/2—just like an IRA.

Medicare—A basic Federal health insurance program that covers people who are 65 or older, people of any age with permanent kidney failure and those under 65 who have been receiving Social Security disability benefits.

Money market—Market for short-term debt instruments, such as negotiable certificates of deposit, commercial paper, bankers' acceptances, U.S. Treasury bills and the like.

Money market fund—An open-end mutual fund that invests in commercial paper, bankers' acceptances, U.S. Treasury bills and the like and pays money market rates of interest. The fund's asset value remains a constant $1 a share—only the interest rate goes up or down.

Municipal bonds—A bond issued by a state or local government body such as a county, city, town or municipal authority. Interest earned on municipal bonds is generally not taxable by the U.S. government, nor in the jurisdiction that issued it. Used to finance long-term projects for cities, towns, villages and even states.

Mutual fund—A mutual fund pools your money with that of thousands of other investors to purchase stocks and bonds in a variety of publicly-held companies.

Nest egg—Assets put aside for a large purchase or a person's retirement. Such assets are usually invested conservatively.

Net—The figure remaining after all relevant deductions have been made from the gross amount.

Net worth—Your net worth is the amount by which your assets (your savings, investments, property owned) exceeds your liabilities (debts owed).

Options—Options come in two varieties: incentive stock options (ISOs) and nonqualified stock options (NQSOs). The difference lies mainly in the tax benefits provided

Ordinary and necessary—A tax term that allows a current tax deduction for business expenses, contrasted with a capital expenditure. An expense is necessary if it is appropriate and helpful to the taxpayer's business, according to the IRS. An expense is ordinary if it is one that is common and accepted in the particular business activity.

Ordinary income property—Property that if sold at its fair market value on the date of its contribution would give rise to ordinary income or short-term capital gain.

Paired investments—Limited partnerships with two distinct businesses. One business generates income and, hopefully, cash. The other business generates losses—at least for tax purposes—to offset that income.

Passive activity—Any rental or other activity in which the investor does not materially participate. With certain exceptions, losses generated by passive activities may not be used to offset active income or portfolio income. Instead, losses from passive activities are suspended until passive income is generated.

Passive Income Generator (PIG)—If you have substantial passive losses from old tax shelter investments, you might consider investing in so-called "passive income generators" (PIGs). A PIG may generate a positive cash flow as well as taxable passive income.

Power of attorney—Instrument by which one person, as principal, appoints another as his agent and confers upon him the authority to perform certain specified acts or kinds of acts on behalf of the principal. The primary purpose of a power of attorney is to evidence the authority of the agent to third parties with whom the agent deals.

Preferred stock—Part of the capital stock of a corporation that enjoys priority over the remaining stock, or common stock, in the distribution of dividends and in the event of dissolution of the corporation. These shares generally pay a higher dividend than common stock but don't have the same price-appreciation potential of common stock.

Premium—The amount that an insured is charged, reflecting an expectation of loss or risk. The insurance company will assume the risks of the insured (length of life, state of health, property damage or destruction or liability exposure) in exchange for a premium payment.

Probate—Probate is a court process in which the executor of an estate, accumulates probate assets, pays debts and taxes and distributes assets to beneficiaries. During the probate process, your executor is responsible for submitting your will to the court as well as preparing an inventory of your estate's assets and liabilities.

Profit-sharing plan—An agreement that allows employees to share in company profits. Annual contributions are made by the company, when it has profits, to a profit-sharing account for each employee, either in cash or in a deferred plan, which may be invested in stocks, bonds or cash equivalents.

Property taxes—Imposed by municipalities upon owners of property within their jurisdiction, based upon the assessed value of that property.

Qualified plan—A pension or profit-sharing plan set up by an employer for the benefit of employees that adhere to the rules set forth by the IRS. An employer receives an immediate tax deduction the trust income is not taxable and the employee is taxed on the income only upon receipt.

Qualified Terminable Interest Property (Q-TIP)—A strategy providing that all income from assets in trust be paid at least annually for the life of the surviving spouse. A Q-TIP trust gives the surviving spouse income for life and possibly some principal but after his or her death, the distribution of the assets is controlled by your wishes as expressed in the trust document rather than by your spouse's will.

Random walk—The theory about the movement of stock and commodity futures prices hypothesizing that past prices are of no use in forecasting future price movements. According to the theory, stock prices reflect reactions to new information coming to the market. Since new information arrives in random fashion, changes in stock prices are no more predictable than the walking pattern or a drunken person.

Real Estate Investment Trusts (REITs)—A real estate mutual fund, allowed by tax law, to avoid the corporate income tax. It sells shares of ownership and must invest in real estate or mortgages. Its unique feature is to allow small investors to participate, without double taxation, in large real estate ventures.

Recession—A downturn in economic activity, defined by many economists as at least two consecutive quarters of decline in a country's gross domestic product.

Repair—Expenditures to keep property in an ordinarily efficient operating condition and which do not add to its value or appreciably prolong its useful life are generally deductible as repairs. Repairs include repainting, tuck-pointing, mending leaks, plastering and conditioning gutters on buildings.

Reverse mortgage loans—Reverse mortgages loans are a relatively new form of mortgage that allow you to eventually convert the equity in your home into installment payments that could provide you with monthly income for life. By taking out a reverse mortgage, you borrow against your property but, instead of getting the proceeds in a lump-sum, they are paid to you in installments.

Risk management—A procedure to minimize the adverse effect of a possible financial loss by (1) identifying potential sources of loss, (2) measuring the financial consequences of a loss occurring, and (3) using controls to minimize actual losses or their financial consequences.

Roll-over—To replace a loan or debt with another. To change the institution that invests one's pension plan, without recognition of taxable income.

The Rule of 72—The approximation of the time it takes for money to double when earning compound interest. The percentage rate is divided by 72 to derive the number of years to double the principal.

Sale-leaseback—A sale-leaseback transaction is typically arranged between retiree-parents and their children. The parents sell their home to the child (or a partnership of two or more children) and then arrange to lease the home and continue to live there.

Savings bonds—U.S. government bonds issued in face value denominations ranging from $50 to $10,000. Issued at discount, these bonds are redeemed at face value at maturity.

Self-directed IRA—Individual Retirement Account that can be actively managed by the account holder, who designates a custodian to carry out investment instructions. The account is subject to the same conditions and early withdrawal limitations as a regular IRA.

Shareholder—Owner of one or more shares of a corporation, real estate investment trust or mutual fund. A shareholder possesses the evidence, usually in the form of certificates, of real ownership of a portion of the property in actual or potential existence.

Short interest—Total number of shares of stock that have been sold short and have not yet been repurchased to close out short position. The short interest figure for securities on the New York Stock Exchange is published monthly.

Short sale—A short sale is a sale of a security without ownership in the hopes of a price decline that will allow repurchase at a lower price. The broker typically borrows the stock from another customer to deliver for the short sale.

Simplified Employee Pension (SEP)—A type of pension plan to which an employer may contribute an amount not to exceed the smaller of 15 percent of net earned income or $30,000 per individual.

Social Security Act—The Federal retirement plan enacted by Congress in 1935. The original purpose of the Act was to adopt a system that required the current working generation to contribute to the support of older, retired workers.

Stockbroker—A employee of a stock exchange member broker/dealer who acts as an account executive for clients. As such the stockbroker or registered representative gives advice on which securities to buy and sell and he or she collects a percentage of the commission income he or she generates as compensation.

Stock option—A stock option is a contract that gives its purchasers the right to buy or the right to sell a fixed amount of stock (usually 100 shares), at a predetermined price and within a predetermined period of time. The contract that gives the purchaser of an option the right to buy the stock is called a "call" option. The contract that gives the purchaser the right to sell is called a "put" option.

Stock rights—Stock rights are usually issued if a company is planning to issue more new shares in the primary market. Prior to the issuance of those new shares the company will give its current shareholders the right to purchase additional shares of the stock.

Stop-loss order—An order to a securities broker to buy or sell at the market price after the security has traded at a specified price called the "stop price"; intended to limit a loss or, in some cases, protect a profit.

Survivors insurance—A program of Social Security that provides a lump sum and monthly benefits for a qualifying worker's surviving spouse, children and even dependent parents. In some circumstances, even a former spouse can collect.

Tax avoidance—Tax reduction methods permitted by law, such as the deferral of income into the following year. Contrast this with the illegal *tax evasion*.

Tax-deferred—Refers to an investment whose accumulated earnings are free from taxation until the investor takes possession of the assets.

Tax evasion—Any method of reducing taxes not permitted by law. It carries heavy penalties. Involves deceit, subterfuge, concealment or an attempt to color or obscure events.

Tax-exempt income—Includes certain Social Security benefits, welfare benefits, nontaxable life insurance proceeds, armed forces family allotments, nontaxable pensions and tax-exempt interest.

Tax exemption—A deduction that is allowed for a taxpayer because of the taxpayer's status or circumstances rather than because of specific economic costs or expenses during the year.

Tax shelter—A device that has been largely restricted by changes to our income tax laws and crackdowns by the Internal Revenue Service. The proper definition of a "tax shelter" is any partnership or other entity, any investment plan or arrangement if the principal purpose of such partnership, entity, plan or arrangement is to avoid or evade Federal income taxes.

Tenancy in common—Ownership of realty by two or more persons, each of whom has an undivided interest without the right of survivorship. Upon the death of one of the owners, the ownership share of the decedent is inherited by the party or parties designated in the decedent's will.

Term insurance—Term insurance provides pure no-frills protection for a particular period of time, usually a year. The price, or premium, reflects the risk to the insurance company of your death during that period.

Time value—The price put on the time an investor has to wait until an investment matures, as determined by calculating the present value of the investment at maturity.

Treasury securities—These securities are the means by which the United States government borrows money. Treasury bills, notes and bonds are issued regularly by the Federal Reserve and are a popular investment for those who want very little risk. Since these are direct obligations of the U.S. government, the interest paid on Treasury bills, notes and bonds is exempt from state and local income taxes.

Trust—A fiduciary relationship in which a person, called a *trustee*, holds title to property for the benefit of another person, called a *beneficiary*. The trustee is usually charged with investing trust property productively. Trusts come in two basic types: (1) *irrevocable*, meaning that you can't amend, revoke or change the trust in any way, and (2) *revocable*, meaning it can be amended or even revoked entirely.

Unified estate and gift tax—The Federal tax imposed on the net value of an estate and on gifts of certain amounts. Usually the transferor is liable for gift taxes, but $10,000 per donee can be given each year tax free and there is a $625,000 lifetime exemption per donee.

Variable annuities—A life insurance annuity whose value fluctuates with that of an underlying securities portfolio or other index of performance. The variable annuity contrasts with a conventional or fixed annuity, whose rate of return is constant.

Warrants—Contractural right of an existing shareholder to purchase additional shares of a new issue of common stock before it is offered to the public. At the time that they are issued, the conversion price of the warrants will be higher than the market price of the stock. Warrants, like listed stock options, are highly-leveraged contracts.

Will—The legal document that serves as a key vehicle of transfer at death.

Workers' compensation—Benefits that usually include hospital and other medical payments and compensation for loss of income. If the injury is covered by statute, compensation thereunder will be the employee's only remedy against his or her employer.

INDEX